PELICAN BOOKS

PAUL'S LETTER TO THE ROMANS

John Cochrane O'Neill was born in Melbourne, Australia, in 1930 and was educated at Melbourne Grammar School. He studied history at the University of Melbourne and theology at Ormond College. He has researched in New Testament at Göttingen and Cambridge. He has published *The Theology of Acts in Its Historical Setting*, *The Puzzle of 1 John*, and *The Recovery of Paul's Letter to the Galatians*. He has also published articles on 'The Silence of Jesus', 'Bultman and Hegel', 'The Synoptic Problem' and 'On the Resurrection as an Historical Problem'. He is a minister of the United Reformed Church, and Professor of New Testament at Westminster and Chestnut Colleges, Cambridge. J. C. O'Neill is married and has three daughters.

J. C. O'NEILL

PAUL'S LETTER TO THE ROMANS

PENGUIN BOOKS

Penguin Books Ltd, Harmondsworth, Middlesex, England
Penguin Books Inc., 7110 Ambassador Road, Baltimore, Maryland 21207, U.S.A.
Penguin Books Australia Ltd, Ringwood, Victoria, Australia
Penguin Books Canada Ltd, 41 Steelcase Road West, Markham, Ontario, Canada
Penguin Books (N.Z.) Ltd, 182–190 Wairau Road, Auckland 10, New Zealand

—

First published 1975
Copyright © J. C. O'Neill, 1975

Made and printed in Great Britain by
Cox & Wyman Ltd, London, Reading
and Fakenham
Set in Monotype Bembo

To my Parents

CONTENTS

ABBREVIATIONS

AV   *Authorized Version of the Bible* or *King James Version*, 1611.

LXX   The Septuagint, the Greek translation of the Old Testament and Apocrypha, thought to have been translated by seventy translators.

NEB   *The New English Bible:* The Old Testament and Apocrypha, 1970; The New Testament, 1961; second edition, 1970.

RSV   *Revised Standard Version of the Bible:* Old Testament, 1952; New Testament, 1946; second edition, 1952; revised, 1959.

(For the manuscripts cited, see pp. 275 ff.)

INTRODUCTION

The reader for whom this commentary is written might well expect that after nearly 2,000 years the experts would have got Paul's Epistle to the Romans straight, and that in these pages he would find a clear explanation of the great man's ideas. If this is what he expects, he will be disappointed.

It is not that there is not a consensus. The acknowledged experts, the commentators as eminent and varied as Chrysostom, Augustine, Aquinas, Calvin, Lipsius, Sanday and Headlam, and Dodd, may disagree fiercely about the interpretation of this verse or that idea, but they are united in believing that the words of the epistle were written by one man at one time to one audience.

In this commentary I have relied very heavily on their insights and interpretations; their skill and devotion cannot be too highly praised. But I believe, with one or two isolated men like Weisse and Loisy, that their whole set of assumptions is mistaken, and that the words of the epistle handed down to us were not written by one man, were not written at one time, were not written to one audience. Therefore this commentary cannot be a simple guide to a subject about which the experts, for all their debates and arguments, basically agree.

It is as if someone should come along and claim that Rembrandt's 'Night Watch' had been over-painted by painters who wanted to introduce the portraits of later town councillors into the original composition. Art critics who had previously identified the figures with Rembrandt's patrons, and who had explained the composition in terms of Rembrandt's mastery of form and colour, would have to put aside all their previous comments until they had taken account of this basic challenge to their assumptions. When they had succeeded in showing that the new claim was wrong they could happily go back to their old positions and continue with their analysis and exposition, but until this challenge was disposed of, their work would have to be suspended.

This commentary, then, is bound to be controversial, and the general reader who has opened this book in the hope of finding a plain guide to the subject may well feel aggrieved. Why should he be bothered with trying to follow a controversy which has hardly begun, and which promises to be long, technical, and bloody?

Yet there are two reasons why a commentary like this one can be offered to the general reader.

First, there does exist already in English a brilliant commentary which does fulfil the requirements the reader who opens this commentary would naturally make. C. H. Dodd's book, *The Epistle of Paul to the Romans*, written for the *Moffatt New Testament Commentary* forty years ago and still available as a paperback in Fontana Books, is an excellent guide to the way *Romans* can be interpreted on the assumption that Paul wrote all the words in our copies of the epistle. Dodd's *Romans* was written by a master of exposition, who is not afraid to let his own voice be heard, who addresses his readers as men and women capable of forming their own judgements about the great matters with which *Romans* is engaged. The very existence of his masterpiece excuses me from trying to repeat what he has done.

But why try to write about *Romans* on my radically new assumptions for the general reader at all? Shouldn't such a commentary be written in a technical style for the experts? Shouldn't the dust of battle have settled before the ordinary reader is invited once again to survey the disputed territory?

If *Romans* were like a play by Sophocles or a code of law belonging to some old civilization I could well agree. But *Romans* is a book of the Bible. Week in and week out *Romans* is read and pondered and appealed to by Christians who believe that the matters about which it speaks make a difference to the quality of their lives, and affect how they stand with God. Partly because of *Romans*, Christians are now divided from one another into Roman Catholics, Protestants, and Orthodox. Partly because of *Romans*, men have stopped being Christians. On the basis of *Romans*, Christian missionaries and apologists are still trying to win back men to the Christian faith or to persuade Moslems and Hindus and Buddhists to become Christians. The interpretation of *Romans* cannot so easily be left to the experts, although any new interpretation must be written in such a way that the expert can see at a glance the arguments that are being advanced so that he can either refute them or find them acceptable.

One thesis of this commentary is that the experts have gravely misunderstood Paul, and that the ordinary Christian who has tacitly ignored certain parts of the epistle and has quietly taken Paul in a different sense from the one adopted by the official theologians of his Church is often nearer the truth. Why, then, should the humble Christian, who cannot understand the subtleties of the official debates, be denied access to a book which shows, in a way he would never have thought of for himself, that he is right?

The ordinary Christian has not been a passive recipient of the theologians' interpretations of *Romans*. He has exercised the same discriminating power over the interpretations as he has over *Romans* itself, quietly accepting one strand while rejecting others. Therefore the ordinary Christian seems to have earned a right to hear directly an interpretation of *Romans* that supports his instinctive preferences. The official confessions of the Roman Catholic and Reformed Churches all declare, in various ways, the doctrine of predestination, which says that God has chosen some men and rejected others before they themselves did anything, and this doctrine is drawn from *Romans*. Few, if any, Christians now believe this doctrine, and no new confession of faith is likely to restate it, but there it is in the Bible and in the writings of the theologians and in the confessions of faith. More important, there it is in Paul. We cannot simply brush the teaching aside as a temporary aberration that can be disregarded, for a man's thought is a unity, whatever the tensions and even contradictions contained. The judgement we make on Paul cannot but be affected by the judgement we are bound to pass on an element as important as this. If he *did* believe that some, and only some, were predestined to eternal life before they had done anything at all either good or bad, we should have to reassess what he said about faith and morality. If we discovered a deep contradiction between the predestinarian part of his thought and the rest, we should have to conclude that he was a tragically split personality upon whose mental balance and wisdom we could scarcely rely – or that he was simply muddled. Yet almost any paragraph from his writings conveys a quite different impression. He can be so simple, direct and compelling that we can scarcely doubt his sanity or his greatness; here is no muddled thinker, playing with contradictions or torn by unresolved conflicts.

The solution put forward in this commentary is that Paul's original letter to the *Romans* has suffered two sorts of corruption, both of which have added new material to the text.

First, scribes, commentators, and editors have written short comments and explanations in the margin of their copies, and these have been copied into the text by mistake in later years. (Until the invention of printing each copy of *Romans* was a unique hand-written copy of an earlier manuscript.)

Second, editors added longer sections to *Romans*, usually drawn from old traditions, in order to supplement the epistle and to make it more suitable for general use. These additions could have been quite long and detailed, although many were short, so short that the line between a *gloss* and an *interpolation* is hard to draw. (A gloss is a short explanatory note, and an interpolation a longer insertion of new material.)

Scholars have long worked on the assumption that books of the Old Testament underwent these two sorts of expansion before they reached the form we have, but they have been reluctant to admit this possibility for New Testament writings.

Admittedly it is hard to see how various additions made to different manuscripts at different times should have produced such a uniformly attested text. How do a paragraph added in one manuscript and an explanatory note added in another come together in the one recognized text? The answer must be that at various stages in the transmission of the text powerful editors collected together as many manuscripts as possible and made a standard edition which became the one uniformly copied thereafter in that part of the church.

Fortunately there are plenty of phrases and short comments that are omitted by a sufficient number of manuscripts of *Romans* for us to see that the process of standardizing and editing had gone on over the centuries; the general reader can see this quite easily by comparing the Authorized Version, which was based on Greek manuscripts mainly representing the edition of the Greek text standardized about the end of the fourth century, with the Revised Standard Version, based on manuscripts mainly representing the edition of the Greek text produced perhaps in the third century. For example, the Authorized Version of Romans 1.3 begins 'concerning his Son Jesus Christ our Lord', for which the Revised Standard Version has simply 'concerning his Son'; a scribe once added the full name of God's Son, either in the margin or as he copied the text, and this addition became part of the official text of *Romans* in the fourth-century revision. All scholars freely admit that such expansions took place, but most are reluctant to entertain the possibility that the process may have gone on in passages where only one or two manuscripts, or even none at all that we possess, provide evidence of corruption. Again, New Testament scholars are much more reluctant than Old Testament scholars to admit just how likely it is that all our manuscripts are affected by editorial additions.

The case for assuming that numerous small (and often trivial) additions have crept into our texts is quite strong, but it may appear more difficult to argue that longer passages – paragraphs or whole chapters – have been added to Paul's letter. Yet even here evidence is not lacking. The doxology printed at the end of *Romans*, 16.25–27, is widely recognized as not written by Paul because of its style, vocabulary, and thought. In this case the evidence in the passage itself is confirmed by evidence from the manuscripts. Most manuscripts contain the passage, although not in the same position, and there are three or four manuscripts that do not contain it at all.

Perhaps another passage, 13.1–7, is also an example. Although it occurs in all our manuscripts, its thought is strangely different from Paul's casual remarks elsewhere on the same subject, and no Christian writer before about A.D. 180 ever refers to it or quotes it.

So there are scraps of evidence from outside *Romans* suggesting that Paul's original letter has been interpolated. In the commentary that follows I have gone on to argue that *Romans* itself, when read attentively, provides clues to indicate that the process of interpolation was much greater than the external evidence shows, and this is much harder to prove. The paucity of external evidence of large interpolations might be taken as indicating that successive scribes and editors guarded the text strictly against addition, but the same evidence could be a sign that many more passages were once added to Paul, and that successive editors made sure that a standard agreed text was eventually circulated as authoritative by the Church. The strictures against omitting anything of value may well have been strong enough to ensure that all evidence of a shorter *Romans* would be suppressed.

We do in fact know that a shorter *Romans* was once promulgated, and that the orthodox theologians combined to denounce this edition as false and misleading. The shorter *Romans* was edited and published by Marcion. He held that the true text of the epistle consisted of, roughly, 1.1–18; 2; 3.1–30; 5; 6; 7; 8; 10.1–4; 11.33–12.21; 13.8–14.23, omitting about six chapters of our epistle. It is very unlikely that Marcion's editing really did recover the original letter, and to that extent the arguments brought against him, that he cut out what did not suit his theology, were correct. But the fact that he felt justified in making the attempt is evidence that the attempt itself was not implausible. The very fury of the attack upon him would ensure that almost all the true evidence that some passages were not present in all copies of *Romans* would be lost.

In the end, the only way to discover whether or not our *Romans* conceals within it a shorter letter from Paul together with later additions is to read the text with all senses alert to the possibility that other words have been added to an original letter.

The dangers of this quest are obvious. A modern editor may, like Marcion, be intent, consciously or unconsciously, on ascribing to Paul only those ideas with which he himself is in sympathy. He may be trying all the time to rescue Paul's logic when Paul's logic was wrong. He may be trying to simplify what should be left complex. He may be trying to turn Paul into a modern man by shearing away everything that offends modern susceptibilities.

These are dangers, but against them can be set the danger of leaving *Romans* so obscure, so complicated, so disjointed, that it is hard to see how Paul could have exerted such an influence on his contemporaries. It is after all suspicious that a document consisting of only sixteen chapters seems to need hundreds of pages of commentary in order to make clear what the author was getting at, and even then it is not entirely clear.

Dangers recognized are dangers guarded against. In this commentary I have tried always to give full weight to everything that is said in the epistle, every sentence and every idea. It could be argued in my support that the approach I have adopted will be freer to allow every idea its full significance, for, unlike the traditional commentators, I will not always be trying to reconcile every thought with the neighbouring thought and every idea with all the other ideas to be found in Paul's writings. The man who is trying to harmonize each detail with the whole set of ideas runs the risk of missing the force of what he is reading, just as the man who assumes that all his friends think like him misses the savour of the variety of his friends, and even positively misrepresents his friends' opinions.

In fact it has long been known that Paul's writings seem to convey two quite different views of how men may be reconciled to God. The scholar who pointed this out most clearly was Albert Schweitzer. He himself thought he could tell a story about Paul's development which would explain how two different theories could live together, and ever since he put forward his daring theory lesser scholars have been repeating and modifying and qualifying his basically simple synthesis.

Schweitzer argued that

in Paul's writings there are two independent conceptions of the forgiveness of sins. According to the one, God forgives in consequence of the atoning death of Jesus; according to the other, He forgives, because through the dying and rising again with Christ He has caused the flesh and sin to be abolished together, so that those who have died and risen with Christ are, in the eyes of God, sinless beings. The former of these doctrines is traditional, the latter is peculiar to Paul, and is a consequence of the mystical being-in-Christ. (*The Mysticism of Paul the Apostle*, p. 223).

Schweitzer was well aware of theories like mine that tried to show that Paul's original letter had been added to by theologians of another cast of mind, and he deals brilliantly (and devastatingly) with them in Chapter 5 of his pioneering work, *Paul and His Interpreters*, but he did not ignore the problem and he worked hard to discover a synthesizing principle to overcome the split in Paul's thought.

He tried and he failed, and the best tribute we can pay him is to put aside his theory and the terms in which he stated the split in order to see whether we can't construct a better story and a better explanation of the nature of *Romans*.

We have to take a larger view of Paul's interpreters than Schweitzer. He confined himself mainly to the work done in the nineteenth century, but we are called on to understand the whole debate through 2,000 years of Church history about Paul's central theme.

Paul's central theme is the *righteousness of God*. (We have to stick to the rather unusual word *righteousness* because of the need not to prejudice the discussion about meaning, but if we think of *righteousness* as true goodness we shan't be far out.) Those two Greek words have fascinated theologians ever since *Romans* has been studied, and the debates about those two words have had a more profound effect on the life of the Church and the intellectual life of the West than any other ideas that have ever been discussed. If we can discover what Paul meant by the *righteousness of God* we shall not only have a measuring rod to judge the most important and divisive events of Christian history, but we shall have found the scarlet thread to guide us through the labyrinth of our present text of *Romans*.

Theologians and commentators have, almost without exception, assumed that Paul meant by the *righteousness of God* God's own righteousness which he graciously gives to sinful men. What man lacks, God gives. The disputes have always been about how God imparts the gift he alone can give.

The Catholic tradition has been that God imparts righteousness by infusing it into men, who thus become righteous and acceptable to him. How he imparts righteousness, when, and how completely, what man can do, must do, and cannot do have all been discussed and disputed, but here is one clear body of tradition about Paul's thought that has always persisted and been wonderfully powerful in helping to make saints out of sinners.

This tradition was sharply challenged at the Reformation. The Reformers took one strand of this tradition, a strand already present, although less prominent, in Augustine, and made it central to Paul and central to the Bible. They argued that God imputed his righteousness rather than imparted it, ascribing righteousness to men who actually were not righteous. He declared that some sinners were righteous, and, according to this view, the sinners who had been so favoured by his grace should look for nothing in themselves and only fix their attention on the author of the unmerited favour they enjoyed.

This tradition, too, has produced lives of great strength and sanctity, and an intellectual system of astonishing brilliance and power.

But what if both systems, the Catholic and the Reformed, have mistaken Paul's basic term and misinterpreted his message? This seems an almost incredible question, given the learning and diligence of the theologians of all ages who have grappled with the problem. And yet the assumption behind both systems leads to a view of God which contains great difficulties and is hard to reconcile with the teaching of Jesus and the teaching of the Old Testament. If God chooses to give his righteousness (either by *imparting* it through *infusion* or by *imputing* it through his *sovereign decree*), he seems to be overruling the wills of men, whom he is supposed to have created free to serve him or to reject him. He seems either to make black white by a mysterious process of change, or to declare black white by an unchallengeable declaration. His justice becomes suspect.

Of course this difficulty was seen and recognized, but the alternative seemed so out of the question that Christian theologians united to reject it. The alternative seems to be that men had to become righteous by their own efforts, and the testimony of human experience, not to mention the explicit statements of Paul, ruled out that possibility from the start. Sinners had to become righteous, and no theologian could solve the problem by supposing that some sinners would actually be righteous. Anyone who has eyes for the human situation can see that.

As I have worked through *Romans* again and again with my students, I have come across key verses, in particular 1.17, where Paul seems to be saying something different from all this. Perhaps Paul *was* saying something quite different. Perhaps theologians couldn't listen to what he was saying because they were trying all the time to reconcile his words with the words of other theologians who had added sections to *Romans* and who conceived of God and sinners differently.

There is another possible translation of the phrase *the righteousness of God*, a translation put forward by Luther and many others. It is possible to take the words to mean 'the righteousness that God approves'. This other translation can, of course, be incorporated into either the Catholic or the Reformed theology, because the righteousness God approves can either be the righteousness he infuses into his chosen ones, or the righteousness he imputes to them. But these interpretations are not the most natural interpretations to put on Paul's words when Paul's words are taken alone without the attempt to combine the ideas in one passage with all the other ideas to be found in *Romans*. The most natural interpretation of Paul's thought is quite different.

Paul taught that the righteousness God approves is attained by the man who lives by faith. If a man trusts God and believes his promises and accepts God's gifts, above all the gift of his Son, he becomes righteous. This is no instantaneous affair but a character of life that is to be lived from day to day. The man who is faithful, who trusts and believes God, is enabled to live righteously despite his weaknesses, his lapses into sin, and his mistakes. He will in the end be found to be righteous, however much he has yet to purge away because of the sins he has committed. God gives men the choice. They may become righteous or may reject righteousness. It would be better if men never sinned, but they do, and God has revealed a way that sinners can become righteous. That is the simple joy of Paul's message, which subtle men in all innocence have obscured, first by overlaying Paul's original letter with commentary, and then by constructing the magnificent systems that have dominated the history of the church. Despite this obscuring of the message, the truth has never been entirely lost. Christians have always gone on reading the passages that ring true; they have concentrated on the gospels rather than on Paul, or on the parts of Paul that seemed most helpful in their daily struggles to live. Great theologians, Tertullian, Origen, Aquinas, Erasmus, have fought tenaciously to preserve man's freedom, however threatened they see this freedom by sin and habit and force of circumstance. They have helped men find the way to *become* righteous, even though hindered by a false idea of what they thought loyalty to Paul's thought required. They played down the awful doctrines of determinism or predestination, and pleaded with men to exercise their God-given freedom to choose the path of righteousness.

We are now in a position, if I am anywhere near the truth, to rediscover Paul's message. That is why this complicated and difficult quest cannot be left to the experts, although all the expertise that the church can muster will be needed for the quest. Nothing less is at stake than the simplicity and credibility of the gospel. Men are searching for God and for his righteousness with an earnestness and persistence that has not been seen for hundreds of years. More men can read and have been taught to think about themselves and their lives than ever before. If Paul has anything still to say, he must be heard and heard clearly. That is the final justification for a commentary that is complicated, difficult, and precarious at every turn.

Although I do set Paul's own message above the work of those who added glosses and longer comments, I do not wish to reject the comments or to deny their value. There are a few passages that seem to me wrongly conceived and hateful (for example, those that teach predestination and the section on the state at the beginning of Chapter 13) – and even here I can understand how they arose, and what truths they were trying, unsuccessfully, to preserve. The additions were drawn from the great body of Jewish and Christian theology, as well as from philosophical reflection that occurred outside the Jewish-Christian tradition, and most of the ideas to be found within these sections are plainly valuable and worth hearing. We can judge; we can distinguish the good from the bad, the true from the false, and there is nothing wrong in trying to discriminate as we read *Romans*. Such discrimination is not an attack on the idea that the words of *Romans* bring us revelation from God. If it is revelation, we may expect to feel the power of the words in our bones, as it were, and the effort to understand and distinguish and to judge can be the way to see that it is God who is speaking. Paul's own ideas as well as those of his commentators must also be subjected to the same scrutiny, and from that scrutiny, I believe, they emerge triumphant.

I have tried to make reading a difficult commentary as easy as possible. At the head of each section is an essay in which the main issues are discussed and the broad conclusions stated. Then follows a series of notes on individual verses in which a more detailed effort is made to argue the case for a particular interpretation. There is no index, but at the end of the book will be found a list of the manuscripts cited, with some explanatory notes, and a list of all the names mentioned with the key facts about the lives of these men and details of important books they have written bearing on *Romans*.

I have added a translation of the letter I suppose that Paul wrote to the Romans. This is followed by a list of the verses I argue are not by Paul and the verses where I suggest a different text from the text on which the Revised Standard Version is based.

I should like to have provided in this commentary an unobtrusive guide to *Romans*; to have been like a skilfully-directed television camera sweeping over the building, with a pause here and there to pick out a significant detail. But *Romans* seemed to demand something different. So here is, rather, a magnifying-glass, with which to detect cracks and joints, and a chisel, with which to test whether stones that had always seemed to belong together can be prised apart. The work of using these tools is much harder than seeing *Romans* through the television camera's eyes, but if *Romans* is as important a book as we know it to be the labour cannot be wasted, whatever the outcome. The work is not destructive – *Romans* cannot be destroyed – but analytic. It is all done in preparation for the moment of vision.

The indirect method of hard work on this ancient document may be the way by which we are surprised into recognition of ourselves and of God.

COMMENTARY

1.1–7

1 Paul, a servant[a] of Jesus Christ, called to be an apostle, set apart for the gospel of God ²which he promised beforehand through his prophets in the holy scriptures, ³the gospel concerning his Son, who was descended from David according to the flesh ⁴and designated Son of God in power according to the Spirit of holiness by his resurrection from the dead, Jesus Christ our Lord, ⁵through whom we have received grace and apostleship to bring about the obedience of faith for the sake of his name among all the nations, ⁶including yourselves who are called to belong to Jesus Christ;

⁷To all God's beloved in Rome, who are called to be saints:
Grace to you and peace from God our Father and the Lord Jesus Christ.

[a] Or slave.

The usual introduction to a letter in Paul's day was as simple as possible. The sender gave his own name first, then the name of the person he was addressing, and finally the one word, 'Greeting': 'Demophon to Ptolemaeus, greeting'.

Affectionate letters could be elaborated a little: 'Apion to Epimarchus his father and lord, heartiest greetings'; but a bare greeting was no sign of lack of affection, as we see from an Egyptian letter of the third century B.C.: 'Polycrates to his father, greeting'. Official letters were naturally more formal, and therefore fuller: 'Claudius Lysias to his Excellency the governor Felix, greeting' (Acts 23.26); 'James, a servant of God and of the Lord Jesus Christ, to the twelve tribes in the Dispersion, greeting' (James 1.1; cf. Acts 15.23).

The first thing that distinguishes Paul's salutation from the common form is that the third part, the greeting from the writer to the recipients, is replaced by a divine blessing. This seems to have been fairly common in the Middle East alongside the more secular form mentioned above. For example: 'Baruch the son of Neriah says to the brothers carried into captivity: Mercy and peace be with you' (2 Baruch 78.2).

Paul always ends his salutations with a blessing. This explains, I think, the additions he usually makes to the earlier parts of the salutation in which he sets out and even defends his credentials and specifies the status of the recipients. The blessing of God is pronounced by one who can rightly pronounce such a blessing, on those who have been called to receive it.

This sort of expansion could make the salutation very long. Nevertheless, it does not explain the length of the salutation in two cases, at the beginning of the *Epistle to Titus*, and here in *Romans*. The expansion is of another kind: these two salutations not only give Paul's credentials, but they also set out the substance of the Christian message. Dodd has already suggested in the case of *Romans* that in vv. 3 and 4 (down to 'by his resurrection from the dead') 'it is probable that Paul is citing more or less exactly a common confession of faith which would be known and recognized at Rome'. Bultmann has followed up this idea and attempted a reconstruction of the confession:

[Jesus Christ] the Son of God,
Come from the seed of David,
Designated Son of God in power by his resurrection from the dead.

(Theology, i.49)

The weakness of the theory that Paul is citing a creed is that he goes on to make no further use of the specific terms of this particular creed in his subsequent argument. This section completely overloads the salutation and makes it a grammatical monstrosity, which no one writer would have perpetrated, and it looks very like a later insertion.

Fortunately we have a Greek manuscript (G) which does not contain the credal statement, and which reveals the proper connection of ideas in the salutation. This manuscript reads: 'Paul, servant of Jesus Christ, called an apostle among all the Gentiles on his behalf.' It is hard to imagine a scribe omitting such a long and important section, even by accident, and therefore I conclude that the long section was a marginal comment or interpolation, which was incorporated very early into the standard texts of *Romans*.

The interpolation is an ancient summary of 'the gospel of God', which originally had no special connection with the office of apostle.

In v. 5 the words 'and apostleship' seem to have been inserted to make such a connection, but they do so at the expense of obscuring the surrounding thought.

What does this ancient creed affirm? Some very important scholars, William Wrede and Johannes Weiss at the turn of the century, and Weiss's pupil Rudolf Bultmann, have extracted from these verses the theory that at least part of the early Church believed that Jesus the son of David became 'Lord' only at his resurrection. The RSV translation rather supports this interpretation.

However, the parallelism between the two clauses 'from the seed of David' and 'Son of God' makes this interpretation hard to sustain, for the first clause ends with the key phrase 'according to the flesh' and we should expect the second clause to end also with the key phrase in parallel, 'according to the Spirit of holiness'. It doesn't. The words 'by the resurrection from the dead' are yet to come, and they completely destroy the otherwise strict symmetry. Pelagius gives evidence of a text which did not contain these words, and I take them to be a gloss by a scribe who could not understand why the central event of the resurrection had been left out. He would recall, perhaps, 2 Tim. 2.8, 'Remember Jesus Christ, risen from the dead, descended from David, as preached in my gospel', and repair the omission in his copy.

The ancient creed possibly went like this:

The Gospel of God is:

That which he promised through his prophets in the Holy Scriptures,
Concerning his Son who was to be of the seed of David according
    to the flesh,
Designated Son of God in power according to the Holy Spirit,
Our Lord through whom we have received grace faithfully to obey.

This creed refers to the two natures of the Son of God, and seems to assume the virginal conception. According to his mother's flesh he was of David's house, and according to the work of the Holy Spirit he was powerfully marked out as Son of God. The work of the Son of God is to call men who acknowledge him as Lord and receive the gift of faithful obedience to God the Father.

There are two similar credal statements preserved in the Epistles of

Ignatius: 'For our God, Jesus the Messiah, was conceived by Mary according to God's plan from the seed of David and of the Holy Spirit' (Ephesians 18.2); '. . . concerning our Lord, that he was truly of the family of David according to the flesh, Son of God according to the will and power of God, truly born of a virgin . . . (Smyrnaeans I.I).

When this creed is set to one side, Paul's original salutation begins to shine out in all its clarity and simplicity. The only obscurity lies in v. 6. Salutations invariably keep off the second person until the blessing. The two parties involved, the writer and his readers, have to be established from outside, as it were, before the writer can address his readers directly. Verse 6, with the words *including yourselves*, breaks this rule, and in a most surprising way. Before the recipients are even mentioned, they are addressed. In fact the remark in v. 6 assumes that the recipients have already been named, and seems to be a comment on the phrase *among all the nations*. Whenever we find a remark which explains something, and assumes that we have already read something that follows, we may suspect a gloss. Glossators are always trying to clear up difficulties, and their remarks are easily copied into the text at a point prior to part of the information they assume to be known. We may suspect a gloss in this case, although there is no textual evidence for this hypothesis.

There is a great deal of textual disturbance in the next verse, which I have tried to sort out in the notes. Assuming the results for which I argue there, Paul's salutation originally read as follows:

Paul, servant of Christ Jesus, by call apostle to all the Gentiles, on his behalf; to all at Rome who are by call saints; grace to you and peace, from God our Father, and the Lord Jesus Christ.

Paul has been called into the service of the risen Lord Jesus Christ to carry his name to the Gentiles so that they may share the blessing which has come to Israel. He writes to the Christians in Rome, a group of Christians for whom he has been in no way responsible, and greets them with an apostolic greeting. 'Grace and peace' means 'the gift of peace'. This gift is not Paul's to give, but he pronounces the blessing in confidence that God will give what his servant says he will give. Jesus promised the disciples just this power (Matt. 16.19; 18.18;

Luke 10.5 f.; Mark 11.23 f.; John 20.23). The gift is from *our* Father –
again in line with Jesus's teaching about God – and from the reigning
Lord, Jesus Christ. 'Lord' is the title of the Messiah (Psalm 110.1), and
the resurrection has confirmed that Jesus is he.

Notes

1
Paul: the writer probably always had two names, the Jewish name Saul
and the Roman form Paul. Acts 13.9 is drawing attention to this fact in
the account of how the first prominent convert, the pro-consul Sergius
Paulus, was defended by 'Paulus' the missionary from the wiles of a
magician.

servant: in ordinary Greek 'slave', but not so in a Biblical context,
where Abraham, Moses, David, and the prophets are called God's
servants.

Jesus Christ: Jesus is an Aramaic name (Joshua in Hebrew). Christ is a
title, equivalent to Messiah in Hebrew, and meaning An Anointed One.
But it has now become a name; when those who believed Jesus was the
final Messiah said 'Christ' they meant Jesus. Wellhausen compares the
way Man in Genesis 1 (*adam* in Hebrew) became a name, Adam. The
double name Jesus Christ is like the Latin double name Julius Caesar.

called to be an apostle: by God.

apostle: two Church Fathers, Eusebius and Epiphanius, tell us that the
word was used in Jewish circles for messengers sent by the rabbinic
authorities to scattered communities with specific tasks. If that is a
proper parallel to the term (and no better, in my view, has been suggested) we must note the decisive shift in meaning brought about by
the Christian context. The Christian Apostles are appointed directly by
God, not by human organizations (Gal. 1.1), and they have a permanent
not a temporary task: to preach Christ (Gal. 1.16). Paul had to fight for
recognition as an Apostle, although the term had not as yet been
restricted to the Twelve. His use of the title here is one more indication
that Paul is writing to the Romans with authority. This is no purely
private letter of greeting, but written to further the plans of God who
called Paul to be apostle to all the Gentiles.

set apart: the term signifies ordination to a ministry which separates one
believer from his fellow believers, and the tense – the Greek perfect –

concentrates attention on the continuing status rather than on the moment of ordination.

for the gospel of God: 'gospel' here means the statement of the key beliefs that a man may hold and so be saved. The word in other contexts can mean 'good news' in a general sense, or even simply 'news'; or it can mean the activity of preaching; and later on it came to be the description of the sort of book in which the whole story of Jesus Christ was set down. I prefer the first meaning in this context to all the other possible meanings, because of the phrase '*concerning* his Son' (v.3). Consequently, the words 'of God' mean that God is the author and giver of this gospel, not that the gospel is about him.

2

which he promised beforehand through his prophets in the holy scriptures: the reference is to specific passages in the Old Testament which are now seen to refer to the incarnation of the Son of God. 'Holy scriptures' appears nowhere else in the New Testament, although the term 'scriptures' is used, and Paul constantly appeals to verses from the Old Testament to illustrate and support his arguments.

his Son: the Messiah of the family of David is to be God's Son according to 2 Sam. 7.14 ff. (1 Chron. 17.13 ff.) and Psalm 2.7. Some parts of later Judaism avoided calling the Messiah 'Son of God', and Origen, *Against Celsus* i.49, thought this was a universal rule. But he himself preserves evidence that this was not universally the case, because he is criticizing the formulation of messianic belief conveyed to his opponent Celsus many years before by a Jew whom we know otherwise to be remarkably reliable. Consequently, the theory of Bousset that the Son of God as a title for Christ first appeared outside the circle of primitive Jewish Christianity is unlikely to be right. Evidence found in the fourth cave at Qumran tends to support the view that the Jews who wrote the writings preserved there spoke of the Messiah as God's Son.

3, 4

who was descended from David according to the flesh and designated Son of God in power according to the Spirit of holiness: I have given above some reasons for taking the two parts of this statement as in parallel. 'The Spirit of holiness' is another way, not found elsewhere in the New Testament, of saying 'the Holy Spirit' (Testament of Levi 18.11), and not a way of referring to Jesus's spirit as opposed to his flesh. I am therefore inclined to paraphrase the statement in these terms: 'who came, according to fleshly descent, of David's seed; marked off, according to the work of the Holy Spirit, as God's Son in power'. The verbs are different in force, and therefore demand that the 'according to' phrases dependent on them be taken differently. The RSV translates the second verb as 'designated'. It can mean 'appoint', but, in parallel to the earlier verb, should probably here receive the root meaning of 'to mark off', meaning from other human beings.

If, as I have argued in the essay above, the following words, 'by his resurrection from the dead', do not belong to the formula at all, there is little doubt that both clauses refer to the conception of Jesus, and not to his birth on the one hand and the later event of his resurrection on the other hand. But if I am wrong about this, it is worth pointing out that the early Church, had it held that Jesus was designated Son of God at the resurrection, would not have concluded that he was less than Son of God before the moment of open announcement. (See Acts 2.36 for the resurrection as God's enthronement of the man whom from the beginning of his ministry he 'attested', Acts 2.22.)

4

by his resurrection from the dead: the Greek is more compressed and cryptic than this rendering: 'from resurrection of dead'. Nevertheless, the RSV translation probably gives the right sense. Some copies of Pelagius's commentary do not have these words at the head of the comment, and they disturb the flow in two ways: they add another phrase after the second 'according to' phrase, with which we should expect the parallelism to end; and they use the preposition 'from' in a confusingly different way from its use in the first half of the parallel. But if this phrase is a gloss, what did the glossator mean by the note? I think he understood the words 'in power' as implying a contrast between an earlier stage when Jesus was Son of God in weakness and hiddenness, and he remarked that the moment of the assumption of power was the moment of resurrection. The words 'in power', however, do not necessarily imply what the glossator thought they implied; they simply modify the verb: powerfully marked off.

Jesus Christ our Lord: this phrase resumes the words 'concerning his Son' in v. 3. The words 'Jesus Christ' occur after 'our Lord' in Augustine (iii.2092), and I suspect that they were originally absent from the creed. In that case this fourth part of the creed would begin with the definite article agreeing with the same article in the earlier parts, all dependent on 'concerning':

> concerning *the* son of his, *the* one who came . . .
> *the* one marked off . . .
> *the* Lord of ours . . .

Lord: there is an implicit reference to the resurrection in the term 'Lord'. The Aramaic-speaking church called the enthroned Messiah 'our Lord' in the prayer 'Our Lord, come', *Marana tha* (I Cor. 16.22; Rev. 22.17,20; Didache 10.6). This address to Jesus was suggested by Psalm 110, where King David is said to announce, 'The Lord said to *my lord*, sit at my right hand until I put your enemies under your feet'. Jesus himself had already drawn attention to this Psalm in order to teach that the Messiah was to be more than David's son; he was to be the Lord whom God would enthrone while the last battles against his enemies were being fought (Mark 12.36, a passage suspected of being made up later by the church, but with little justification; a later fabricator would have been more careful to exclude the possibility that Jesus might have been denying descent from David).

5

grace: both in ordinary Greek and in the Greek of the LXX translation of the Old Testament grace means primarily favour, kindness, or the expression of kindness, a gift. Here favour is the dominant meaning. God's favour is meant, received through our Lord.

and apostleship: to the argument in the introductory section above that these words are a gloss, add the consideration that they confuse the issue terribly when we come to decide the reference of the next phrase. Who are to obey, those who have received apostleship, or those to whom they are sent? Without these words, it is pretty clear that those who have received grace are to obey; with these words, it seems the Gentiles are to obey, but the decision is difficult because the Gentiles do not come in until after the doubtful phrase. The insertion was made in order to link the creed to Paul's original salutation.

to bring about the obedience of faith: we who have received God's favour through our Lord Jesus Christ consequently obey that Lord. The pre-1959 RSV translation, *to bring about obedience to the faith* (cf. AV) which makes the faith that which is obeyed, is not so likely as the translation adopted after 1959 which allows that the Lord is the one obeyed. We may translate the Greek, which is literally 'the obedience of faith', as 'the obedience that consists of faith': Our Lord through whom we have received grace so that we obey him in faith.

among all the nations: as I have argued in the introductory section, Paul's original salutation resumed with these words, which followed 'called to be an apostle' in v. 1. Everything in between was a cited creed, made originally by a commentator who wished to set out the message an apostle would proclaim, and whose remark was later copied into the text. 'Nations' is a technical term for the non-Jewish nations, the Gentiles. Paul believed he had been entrusted with the special task of calling Gentiles as Gentiles to become children of Abraham by receiving God's grace through the Lord Jesus Christ. They were to remain Gentiles, and had not first to become proselytes, that is, Jews, or even to attach themselves to the Jewish synagogues that believed Jesus was Messiah.

for the sake of his name: probably an idiom meaning 'on his behalf'. Paul acts for Jesus Christ, who has commissioned him.

6

including yourselves who are called to belong to Jesus Christ: I have argued in the introductory section above that Paul could hardly have addressed the recipients of the letter in the second person before the formal naming of them in the third person, which has yet to come. The verse is, therefore, a gloss, which was later copied into the text. As it stands, this verse implies that the Roman Christians are Gentiles. Some of them may have been, but the form of this remark would imply that the bulk of them were. That is impossible, because Paul never mentions any forerunners in his special task of establishing Gentile congregations as such (see especially Gal. 2). It follows that the words 'including yourselves' originally referred to some other part of the text. I think the reference was to v. 7, possibly in its universal form; v. 7 in this form reads, 'to all those who are in the love of God called saints', and a commentator added, for his own audience, 'among whom are you also, you called of Jesus Christ'. The phrase 'called of Jesus Christ' is strange. The word 'called' never has a genitive after it like this in the New Testament. On the Old Testament analogy of 1 Kings 1.41,49 the phrase would mean 'guests of Jesus Christ', which does not seem to fit here. I think 'called' has become a technical term for Christians, as in Barnabas 4.13, and the whole phrase is in the vocative, 'O you called of Jesus Christ'.

7

To all God's beloved in Rome, who are called to be saints: most manuscripts read (1) To all those being in Rome beloved of God called saints. One Greek manuscript, G, reads (2) To all those being in the love of God called saints. Origen on *Romans* probably reads (3) To all those being beloved of God (called saints?); some Latin manuscripts, Ambrosiaster, and Pelagius read (4) To all those being in Rome in the love of God called saints; and finally the Greek and Latin manuscript Ee reads (5)

To all those being in Rome called saints. Some notable scholars, including Theodor Zahn and Adolf von Harnack, have thought that the reading (2) was original, although they still held that the epistle was meant for Rome, accepting the universal ancient testimony, as well as the reading 'in Rome' in 1.15. Alexander Pallis, in omitting all reference to Rome, goes further, and argues that the epistle was originally pseudonymous and not addressed to Rome at all. Hans Lietzmann is more likely to be right, that 'in Rome' was omitted by a later scribe to show that the letter was of universal application. The probable stages in the story of the text, to produce the five readings above, were these: reading (5) represents what Paul originally wrote; an editor who copied the epistle for universal use substituted 'in the love of God' for 'in Rome', to produce reading (2); this change was taken as an addition to the original text in reading (4); the change was assimilated to the form of 'called saints' and became 'beloved of God' (see reading 2); and finally, in the assimilated form, came to rest in the overwhelming number of manuscripts representing the standard text (1).

called to be saints: God's call is to holiness, 'for we must all appear before the judgment seat of Christ to receive each as he did while in the body, whether good or ill' (2 Cor. 5.10).

Grace to you and peace: perhaps two nouns to represent what we would express as 'the favour of peace'. Peace is primarily peace with God; if God has in his favour established peace and reconciliation with them, there is nothing that can disturb their joy. The blessing is pronounced by Paul in confidence that God bestows what his servants ask for.

from God our Father and the Lord Jesus Christ: Jesus Christ is the Lord because God has raised him from the dead to reign 'at his right hand'. Those who acknowledge him as Lord become sons of God and call him 'our Father'.

1.8–17

⁸*First, I thank my God through Jesus Christ for all of you, because your faith is proclaimed in all the world.* ⁹*For God is my witness, whom I serve with my spirit in the gospel of his Son, that without ceasing I mention you always in my prayers,* ¹⁰*asking that somehow by God's will I may now at last succeed in coming to you.* ¹¹*For I long to see you, that I may impart to*

you some spiritual gift to strengthen you, [12]*that is, that we may be mutually encouraged by each other's faith, both yours and mine.* [13]*I want you to know, brethren, that I have often intended to come to you (but thus far have been prevented), in order that I may reap some harvest among you as well as among the rest of the Gentiles.* [14]*I am under obligation both to Greeks and to barbarians, both to the wise and to the foolish:* [15]*so I am eager to preach the gospel to you also who are in Rome.*

[16]*For I am not ashamed of the gospel: it is the power of God for salvation to every one who has faith, to the Jew first and also to the Greek.* [17]*For in it the righteousness of God is revealed through faith for faith; as it is written, 'He who through faith is righteous shall live.'*[b]

[b] *Or The righteous shall live by faith.*

In our present text, this passage gives the impression that Paul first hypocritically flatters the Romans, in order then to persuade them to listen to his arguments, which really cut against their own cherished understanding of the faith. This, however, is a misleading interpretation of Paul's true attitude to the Roman Church; the opening statement, 'I thank my God through Jesus Christ for you all, because your faith is proclaimed throughout the whole world', is a perfectly genuine expression of Paul's gratitude, and the whole section does nothing to detract from this initial warmth. The epistle is not written to change the mind of the Roman Church, but to win their support for his work among Gentiles.

The usual renderings of this passage suggest, however, that Paul is coming to Rome to preach to the Roman Christians, to admonish them, with the implication that they need to know the gospel. Of course, the very length of the epistle shows that Paul must argue his case, but the opening thanksgiving for their faith is a sign that he can assume agreement about the fundamentals: the saints in Rome, as everywhere, live by faith.

Paul calls God to witness that the name of the Romans is constantly in his prayers, because he is always praying God to open the way for him to come to them. Paul's desire is to see the Romans, to impart to them some spiritual gift from God, but above all to be strengthened with them, so that, with their support, he could preach to Gentiles in Rome too. His special apostolic task and duty was to preach to Gentiles. This point has been obscured by a scribal error in v. 15, which suggests that the Roman Christians needed the gospel preached to them; the original text of vv. 14 and 15 read, 'to Greeks and non-Greeks, to educated and uneducated I have a duty, hence my desire to preach to those in Rome as well'.

It needed a brave man to preach to Gentiles, but Paul ascribes his confidence to the power of God inherent in the gospel. This power can save a man from destruction, if only he believes. In the gospel is revealed to the man who goes from faith to faith the righteousness acceptable to God. As it is written in the Bible, the righteous man shall live by faith (Habakkuk 2.4).

The whole section is dominated by the word 'faith'. Clearly Paul here means by faith the loving and trusting confidence in God which men display when they forget themselves and fix all their attention and expectation on him for what he has done for them and will do for them in Christ. The gospel calls for this faith, and the men who live by faith live righteously in God's sight, and will therefore be saved from destruction.

Notes

9

in the gospel of his Son: in the activity of preaching the gospel concerning God's Son.

9, 10

that without ceasing I mention you always in my prayers, asking that . . .: it is better to punctuate with a comma after 'I mention you' so that one adverb, 'without ceasing', goes with the first verb, and the other adverb, 'always', goes with the second verb. 'For God is my witness whom I serve . . . in preaching the gospel of his Son, that I am constantly making mention of you, always in my prayers asking whether I will finally succeed, by God's will, in coming to you'.

11 f.

to strengthen you: literally, 'so that you might be strengthened'. Something has gone wrong with the text. Verse 12, *that is,* implies a connection, or the substitution of a more felicitous expression. However, the suggestion of another verb, 'mutually encouraged', for the first verb, 'strengthened', does not help if the subject of the first verb

remains 'you'. I conjecture that the pronoun 'you' at the end of
v. 11 is a scribal gloss. Paul wrote, 'For I long to see you in order to
impart to you some spiritual gift (from God), so that there may be
strengthening, I mean, the reception of mutual comfort in your company, through the faith which is in each of us, yours and mine'. Paul
has, by the grace of God, something to give; but he also has something
to get.

13

some harvest among you as well as among the rest of the Gentiles: Paul
excludes the possibility of preaching where others have preached
before, in his important remarks at the end of *Romans* (15.15–25). He
cannot, then, mean that he wants to preach to the circle of the Roman
congregation. That circle, I take it, would be the rest of the Jews in
Rome, who had not accepted Jesus Christ. *Among you* must mean
something like 'in your city'. He is referring to the Gentiles of Rome.

14

I am under obligation: not in the sense 'I owe them something', but in
the sense 'I have a duty'.

15

The Roman Church does not need the gospel in this sense; they have
already received the gospel and were living by it, however much Paul
might want to enlarge their understanding of its implications. Furthermore, the Roman Christians were Jews for the most part; perhaps a
few would be proselytes, but that is all. This sentence must apply to
Gentiles, in view of v. 13. The grammatical construction of the text
translated in the RSV is odd, and I conjecture that Paul originally
wrote: 'hence my eagerness to preach also among those (Gentiles of
various kinds) in Rome'. This is the text of Minuscule 255; it omits
to you and reads instead the word 'in', 'among'.

16

For I am not ashamed of the gospel: this is neither a hit at the Roman
Christians nor a defence against a charge levelled at Paul, but a statement that he can and does face hostile and incredulous audiences;
hostility is one indication that the gospel is powerful and works (cf.
Mark 8.38; 2 Tim. 1.8,12).

it is the power of God for salvation: the gospel believed and trusted brings
the power of God which it speaks about. Salvation is preservation in
God's peace during this life, whatever else happens, and the gift of
eternal life at the day of judgement (8.24).

to every one who has faith, to the Jew first and also to the Greek: Marcion, and B, G, and sa, omit 'first', an ideological omission which cannot change the sense, because the very mention of the terms 'Jew' and 'Greek' (= heathen, not 'Greek-speaker' as in v. 14) makes the point that God's Messiah came to God's people, the Jews, and that they had the first opportunity to welcome him. Paul always acknowledged this special place of the Jews. He wishes to maintain that Gentiles *also* can be saved by faith, and Jews can *only* be saved by faith. (The same point was made by Peter, Acts 15.9.)

17

For in it the righteousness of God is revealed through faith for faith: 'it' refers to the gospel. 'The righteousness of God' may mean broadly (a) God's own quality of righteousness in himself (Romans 3.5); (b) God's righteous activity towards men by which he makes them righteous, God's victory over his people's enemies by which he delivers them and saves them (Is. 46.13; 51.5,6,8); (c) God's gift which he gives to believers (perhaps Phil. 3.9); or (d) the righteousness which is approved by God, godly righteousness (Romans 10.3; Psalm 119.106; Test. Dan 6.10; I QS X.24 f.; Matt. 6.33; Jas. 1.20). Meaning (a) is ruled out by the context, which refers to men who believe. Meanings (b) and (c) receive support from the phrases 'the power of God' and 'the wrath of God' in vv. 16 and 18. There seems to be little difficulty, however, in passing from 'the power of God' (given) to 'the righteousness of God' (approved) to 'the wrath of God' (manifested) if that is the required sense of v. 17.

The whole logic of the passage argues in favour of meaning (d), the righteousness God approves. Verse 16 says that the believing of the gospel leads to salvation, and Paul assumed that salvation is for the righteous (Rom. 9.30). At the end of v. 17 Paul quotes from the Old Testament, and this passage is about 'the righteous man'. God's righteousness in senses (a) and (b) is undoubted; the great problem is how men are to be accepted by the righteous God. To the objection that Paul wants to speak only of God's action and not at all of man, I answer that this context is about faith, what man has to do if he would live before God.

The translation which states that this righteousness is revealed *through faith for faith* can hardly be right. The Greek says 'from faith to faith', and this is a standard sort of expression, like 'from strength to strength' (Psalm 84.7; cf. Jer. 9.3 and 2 Cor. 3.18). The phrase can hardly go with 'the righteousness of God', which is too remote in the Greek sentence. It must somehow follow on to 'is revealed'. Yet the passive verb 'is revealed' cannot take such a phrase directly; there must be a person or thing understood, to be or change from faith to faith. The natural understanding would be that God's righteousness is revealed in the gospel *to the man who lives* from faith to faith, or to the man who goes from faith to faith. 'To go from faith to faith' means 'to go forward with ever-increasing trust and belief'. Note the present tense of the verb 'to be revealed'. The revelation of the nature and demands and the character of righteousness is made known day by day in the gospel, together with God's power, to those who live by faith.

as it is written, 'He who through faith is righteous shall live': the translation of this quotation from Habakkuk 2.4 is better rendered 'The righteous man shall live by faith'. The question is, How shall the righteous man live? not Who shall live? for it is assumed that only the righteous man shall live. Scholars argue about the original meaning of Hab. 2.4, but the NEB translators give what I take to be Paul's exegesis, 'the righteous man will live by being faithful'. Paul has no wish to be novel in his theology, and some hundreds of years later a Jewish rabbi, Rabbi Nachman ben Isaac, could sum up how to live by citing the same one word of Habakkuk (b. Talmud, Makkoth 23b).

1.18–32

18For the wrath of God is revealed from heaven against all ungodliness and wickedness of men who by their wickedness suppress the truth. 19For what can be known about God is plain to them, because God has shown it to them. 20Ever since the creation of the world his invisible nature, namely, his eternal power and deity, has been clearly perceived in the things that have been made. So they are without excuse; 21for although they knew God they did not honour him as God or give thanks to him, but they became futile in their thinking and their senseless minds were darkened. 22Claiming to be wise, they became fools, 23and exchanged the glory of the immortal God for images resembling mortal man or birds or animals or reptiles.

24Therefore God gave them up in the lusts of their hearts to impurity, to the dishonouring of their bodies among themselves, 25because they exchanged the truth about God for a lie and worshipped and served the creature rather than the Creator, who is blessed for ever! Amen.

26For this reason God gave them up to dishonourable passions. Their women exchanged natural relations for unnatural, 27and the men likewise gave up natural relations with women and were consumed with passion for one another, men committing shameless acts with men and receiving in their own persons the due penalty for their error.

28And since they did not see fit to acknowledge God, God gave them up to a base mind and to improper conduct. 29They were filled with all manner of wickedness, evil, covetousness, malice. Full of envy, murder, strife, deceit, malignity, they are gossips, 30slanderers, haters of God, insolent, haughty, boastful, inventors of evil, disobedient to parents, 31foolish, faithless, heartless, ruthless. 32Though they know God's decree that those who do such things deserve to die, they not only do them but approve those who practise them.

This section begins an argument to show that immorality will be punished by God in the end, springing as it does from culpable refusal to recognize God as Creator. The whole argument extends to the end of Chapter 2.

The first verse of the section now in front of us sums up the complete case, and vv. 19–32 state that those who turn from God and worship idols inevitably sink into unnatural vices and all sorts of immorality.

The language in which the argument is expressed is unlike Paul's usual language in both vocabulary* and style, and I doubt very much whether Paul wrote these verses. Language apart, it is very hard to see how the argument would fit into the train of thought so strikingly begun in 1.1–17. If the argument in 1.18–2.29 had been that all Gentiles were sinners, one could perhaps have seen a connection between this and the larger argument later on, that all men are sinners (3.23), but the writer is not arguing that all Gentiles are sinners. The argument is that idolaters are prone to immorality, not that all Gentiles are immoral. The proof is made acceptable to Gentile ears by the skilful bringing-in of Stoic moral judgements to prove convincingly that immorality is immorality, but the very use of accepted moral standards implies that morality is a well-known possibility. Similarly, a standard Gentile argument against idolatry is employed to back up the much clearer Jewish doctrine of creation.

We possess in Acts 17 an old and trustworthy account of a speech Paul made at Athens against idolatry, so that we cannot say that it is inconceivable that this passage was written by Paul. My case is rather that there seems to be no point to the argument in this context.

Paul wants to prove to the Roman Christians, who were mostly Jews, that because the only way to the righteousness revealed to them day by day in the gospel was by faith they should support him, when he came to them, in his mission to the Gentiles in the city, for Gentiles too could come to the same righteousness by the same path.

Naturally, a later commentator could easily feel the urge to say just how much Gentiles needed to become righteous; it seemed an obvious supplement to Paul's argument to point out that refusal to worship the Creator led to immorality. But these things did not have

* At least twenty-nine words in 1.18–32 occur nowhere else in Paul's writings; at least forty-nine such words in 1.18–2 29. Compare this with the total of nineteen words not found elsewhere in Paul which occur in an equal stretch of *Romans* around this chapter and a half (excluding the explicit Old Testament quotations).

to be proved to the Romans Paul was addressing. He and they could simply agree that Gentiles were sinners (Gal. 2.15). Paul's argument, in any case, is that *all* men need to find the way to righteousness, not that *some* forms of Gentile life were particularly bad.

It could perhaps be urged that Paul wishes to revive these familiar arguments against Gentile immorality in order in the next chapter to turn the tables on the Jews. There is indeed a turning of the tables in Chapter 2, but it is done in a way that is so alien to Paul's purpose in writing to the Christians of Rome, applying as it does to Jews who are alleged to be immoral, that we can hardly regard the argument as part of Paul's original epistle, any more than the passage now before us.

Notes

18

the wrath of God is revealed from heaven: in v. 17 Paul says that the righteousness of God is revealed day after day in the gospel. The verbal similarity between v. 18 and v. 17 would lead us to expect that God's wrath is also revealed day after day. Perhaps we could argue that the moral degradation to which idolaters are prone is a manifestation of God's wrath, but that would be to split this passage from Chapter 2, where God's wrath is revealed at the end, on the day in which he judges the secrets of men (2.16; cf. 2.8). If we reject this interpretation, and maintain the unity of 1.18–32 with 2.1–29, we are left with two possibilities: either 'it is revealed (in the gospel) that God's wrath will eventually come from heaven', or 'God's wrath will be revealed from heaven'. The first of these possibilities is scarcely possible as a translation of the Greek, since the phrase 'from heaven' goes with the verb 'is revealed', and revelation from heaven most naturally refers to a future event. The second is perfectly natural, since present tenses in Greek can refer to future events. The only valid objection to this interpretation is that it forces us to take two constructions quite differently from the way they are taken in the verse before: *the wrath of God* is taken to be God's own wrath, whereas *the righteousness of God* in v. 17 was taken to be righteousness acceptable to God; *is revealed* is taken to mean 'will be revealed', whereas *is revealed* in v. 17 was taken to refer to the present time.

My answer to this objection is that the difficulties in the way of taking either v. 17 or v. 18 in any other way are so great that we must accept the force of this state of affairs and see if there is some other explanation to be found. The explanation I wish to put forward is that 1.18–2.29 was written by some later commentator on Paul. He used a verbal similarity, in writing v. 18, to make a bridge between Paul's argument and his own. Of course, he believed that his supplement was perfectly in tune with Paul's thought; by providing arguments to show that God's wrath descended only on those who could have known the truth, and who acted unnaturally by their immorality, the commentator believed he was supporting the statement that God's *righteousness* (i.e. his justice) was revealed in the gospel. I think, however, that he has missed the true force of Paul's statement in v. 17.

the wrath of God: there is little reason to suppose that the Bible regards God's wrath as some impersonal mechanism within the universe, to be distinguished from his personal mercy, as Dodd has argued at some length in his commentary (pp. 47–50). In this context the phrase refers to God's condemnation of men's ungodliness and unrighteousness in unrighteously holding down the truth, and the words probably refer to God's specific condemnation on the day of judgement, rather than to his disapproval of such behaviour at present.

Dodd argues that 'in the long run we cannot think with full consistency of God in terms of the highest human ideals of personality and yet attribute to Him the irrational passion of anger'. In answer I would say that even the highest human ideals of personality require an honest recognition of evil and wickedness for what it is. If men are commanded not to judge others, that is because of their own limitations and sins. If God, who knows the secrets of men's hearts, were not to judge men justly, he would be denying the special status he gave to men, and treating them not as responsible creatures but as an irresponsible part of creation. The teaching of Jesus, to which Dodd appeals, certainly speaks of God's limitless forgiveness and his fatherly kindness to the unthankful and evil, but it also speaks of an end to this age, an end to the possibilities for repentance, and of an essential condition, that men should repent and ask for forgiveness.

The Bible everywhere assumes that God will judge men for what they have done in this life, and that God's punishment will fall on the unjust.

men who by their wickedness suppress the truth: not all men, but those who do actually restrain (or perhaps even, do hold back from others) the truth about God.

19

For what can be known about God is plain to them . . .: The first stage of the argument is to show that God's wrath is a just punishment, because the men who are punished could have recognized the Creator in creation, and did not.

20

This is a concise summary of an argument for the existence of God that was already at least 500 years old when *Romans* was published, having been stated by the Greek philosopher Anaxagoras. By thinking about the world, the invisible qualities of God, his eternal power and divine nature, are, as it were, made 'visible'. The argument had been taken over into Jewish apologetics by Jews who were living scattered in the Hellenistic cities, where they spoke Greek and attempted, with some success, to win their Gentile neighbours to Judaism. The argument is more like a call to reflection than a proof in geometry. The counter-arguments against this argument are usually attempts to ban the possibility of reflecting in a way that might lead to God, but I cannot see how this possibility is logically to be denied. If the possibility is left open, the logical conclusion is that the invisible God did create all changeable things. I think the proof here summarized is valid.

21–23

The thoughtful men, leaders of their communities, who could and should have known that God is unchangeable, put in God's place an image of something corruptible, a man, or even images of birds and beasts and reptiles. They worshipped part of creation and did not give thanks to the Creator.

24

Therefore God gave them up . . . to impurity: the idea of God's handing men over to immoral ways of life (24, 26, 28) strikes us as strange. The difficulty may lie in our not taking the difference between men and God seriously enough. If a man permits natural processes to take their course he cannot necessarily be held responsible for the results, but the natural processes to which God abandons an idolater are processes for which he is responsible. Therefore, in the case of God, it is better to say commits than permits. To the objection that the loving Father should not be thought of as committing his creatures to immorality, the only answer is that human freedom and responsibility would be meaningless if human choice could not be followed by evil consequences.

24, 25

Idolatry, which is worship of what changes, implies that there are no unchanging norms of behaviour and no divine moral laws. Idolatry may, therefore, lead to the unnatural practices to be listed in vv. 26–27, which are here summed up as the dishonouring of men's bodies.

The argument assumes that the distinction between natural and un-natural, proper and improper, is well understood. It is alleged today that these distinctions are meaningless, but that cannot be true. Since the very terminology implies that not all behaviour is natural, it is not enough to *assert* that something is natural. The case must be argued.

28–31

Children were taught lists of virtues and vices, and such lists were the stock-in-trade of philosophers and rhetoricians in the Hellenistic world. The heading given to the vices here enumerated is 'the things not fitting to do' (RSV, *improper conduct*), and this was a key ethical term in Stoicism.

32

that those who do such things deserve to die: the vices just listed were not punishable by death in any known code of morality. Perhaps spiritual death is meant, or the general judgement that 'the wages of sin is death'. I agree with Weisse that the whole clause should be omitted, as a gloss that has crept into the text from the margin. When the words are included, the train of thought must be: although they know God's decree that those who do these things are worthy of death they not only do them, but also approve of those who do them and thereby encourage others to do what is worthy of death. This is possible, but note that the key move is not expressed in actual words, but has to be supplied by the reader. If, however, the words 'that those who do such things deserve to die' are put back into the margin where they belong, the train of thought in the text is perfectly straightforward, and nothing needs to be supplied by the reader: although they know God's principle of right they do not only do these things (bad enough) but even philosophically approve of those who do them (much worse: *trahison des clercs*).

2.1–16

2 Therefore you have no excuse, O man, whoever you are, when you judge another; for in passing judgment upon him you condemn yourself, because you, the judge, are doing the very same things. ²We know that the judgment of God rightly falls upon those who do such things. ³Do you suppose, O man,

that when you judge those who do such things and yet do them yourself, you will escape the judgment of God? 4*Or do you presume upon the riches of his kindness and forbearance and patience? Do you not know that God's kindness is meant to lead you to repentance?* 5*But by your hard and impenitent heart you are storing up wrath for yourself on the day of wrath when God's righteous judgment will be revealed.* 6*For he will render to every man according to his works:* 7*to those who by patience in well-doing seek for glory and honour and immortality, he will give eternal life;* 8*but for those who are factious and do not obey the truth, but obey wickedness, there will be wrath and fury.* 9*There will be tribulation and distress for every human being who does evil, the Jew first and also the Greek,* 10*but glory and honour and peace for every one who does good, the Jew first and also the Greek.* 11*For God shows no partiality.*

12*All who have sinned without the law will also perish without the law, and all who have sinned under the law will be judged by the law.* 13*For it is not the hearers of the law who are righteous before God, but the doers of the law who will be justified.* 14*When Gentiles who have not the law do by nature what the law requires, they are a law to themselves, even though they do not have the law.* 15*They show that what the law requires is written on their hearts, while their conscience also bears witness and their conflicting thoughts accuse or perhaps excuse them* 16*on that day when, according to my gospel, God judges the secrets of men by Christ Jesus.*

In 1.18–32 the argument went that Gentiles could know God and avoid idolatry, and that refusal to worship the Creator led inevitably to unnatural sexual and social relationships. Now the argument is taken a stage further. Men who behave unnaturally and unjustly cannot hope to escape judgement for what they do.

The final stage of the argument, which is fully treated in vv. 17–29, is foreshadowed in this section. God's judgement is according to men's works, and this applies to Jews as much as to Gentiles. So the basis is laid for the proposition that the Jew who does not obey the Law will not escape God's condemnation simply because he is a Jew.

Most commentators say that our present section contains much more than a foreshadowing of the argument against the Jew, and that the Jew is already in view in v. 1. This conclusion seems fairly likely, if our version of vv. 1 and 3 represents the original text, for they speak of the man who condemns the wickedness of others while committing the very same sins himself, and that is precisely the failing of the man who prides himself he is a Jew (2.21–3). But the main point of our present section, taken as a whole, is that God will judge men according to their deeds, and this is a necessary step in the argument. This has first to be established before the even greater crime, of the man who knows the Law and condemns others who transgress God's commandments but yet himself breaks the Law, can be exposed for the enormity it is. The solution I would put forward is that a glossator, who assumed that the man addressed rhetorically as 'O man' in vv. 1 and 3 was the same as the one addressed as 'you, a Jew' in v. 17, added words that attributed the hypocrisy of the Jew to the man in vv. 1 and 3. But the man in vv. 1 and 3 is simply being warned, as becomes quite clear in vv. 4–16, not to presume that he can escape the consequences of his actions. It is complacency that is attacked here, not inconsistency.

If we remove the glosses, v. 1 would read, 'Consequently you are without excuse, O man, whoever you are who do the same things', and v. 3 would read, 'Or do you think this, O man who do these things, that you will escape God's judgment?' Then the beginning of this chapter logically follows the end of the last chapter, and the great hiatus observed by most commentators disappears.

Men can know the Creator, and should worship him. From their refusal to acknowledge God there flow, inevitably, immoral practices and attitudes. They might seem to be able to act immorally with impunity, but their present freedom from punishment should be regarded not as a sign that all will be well but rather as an opportunity provided by God's goodness during which they have time to repent. Repentance would lead to a life of patient well-doing, aiming at honourable behaviour, and God will reward such a life with eternal life. Punishment will be meted out on those who do evil. Mere possession of the Law will be no defence; God is not partial, and he will recognize only those who have kept the Law, regardless of whether or not they knew what they were doing. This judgement of God will be administered by Christ Jesus.

It is perfectly possible to imagine that Paul could have mounted such an argument in certain circumstances. The conclusion of the report of his speech at Athens in Acts 17 is not so very different: God is bringing his time of forbearance to an end, and will judge men by the man he has appointed. However, Paul could hardly have put forward the argument in this form at this point in his epistle to the Romans. First, he was addressing Christians in his epistle, whereas this section is addressed to mankind in general, and then addressed to those Jews who were breaking the commandments they proclaimed. Second, in addressing Christians, Paul is trying to show them that even though they might seem to be keeping the requirements of the Law pretty successfully the Law itself says that this way of being righteous will not succeed, and that the whole approach is wrong (see Chapter 3). But the section in front of us is unaware of that problem, and assumes that the only question is whether or not a man keeps the Law. Paul can of course tell the difference between a man who steals and a man who doesn't steal, a man who commits adultery and a man who doesn't commit adultery, but his problem in trying to persuade the Jewish Christians in Rome to support his mission to the Gentiles is that of the man who neither steals nor commits adultery but who nevertheless has missed the way to righteousness. He wants them to face the awful paradox, that Gentiles who were not pursuing righteousness have attained righteousness, a righteousness that started from faith, while Israel, in pursuing the law, did not attain it (see Romans 9.30f.). If they face this fact, then they will be willing to give him full support in his work among Gentiles, and will recognize that Gentiles do not have to become Jews in order to be righteous. The present argument leads to the same conclusion, that Gentiles as much as Jews can be rewarded with eternal life by God, but it gets there by ignoring Paul's main problem. Of course God will reward righteousness, but, on the basis of the present passage, the best way to help Gentiles to be righteous would be to preach to them the Law. The assumption here is that Gentiles can already escape God's wrath by keeping the Law, and indeed they are in a position to know enough about God to avoid immorality, but it would clearly be better if they were explicitly taught the truth as revealed in the Law. But Paul's whole case rests on the argument that the preachers of the gospel must not start with the Law.

The assumption behind the present passage is shared by Paul, that all men will be judged according to their works, but the writer of this section is not aware of Paul's dilemma, which it is so important he persuade the Jewish Christians at Rome to see, namely, that even men who know and strive heroically to keep the Law do not succeed in discovering the righteousness acceptable to God.

Notes

1

Therefore: as the verse stands, this strong logical connective is 'a colourless transitional particle which appears quite illogical' (Lietzmann), because the chapter begins an entirely new train of thought: 1.20–32 states that men are without excuse in their immorality, and 2.1–11 that they are without excuse in their condemnation of an immorality which they themselves share. However, if the references to judging others be removed from vv. 1 and 3 as glosses, we are left with a perfectly logical *therefore:* the man who does these things is without excuse, because he could have known the Creator and could have acted morally.

O man: a stylistic device used by Stoic philosophers to enliven the argument by conjuring up an objector.

whoever you are, when you judge another; for in passing judgment upon him you condemn yourself, because you, the judge, are doing the very same things: this argument seems to be out of place. Certainly, a judge who does what he condemns is without excuse, but both before, in 1.18–32, and after, in v. 2 and vv. 4–11, the inexcusableness of men rests on their ability to know what is required of them, and their knowledge that what God requires must be right. Their relationship to external standards of morality, not their consistency in applying those standards to themselves, is what is first of all in question. I therefore take the original text as reading: *whoever you are (who) . . . are doing the . . . same things.* There is one tiny scrap of evidence in the textual transmission of this verse which gives a little support to my conjecture. One manuscript, 1827, reads a participle instead of an indicative form for the verb 'to do'. I can see no reason for any scribe's making such a change, and this reading is perhaps a clue to the original text.

Bultmann has suggested that v. 1 was a summarizing gloss which really belonged as a comment after v. 3. See the comment on vv. 3 and 4 below.

3, 4
Do you suppose, O man, that when you judge those who do such things and yet do them yourself, you will escape the judgment of God? Or do you presume upon the riches of his kindness and forbearance and patience? Do you not know that God's kindness is meant to lead you to repentance? As it stands, the argument does not quite fit. The kindness and forbearance of God refers to the present time, in which men who do evil are not punished and may, in fact, flourish. The argument at the end of v. 4 is that this time is not a time for complacency, but a time given by God to allow men an opportunity to repent. But such an argument, which is designed to make a man reflect about God's requirements and God's eventual judgement, is not the sort of argument to employ against a men who knows all about God's judgement, and who delights in condemning the behaviour of others on the basis of this criterion. Such a man is the Jew (vv. 17–24) who needs to be told to be consistent. The argument in vv. 2 and 4–11 is directed rather to the man who is not without moral insight and philosophical nous, who can be led to the point of repentance. He is the Gentile. God had justly given him time to repent, because he needed time to reflect. The hypocrite does not deserve time, and can hardly be said in God's goodness to be given time.

Again, the solution to logical lameness is to suppose that the case of the Jew in the next section has been read back into our text; a marginal gloss identifying the 'man' and 'you, the Jew' has become incorporated into the argument, to produce the present difficulties.

If the first question (v. 3) be read as follows, the rest of the argument flows forward with complete logic and great effectiveness: 'Do you suppose this, O man, when you do such things, that you will escape the judgement of God?'

7
to those who by patience in well-doing seek for glory and honour and immortality, he will give eternal life: another possible translation, 'to those who seek eternal life, (he will bestow) glory and honour and immortality according to their patience in well-doing', should probably be rejected on grounds of both order and construction. *Patience in well-doing* is the way they seek *glory and honour and immortality*, and God rewards such lives with eternal life on the day of judgement. There is no suggestion here that the way of the 'good work' is transcended (*pace* Barrett); Paul's problem of faith and works is not even on the horizon.

13
who will be justified: i.e. adjudged righteous.

14, 15

Moffatt, in his translation of the New Testament, brackets off these two verses as 'either a marginal note or an awkward insertion'. I think his first suggestion, that they are a marginal note, is more likely to be right, because the whole point of the little paragraph is to remove a possible misconception raised by vv. 12 and 13, and such attempts to remove misconception are often the work of glossators.

Verses 12 and 13 might be taken to mean that Gentiles who are 'doers of the Law' are actually 'without the Law', the description used in v. 12 for their fellow-Gentiles who sin, but in fact, says the glossator, they have been granted by God a sense of *what the law requires; they are a law to themselves* (v. 14). They have the ability to be pricked by conscience when they go wrong; their thoughts can discriminate between various courses of action open to them, forbidding some and approving others. This view of man's nature was widespread in popular Greek thought of the time. Cicero summed up the notion with the words, 'The law is the supreme reason implanted in nature which approves the things that ought to be done, and prohibits what ought not to be done' (*De Legibus* 1.6.18).

Of course, the work of conscience will be superseded on the day of judgement, and the 'bearing witness' or the 'accusing and excusing' will not need to operate *on that day when . . . God judges the secrets of men by Christ Jesus.* It therefore makes little sense to run v. 16 on straight after v. 15, and Moffatt is surely right to put v. 16 after v. 13: *for it is not the hearers of the law who are righteous before God, but the doers of the law who will be justified on that day . . .*

16

according to my gospel: not a reference to Paul's particular version of the gospel, but an indication that the messenger to the Gentiles has additional news, that God has already appointed his agent at the judgement, Jesus Christ. This is fresh news, which adds urgency to the usual Jewish warning to the Gentiles that they had to face judgement at the last.

2.17–29

¹⁷*But if you call yourself a Jew and rely upon the law and boast of your relation to God* ¹⁸*and know his will and approve what is excellent, because you are instructed in the law,* ¹⁹*and if you are sure that you are a*

guide to the blind, a light to those who are in darkness, ²⁰a corrector of the
foolish, a teacher of children, having in the law the embodiment of knowledge and truth – ²¹you then who teach others, will you not teach yourself?
While you preach against stealing, do you steal? ²²You who say that one
must not commit adultery, do you commit adultery? You who abhor idols,
do you rob temples? ²³You who boast in the law, do you dishonour God by
breaking the law? ²⁴For, as it is written, 'The name of God is blasphemed
among the Gentiles because of you.'

²⁵Circumcision indeed is of value if you obey the law; but if you break the
law, your circumcision becomes uncircumcision. ²⁶So, if a man who is uncircumcised keeps the precepts of the law, will not his uncircumcision be regarded as circumcision? ²⁷Then those who are physicially uncircumcised but
keep the law will condemn you who have the written code and circumcision
but break the law. ²⁸For he is not a real Jew who is one outwardly, nor is
true circumcision something external and physical. ²⁹He is a Jew who is one
inwardly, and real circumcision is a matter of the heart, spiritual and not
literal. His praise is not from men but from God.

This is a fine appeal to a Jew from a fellow-Jew to keep the Law
which they both profess. I do not think any sarcasm is meant in the
list of the things in which the Jew prides himself: guide to the blind, a
light to those who are in darkness, a corrector of the foolish, a teacher of
children. They do have in the Law the embodiment of knowledge and truth.

The tragedy is that some Jews betray their high calling by doing
the opposite of what they stand for as a nation. They say: Do not
steal, and steal; Do not commit adultery, and commit adultery; they
abhor idols, but manage to conquer their abhorrence if they see the
chance to steal idols from temples. God is thereby dishonoured, for
Gentiles can only hold in contempt the God in whose name such
hypocrisy is practised.

Verses 25–29 have been taken to mean that circumcision is a matter
of indifference, but I do not think this can be the force of the passage.
The first verse in fact begins by affirming the value of circumcision:
circumcision indeed is of value; and the remark at the end of the same
verse, if you break the Law, your circumcision becomes uncircumcision, is
meant as rhetoric rather than a sober statement of legal fact: your
circumcision is in danger of becoming uncircumcision. Circumcision

is the sign of a Jew who has been entrusted with the Law, and this is an appeal to him to be one truly, in secret, for which God will praise him (cf. Matt. 6.1–18). There is, perhaps, a suggestion in vv. 28 and 29 that circumcision as an outward ordinance is superseded, but I do not think the rhetorical contrast between outward circumcision and true circumcision should be pressed. (Perhaps there is even some disturbance to the original text, by a scribe who wished to say that outward circumcision had been abolished; see the notes.)

The whole assumption of this section, as of the last, is that Jews and Gentiles can keep the Law, and can act in a manner to deserve God's praise by obeying the commandments. There is no suggestion that righteousness is elusive, or that *none is righteous, no, not one* (Psalm 14.1; Romans 3.10). One Jew is addressing another in confidence that he can be shamed into becoming worthy of his high status, and this section is not attempting to show the utter moral bankruptcy of Judaism.

Can Paul have written this passage? I do not think his authorship can be ruled out simply because the argument assumes that God's commandments can be kept. Paul himself seems to assume that commandments can be kept, and is content to accept the assumption that Jews are in general morally better than Gentiles (Gal. 2.15). The real reason why this passage can hardly have been written by Paul is that it has no inkling of Paul's problem. Paul's problem is that even the Jew who conscientiously keeps the Law fails in the end to attain the righteousness acceptable to God, fails to become a truly righteous man. The argument before us in vv. 17–29 has no understanding of the problem Paul is concerned with in writing to the Roman Christians.

If this section, 2.17–29, and the two previous sections, 1.18–32 and 2.1–16, are not by Paul, we could perhaps understand it if they were elaborations and extensions of Paul's arguments in the interests of some later ecclesiastical position or other. But I have been arguing that they are oblivious of Paul's problems, that their line of argument is irrelevant to his immediate purpose. How can I explain that some material added *to* Romans puts forward ideas that take not the slightest account of the most pressing issues dealt with *in* Romans?

I think the answer is that perhaps none of this material was com-

posed especially for insertion into *Romans* at all. We have here a
traditional tract which belongs essentially to the missionary literature
of Hellenistic Judaism. The only distinctively Christian piece is the
note that God has now appointed his agent of judgement, Jesus Christ
(2.16), and otherwise the passage is a straightforward example of the
arguments employed by Greek-speaking Jews scattered in communities throughout the Hellenistic world, now under Roman rule, who
were trying to convert their Gentile neighbours. Perhaps the opening
remark, in 1.18, is so similar to 1.17 that we must agree that the
interpolator who inserted this section into his copy of *Romans*
deliberately designed the connection, but even here we may have the
wording of the old tradition, whose striking similarity first suggested
the happy juxtaposition of the two venerable documents.

Whatever the true story of how and why the interpolator first
added his long excursus, there is little doubt that his motive was not
to correct Paul but rather to incorporate into Paul's epistle another
old and revered document which, he thought, bore on the same
problem. And the coincidences in subject matter are striking: revelation, sin, righteousness, justification, circumcision, not to forget the
great over-arching problem of Jew and Gentile. Yet at every point
there is tension, as all commentators have perceived. Dodd has tried
to escape the difficulty by supposing that Paul is working in old
material which he had used many times before, but I myself think
that the difference in presupposition between the argument in the
genuine *Romans* and this passage is too fundamental to allow Dodd's
solution. We have before us the work of two different minds working
with a different understanding of the issues at stake.

Notes

17
But if you call yourself a Jew: the argument about whether this is a
Christian Jew (Zahn) or an unbelieving Jew (Kühl) is beside the point.
The whole discussion is taken over bodily from pre-Christian Hellen-
istic Judaism. The Jewish attempt to win Gentile converts is being
badly hampered by the occasional Jew who finds rest in the Law (the
Mosaic Law) and boasts in God, who yet disobeys the commandments

he is claiming to be able to teach the Gentile. The discussion can be taken over bodily from Hellenistic Judaism because the synagogues that believe in Jesus Christ still feel themselves an integral part of Judaism. Their approach to Gentiles is the same as the usual Jewish approach, except that they can announce that now the Messiah has come, and will come to judge all men.

21

– *you then who teach others:* these words destroy the grammatical flow of the sentence that began at v. 17. They were possibly falsely introduced into the text from the margin. The marginal note was originally designed to make the words, *will you not teach yourself?*, parallel to the next three questions: *do you steal?* is preceded by *while you preach against stealing; do you commit adultery?* is preceded by *while you say that one must not commit adultery; do you rob temples?* is preceded by *you who abhor idols*; should not then *will you not teach yourself?* be preceded by *you then who teach others?* (The Greek constructions are far more similar in all four cases than the English can conveniently be made.) When these words are removed from our text, we get a long and effective sentence without a grammatical break.

22

You who abhor idols, do you rob temples? the argument strikes us as odd, because we could understand how a man who abhorred idols might feel justified in robbing temples. Richard Bentley (1662–1742), the great textual critic and tyrannical master of Trinity College, Cambridge, conjectured that the original text read 'do you offer sacrifices?' J. B. Lightfoot has argued that the broader meaning of the verb should be preferred: 'do you commit sacrilege?' (= the Vulgate). The conjecture is unlikely (for why should a scribe have changed the conjectured word for the more difficult one that stands in our present text?), and the wider meaning probably should be ruled out on the grounds that the strict meaning would most naturally follow a mention of idols. I think we can see the sense of our present text if we remember that, however firmly it was held that idols were simply helpless statues made from wood and metal, no Jew would want to have anything to do with such objects of worship. Josephus said that stealing from pagan temples was forbidden (*Antiquities* iv. 8.10 = §207).

24

A fairly exact citation of the LXX version of Is. 52.5. The Hebrew original does not say explicitly why God's name is despised; the LXX suggests that it is despised by the Gentiles *because of you;* and this writer is arguing that it is the inconsistency of the occasional bad Jew in the Dispersion that leads Gentiles to turn away from the lofty ethical teaching contained in the Mosaic Law.

28, 29
The point is that the real Jew must be a Jew through and through. I have argued in the essay at the head of this section that there is no suggestion that circumcision could be dispensed with. Circumcision without the accompanying obedience to the Law of course counts for nothing on the day of judgement, and the Gentile who keeps the Law will condemn the Jew who doesn't, but the Jew is still the custodian of the Law and *a light to those who are in darkness*. His aim must be to be a Jew in secret (*inwardly*) as well as in the open (*outwardly*).

This point is somewhat obscured by the suggestion that *true circumcision* is not *something . . . physical*, and that *real circumcision is a matter of the heart, spiritual and not literal*. This could be mere rhetoric, not designed to denigrate physical circumcision, designed to suggest, rather, that inward circumcision is the more important part of the sacrament, but the grammatical disorder of v. 29 leads me to suspect that again a gloss has been introduced from the margin into the text. The last sentence in the RSV is actually a relative clause which is separated from its true reference, *he is a Jew*, by the remark concerning circumcision. If we remove the three Greek words represented by *and real circumcision is a matter of the heart* we restore both grammar and sense. Similarly, the words represented by *and physical* at the end of v. 28 are an awkward appendage in the Greek and should also be set aside. Then we may translate the two verses as follows. 'For not in outward appearance is a man a Jew, nor in outward appearance is circumcision circumcision, but in secret is a man a Jew, in spirit not in letter, and his praise is not from men but from God.'

His praise: Gifford suggests that this may be a punning reference to the supposed etymology of the name Judah, from which the word Jew is derived (Gen. 29.35; 49.8.)

3.1–8

3 *Then what advantage has the Jew? Or what is the value of circumcision?* ²*Much in every way. To begin with, the Jews are entrusted with the oracles of God.* ³*What if some were unfaithful? Does their faithlessness nullify the faithfulness of God?* ⁴*By no means! Let God be true though every man be false, as it is written,*

　'*That thou mayest be justified in thy words,*
　and prevail when thou art judged.'

⁵*But if our wickedness serves to show the justice of God, what shall we say? That God is unjust to inflict wrath on us? (I speak in a human way.)* ⁶*By no means! For then how could God judge the world?* ⁷*But if through my falsehood God's truthfulness abounds to his glory, why am I still being condemned as a sinner?* ⁸*And why not do evil that good may come? – as some people slanderously charge us with saying. Their condemnation is just.*

These verses are so obscure, and my own interpretation of the Greek differs so much from the RSV, that it seems best to print the following paraphrase as an alternative rendering.

　1. What then is the Jew's advantage, or what is the value of circumcision? 2. Much in every way. For, above all, (the Jews) were entrusted with the oracles of God. 3. What then? If *some* were faithless, their faithlessness does not destroy God's faithfulness, does it? 4. Not at all. Let God be faithful, even if *every* man is a liar, as it is written in scripture (Psalm 116); ['So that you may be pronounced righteous in your words, and prevail in administering justice', Psalm 51.]

　5. But if our unrighteousness adopts the righteousness acceptable to God, what shall we say? Surely not that God in inflicting wrath upon men is unrighteous? 6. Not at all. [Else how will God judge the world?] 7. But if the truth of God together with my lie abounds to his glory what (shall we say)? I too am after all still judged as a sinner. 8. And this is not, is it (as we are slandered with saying, and as some affirm we

57

actually say), 'Let us do evil that good may come'? The condemnation of those who say *that* is just.

I have argued that 1.18–2.29 is a long insertion added later to the original text of *Romans*. The insertion not only begins with a strikingly similar statement to Paul's own assertion 1.17; it also ends with a passage about the true Jew that at first sight seems to require the question with which Paul begins Chapter 3: *Then what advantage has the Jew?* The coincidence is, however, more apparent than real. Chapter 2 assumed the natural superiority of the Jew, and was a rhetorical appeal to all Jews to live up to their profession of the Law. Chapter 3, on the other hand, is argument of another kind. The tone is much more staccato, and the argument is not with stylized opponents (the typical Gentile, addressed as *O man*, and *you who call yourself a Jew*, 2.1, 3, 17) but with the objections of genuine opponents, and in the presence of the congregation to which he is writing, whose help and support he hopes to win for his particular mission to the Gentiles.

In Chapter 1, up to v. 17, Paul has been maintaining that in the gospel the righteousness God will accept is revealed to the man who lives from faith to faith. The righteous man shall live by faith, and therefore salvation is open to Jew and Gentile on exactly the same terms: that they are prepared to live trusting only in God.

This position, which allows Paul to call Gentiles who still remain Gentiles to form their own Christian congregations alongside the Jews who have believed, was open to objection, and in vv. 1–8 Paul states four of these objections and attempts to defend himself from these charges levelled at him by fellow Jewish theologians.

The first objection is that Paul robs the Jew of any advantage in the divine dispensation, and denies the value of circumcision, by which the distinctiveness of the Jewish people was preserved and passed on. Paul answers this charge by affirming that the chief claim to honour of Israel was that God had entrusted her with his *oracles*, that is, Old Testament scripture. This was enough to guarantee the status of Jews and the value of circumcision.

The second objection is that Paul's teaching that all Israel had been faithless and sinned seems to threaten God's faithfulness; if God is faithful and has promised to preserve Israel, no theology can start from the assumption that all Israel has sinned. Paul's first defence is to get his opponents to admit what is obvious, that if *some* of the Jewish people proved faithless that would not nullify God's faith-fulness. Then he presses home the advantage he has won by this admission and extends the argument to the case where every man is untrue. Surely, even then, God is faithful! He is on good ground in bringing this argument forward, because he can cite the Psalmist who was at one stage forced to cry out that *every man is a liar* (Psalm 116.11); the Psalmist's whole experience, when he came to this realization, was that God had remained faithful and delivered him.

The third objection, in v. 5, is that Paul seems to be threatening the justice of God by supposing that God accepts some unrighteous men while condemning others. Paul cannot for one moment allow this conclusion to be drawn from his argument, although some Christian theologians have come pretty close to finding the difficulty tolerable. Paul, however, will have nothing to do with a view that holds that God would accept some men as righteous by a legal fiction, according to his inscrutable good pleasure. He states his position here in a way that excludes the legal fiction, by asserting that unrighteousness can adopt a righteousness acceptable to God; men who know they are unrighteous can become righteous. (See the notes, for this reading of v. 5.) God is not unjust to accept such unrighteous men, for they have learnt to become righteous.

The fourth objection is a variant of the third. Paul seems to be saying that his being untrue to God has somehow ended up by serving God's greater glory. This he admits, but also states quite flatly (on my reading of v. 7, for which see the notes) that he will still be condemned as a sinner; he has still to be purged of all the wrong he has done in the body, although accepted at judgement for the righteous man he has become.

Therefore he repudiates his opponents' charge. They have actually accused him of teaching, *Let us do evil that good may come*, and this aphorism he rejects with the utmost scorn.

We do not find this aphorism as damaging as Paul and his objectors did, since it is the slogan favoured by our own moral philosophers. They argue that moral choices should be governed only by our assessment of the likely outcome in satisfying the highest number of people. We may do evil, if good will follow. But I think we should try to see Paul's point, and the point of the people who slandered Paul by putting it around that he taught 'Let us do evil that good may follow'. The morality of 'Let us do evil that good may come' can claim to be neither moral nor Christian, since all actions, even if they are patently unjust or false or shameful, may be bravely justified by this philosophy. It all comes down, in the end, to how we foresee the consequences, and who can see furthest, and that is impossible to decide, especially since no one is allowed to be condemned morally for consequences he did not foresee.

Paul will not allow his position to be, *Let us do evil that good may come*, and neither should we. But how are we to avoid this conclusion, if we hold that bad men may be good in God's sight? Paul has already sketched out an answer, but in the next section he begins to argue more systematically for the truth and morality of saying that 'the righteous man shall live by faith'.

Notes

1
Or what is the value of circumcision? Paul assumes that Jewish Christians will go on circumcising their male children.

2
To begin with: this translation suggests that Paul is beginning a list, and I prefer the translation 'first of all', or even 'above all', suggested by an old commentator whose words were preserved by Eusebius of Emessa and Severian. Cf. the use of 'first' in Josephus, *Antiquities* 10.213, and Hermas, *Mandates* 4.2.3. Possession of the *oracles of God* is the chief reason for the *advantage* of the Jews.

the oracles of God: probably the words of scripture (our Old Testament), rather than any specific part of scripture like the laws or the promises. God has inspired men to speak and write the words contained in scripture, and this is something the Gentiles do not themselves have. Paul could not conceive of the scriptures' being venerated without the people of the scriptures being honoured, for they were *entrusted* with the oracles of God.

4
Let God be true though every man be false, as it is written: these words are

an appeal to Psalm 116.11 and the whole context of the Psalm; although the Psalmist was forced to cry out that 'Men are all a vain hope', God has remained faithful and rescued him from death. Paul uses this passage to buttress his argument that even the faithlessness of all men does not disprove or nullify the faithfulness of God. *Let God be true* means: you must recognize that God remains true even though every man be false. The words *as it is written* refer back to the citation from Psalm 116 (as they do in 2.24), not forward to the citation from Psalm 51, which I take to be a gloss.

> *That thou mayest be justified in thy words,*
> *and prevail when thou art judged.*

An exact quotation from the LXX version of our Psalm 51.4 (LXX 50.6). The RSV translation suggests that when men judge God he will *be justified* and *prevail*. The Greek probably should, however, be translated '. . . and prevail when thou enterest judgment' (cf. 1 Cor. 6.6). The thought is that we should all acknowledge that God is true and every man a liar, and so acknowledge that God is justified in his words of sentence on our sin and that he is clearly right in exercising justice against sinners. This is in harmony with the force of the original Psalm. Nevertheless, such a proper pious comment is out of place in Paul's argument. The citation of Psalm 51 implies that the point at issue is God's rightness in exercising justice, whereas the real issue is whether the unfaithfulness of *men*, in this case all of Israel, can possibly be maintained, in view of God's promises to be faithful. Psalm 116 serves that argument beautifully, whereas Psalm 51 does not.

Perhaps a pious scribe thought *as it is written* could do with a long and explicit illustrative quotation, not realizing that it already referred back to a most apposite allusion.

5

But if our wickedness serves to show the justice of God, what shall we say? As our text stands, it is hard to see the force of the argument. Paul cannot mean, If our wickedness shows up the justice of God by the contrast between his justice and our wickedness, for no one could possibly draw the conclusion from this that *God is unjust*. Then perhaps Paul meant, If our wickedness shows the amazing power of God to justify sinners who still remain sinners, what shall we say? The trouble with this reading of the question is that the conclusion *God is unjust* is unavoidable, because the God who justifies sinners who remain sinners also condemns sinners who remain sinners, and that cannot be just.

If he is going to justify some sinners who remain sinners, he must justify all. Many theologians have drawn that conclusion, of which the greatest, I suppose, is Karl Barth. But Paul implicitly excludes this possibility, in speaking of *wrath*, by which he means the condemnation of some.

I think Paul's sentence has to be taken in a way that allows that unrighteous men can become righteous. Then the objection that God is unjust in condemning other unrighteous men can properly be brushed aside with a *By no means!* The unrighteous have, somehow, become actually righteous.

The verb translated *serves to show* (*synistēsin*) can bear the meaning given in the RSV, but its basic force is 'to place or set together'. It may, then, mean 'to combine', as in the LXX version of Proverbs 26.26, 'The man who (wishes to) hide hostility combines (it with) guile or adopts guile, but his sins are revealed in the assembly'. That meaning fits the context in *Romans*, and also allows us to refer both the unrighteousness (RSV: *wickedness*) in the subject, and the righteousness (RSV: *justice*) in the object to human qualities of life, and again to adopt the sense 'the righteousness acceptable to God' for the ambiguous phrase 'the righteousness of God', as we have done earlier in 1.17. The sentence should then be translated: 'If our unrighteousness combines itself with or adopts the righteousness of God (the righteousness acceptable to God) what shall we say?' On this translation it is clearly possible to avoid the charge that God is unjust in condemning unrighteous men, because those who are not subject to the wrath of God have managed to combine their unrighteousness with a righteousness he will accept. And yet, on this translation, the possibility of the charge is still apparent; Paul does seem to be saying that God accepts some unrighteous men, while rejecting other unrighteous men. He does have a case against him to answer.

(*I speak in a human way*): as it stands, this is probably an apology for even entertaining the possibility that God should be *unjust*; the phrase, or something like it, is quite common in Paul (1 Cor. 9.8; Gal. 3.15; cf. Rom. 6.19; 1 Cor. 3.3.; 15.32). But it is hard to see why Paul should apologize for a rhetorical question which both he and his opponents would immediately agree was unacceptable. Origen knew of another reading to be found in Greek manuscripts of *Romans*, which omitted *I speak* and had 'against men' instead of 'according to man' (see Zahn, pp. 618 f.). This gives a much better sense: 'If our unrighteousness adopts the righteousness acceptable to God, what then shall we say?

That God who inflicts wrath on men is unjust? By no means!' The change was possibly made because a pious scribe could not bear the apostle even to ask whether God could be unjust, and he assumed that Paul had used his customary phrase, *I speak in a human way.*

6

For then how could God judge the world? This remark begs the question, which is, How can God be just in judging the world if he accepts some unrighteous men and rejects others? It assumes that the objection is unanswerable according to human logic. It seems to say, God must be just, but I can't see how, for he condemns some unrighteous men and accepts other equally unrighteous men, yet unless he is allowed to do this unjust thing, he will not be able to judge the world at all.

However, on my reading of v. 5, the difficulty does not really exist, even if the reader is bound to expect Paul to explain himself more fully later on in the epistle. Paul agrees that God accepts unrighteous men, but he argues that these men are distinguished from the unrighteous men God rejects by having been able to adopt a righteousness acceptable to God. Paul can escape the charge that his view of how God will judge the world would make God unjust, although he has still to unfold a full and convincing argument that unrighteous men are able to become righteous in the way he believes possible.

I am very much inclined to think, therefore, that this question-begging remark is the work of a glossator who couldn't for the life of him see how Paul could escape the charge that his theology would make God unjust. His only answer is to confront the objection with the blank assertion: God will judge the world. But Paul uses arguments, and expects them to hold.

7, 8

Verse 8 presents difficulties in the Greek, which the RSV has attempted to iron out. The danger of the smooth rendering which the revisers have achieved with some skill is that it suggests that the question, *And why not do evil that good may come?* is simply another formulation of the previous question, *But if through my falsehood God's truthfulness abounds to his glory, why am I still being condemned as a sinner?* Many commentators have taken it as such a continuation, as a sort of sharpening up, to show into what a ridiculous position an already ridiculous formulation in v. 7 gets you. But the actual Greek order in v. 8 suggests rather that the second question is a perversion of a perfectly genuine statement in v. 7, just as the second question in v. 5 was a perversion of the first.

A fairly literal rendering of v. 8 would be: 'And this is not, is it (as we are slandered with saying, and as some men affirm we have said), "Let us do evil that good may come"?'

However, this rendering of v. 8 seems not to follow on from v. 7, for v. 7, as it is translated in the RSV, does not seem to express a position that could be misrepresented by 'Let us do evil that good may come'. On the contrary, v. 7 seems to express a complaint against God by an unrighteous man who wonders why he is being condemned when other unrighteous men are getting off scot free.

This cannot be right, because the 'I' of v. 7 can hardly be different from the 'we' of v. 5, since there is no indication of a change of speaker. However, the 'we' of v. 5 were not to be condemned by God at all; on almost any rendering of those difficult opening words, 'we' are not to be condemned, but escape the wrath of God. (The RSV does suggest that God's wrath is inflicted *on us* by adding those two words to the translation of the second sentence in v. 5, but there is no basis for that addition in the Greek.)

We should expect v. 7 to raise the problem of the justified sinner, rather than voice the complaint of the condemned sinner; that would preserve the connection with the question in v. 5. We should also expect v. 7 to contain a statement capable of proving that the slogan in v. 8, 'Let us do evil that good may come', is a patent slander.

One Latin manuscript, codex Amiatinus, preserves an ancient suggestion about punctuating this verse which gives a rendering that satisfies our two expectations. On this punctuation the verse would read: 'If the truth of God together with my lie abounds to his glory, what (shall we say)? I too as a sinner am still condemned.' (The first question is grammatically an elliptical form of the first question in v. 5. This obvious parallel has been overlooked because *why . . . still* is a common Pauline construction.)

The point Paul is making is that God in his faithfulness ('the truth of God') has taken up Paul's faithlessness ('my falsehood') in a way that has recovered a righteous man for himself, and thus served his glory by restoring creation one step nearer its proper state. But that does not mean that Paul is content to remain false and expects no judgement on his sin. On the contrary, although he has become righteous, he too will still be judged as a sinner. He means he will still have to face God's judgement, and be purified from all the ill he has done in the body, although he has become righteous and can confidently expect to be saved after purging, 2 Cor. 5.10; 1 Cor. 3.10–15. Therefore, it is slanderous to suppose that he would subscribe to the sentiment, 'Let us do evil that good may come', even though a superficial acquaintance with his position might lead one to deduce that conclusion, from hearing that unrighteous men were to be accepted by God as righteous.

Verses 7 and 8 together may, then, be rendered as follows: 'If God's trustworthiness in dealing with my falsity has abounded to his ultimate glory, what shall we say? It still remains true that I too will be judged as a sinner. And this is surely not, is it (as we are slanderously accused of implying, and as some men affirm we actually say), "Let us do evil that good may come"? The condemnation of those who subscribe to that principle is, of course, just.'

3.9–20

⁹*What then? Are we Jews any better off?ᶜ No, not at all; for Iᵈ have already charged that all men, both Jews and Greeks, are under the power of sin,* ¹⁰*as it is written:*

'None is righteous, no, not one;
¹¹*no one understands, no one seeks for God.*
¹²*All have turned aside, together they have gone wrong;*
   no one does good, not even one.'
¹³*'Their throat is an open grave,*
   they use their tongues to deceive.'
'The venom of asps is under their lips.'
¹⁴*'Their mouth is full of curses and bitterness.'*
¹⁵*'Their feet are swift to shed blood,*
¹⁶*in their paths are ruin and misery,*
¹⁷*and the way of peace they do not know.'*
¹⁸*'There is no fear of God before their eyes.'*

¹⁹*Now we know that whatever the law says it speaks to those who are under the law, so that every mouth may be stopped, and the whole world may be held accountable to God.* ²⁰*For no human being will be justified in his sight by works of the law, since through the law comes knowledge of sin.*

ᶜ *Or at any disadvantage?*   ᵈ *Greek we.*

In 3.1–8 Paul has tried to defend his position from the main objections that his fellow theologians could bring against him – that he would destroy the special position of the Jewish people; that he would nullify God's faithfulness if it were true that all Israel had proved faithless; that he would make God unjust if God were to choose some unrighteous men and reject others; and that he would encourage men to sin by assuring them that all would be well in the end.

He now turns to a positive statement of his case.

The first proposition is that all men are subject to sin. No one is righteous. The Law itself says so, therefore no attempt to keep the precepts of the Law is at all likely to make a man righteous. The Law itself is the clearest revelation of sin.

Unfortunately for Paul's case, many of the quotations from the Old Testament he uses to support the position that all men are sinners suggest just the opposite. Verses 13, 14, and 18 come from Psalms in which a clear distinction is made between the righteous and the unrighteous.

I do not think it possible that Paul cited these verses in the original Epistle to the Romans and, in this case, the proof is relatively easy.

There is a clear distinction, in vv. 10–18, between those parts that are taken word for word from the LXX version of the Old Testament, the standard Greek translation used in the Mediterranean cities where Jews of the Dispersion normally spoke Greek, and those parts that are free translations from the original Hebrew. Paul himself used the Hebrew of the Old Testament direct, and the later glossators and commentators the standard Greek translation.

The following table sets out the differences.

Romans	A	B
10b	Psalm 14.3	
11	Psalm 14.2b	
12		Psalm 14.3
13a		Psalm 5.9
13b		Psalm 140.3b
14		Psalm 10.7a
15		Isaiah 59.7a
16		Isaiah 59.7c
17		Isaiah 59.8a
18		Psalm 36.1b

[The Psalm numbers and the verse numbers are those of the RSV; the LXX numberings differ slightly.]

Column A contains free citations from the original Hebrew; column B a catena of verses from the Psalms and Isaiah, which follows the LXX version more or less closely.

The collection of verses in column B had an independent existence before it was added to Romans. It was put together to illustrate from scripture how every part of man's body is prone to wickedness: his throat, his tongue, his lips, his mouth, his feet, and his eyes are all bent on evil.

Although the collection actually weakens Paul's case, by drawing attention to passages from the Psalms that contrast the ways of the righteous with the ways of the unrighteous, it is easy to see how it came to be incorporated here. The catena began with a verse from Psalm 14 that Paul had already cited in his own translation, and of course the verses seemed to support Paul's case about the wickedness of man.

If a reader is doubtful whether such long passages could come to be incorporated into a Biblical text in this way, let him turn to the Prayer Book version of Psalm 14. There he will find that the opposite process has been at work: Romans 3.13–18 has been incorporated back into the Old Testament in Psalm 14.3–8 (LXX 13.3).

Paul's original citations are brief and telling references to Psalm 14 that support his case for saying that all men are unrighteous. He concludes with a reference to another verse, from Psalm 143, to show that no flesh shall be justified before God. The Old Testament does not leave any hope that a man can fulfil its precepts and become righteous, and, since nothing better can be expected from the Gentiles, every mouth is stopped and the whole world is accountable to God (verse 19).

Notes

9

What then? Are we Jews any better off? No, not at all; for I have already charged that all men . . .: This translation, down to *not at all*, represents merely five Greek words, and the length of the paraphrase is a measure of the difficulties involved in making sense of Paul's seemingly cryptic remark. The makers of the RSV have translated the Greek in this sense:

'What then? Are we excelled? Not at all?' They have then referred the 'we' to the Jewish objectors who asked, 'Then what advantage has the Jew?' in v. 1. Barrett explains this interpretation very clearly. He writes, 'The Jew has an advantage, and he has not an advantage ... The advantage of the Jew is real, but it is an advantage which is (or may at any moment become) at the same time a disadvantage. It consists in knowing (out of Scripture) that before God all talk of "advantages" is folly and sin.'

The greatest difficulty in accepting this reading is that the 'we' in both v. 8 and later on in v. 9 refers to Paul himself, and is difficult to take otherwise here. The other difficulty is that Paul could hardly have so flatly denied that the Jew had any advantage so soon after affirming the greatness of his advantages in v. 1.

The five Greek words in question may, however, be translated like this: 'What then do we put up as a defence? Not completely.'

As it stands, this is nonsense, but I hope to show that the true sense lies hidden in this rendering. In its favour, 'not completely' is a more natural translation than 'no, not at all', even if the latter be perfectly possible (cf. 1. Cor 5.10 for 'not completely'). Furthermore, it is very unusual in Paul to find one verb standing alone in a sentence, as the RSV takes the verb here; we should expect there to be more to the sentence. If we make one sentence of the first three words, the 'what' becomes the object of the verb taken in its middle sense, 'we hold something before us for our protection'; the passive sense, 'we are excelled', could not, of course, take an object, so that the verb had to stand alone.

'What, then, do we put up as a defence?' is a beautifully apt step in the argument. In the previous verse Paul has said 'we have been slandered' and in the rest of the chapter he goes on to make a reasoned defence against the charges levelled against him. The only difficulty in the way of accepting this rendering is the nonsensical remark, 'Not completely'. However, these two words do not appear in a host of manuscripts (D*, G, P, Ψ, 104, eth, Origen), and the exact reading we require is positively given by P: 'What, then, do we put up as a defence? We have argued previously that Jews and Greeks are all under sin'.

The words 'not completely' were originally a gloss, possibly to the next word, 'we have previously argued'. The glossator noted, rather pedantically, that Paul seemed only to have argued previously that *Jews* were under sin, assuming, rather than arguing, that Gentiles were under sin. Whatever the true explanation of the gloss, the intrusion of the words into the text in most manuscripts has caused commentators a great deal of trouble.

10

none is righteous, no, not one: this is Paul's own translation of the Hebrew original, which runs literally, 'There is no one doing good; there is no one, not even one'. The righteous man is the man who does good – a further indication that Paul cannot be thinking of imputed righteousness when he quotes Habakkuk, 'The righteous man shall live by faith' (Romans 1.17). No one does good, and God has revealed in the gospel how a man may do good and live.

19

The argument is not entirely clear, and a step seems to have been omitted. If the Law (the whole Old Testament) is for the Jews, it can only be understood to lead to the conclusion that the whole world of Jews and Gentiles is accountable to God provided the further argument, that the Gentiles are accountable to God anyway, is assumed. But why should Paul have used the strong logical connection, *so that*, if the conclusion does not completely follow from the premiss? I suspect that the words *to those who are under the law* were originally a gloss by someone who did not hold that Christians were under the Law. Paul wrote, 'Now we know that all that the Law says it speaks in order that every mouth be stopped and all the world be answerable to God.' He was making an assertion, with which all Jewish theologians would agree, that the Old Testament moral law was meant to apply to all men; therefore, the affirmation that no one is righteous applied to Gentiles as well as to Jews.

There is no textual evidence for this omission.

3.21–31

²¹*But now the righteousness of God has been manifested apart from law, although the law and the prophets bear witness to it,* ²²*the righteousness of God through faith in Jesus Christ for all who believe. For there is no distinction;* ²³*since all have sinned and fall short of the glory of God,* ²⁴*they are justified by his grace as a gift, through the redemption which is in Christ Jesus,* ²⁵*whom God put forward as an expiation by his blood, to be received by faith. This was to show God's righteousness, because in his divine forbearance he had passed over former sins;* ²⁶*it was to prove at the present time*

that he himself is righteous and that he justifies him who has faith in Jesus.
²⁷*Then what becomes of our boasting? It is excluded. On what principle?
On the principle of works? No, but on the principle of faith.* ²⁸*For we hold
that a man is justified by faith apart from works of law.* ²⁹*Or is God the
God of Jews only? Is he not the God of Gentiles also? Yes, of Gentiles also,*
³⁰*since God is one; and he will justify the circumcised on the ground of their
faith and the uncircumcised through their faith.* ³¹*Do we then overthrow the
law by this faith? By no means! On the contrary, we uphold the law.*

If my understanding of Paul's epistle to his fellow Jewish Christians
at Rome has been at all on the right lines, we should expect at this
point in his argument a clear statement that God will declare righteous
at the end those who have discovered the righteousness acceptable to
him. All men, even Jews who do their best to keep the precepts of the
Law, fail to be righteous, yet, if Paul's case in 3.1–8 is to have any
basis of truth, there must be a way for them to be righteous, and this
way must have been shown by God to men.

That is what we should expect Paul to say, and say clearly.

Certainly, the passage ends, in vv. 27–31, with a clear enough
conclusion to the sort of argument we should have expected: since
only the man who trusts and who does not boast in his own prowess
at keeping the precepts will be declared righteous, the Gentile has the
same right to the gospel as the Jew. But vv. 21–26 are so overloaded
with ideas that it is hard to see clearly what Paul is getting at.

Much of vv. 21–26 is a defence of *God's* righteousness – vv. 25b
and 26 seem to be entirely a statement justifying God in ignoring past
sins, and in declaring righteous the men who are not righteous but
yet have faith in Jesus. But, if that is what Paul is saying here, his case
could hardly stand against the objections he has already discussed in
3.1–8, and would conflict with the argument he is about to launch in
Chapter 4. In 3.1–8 he maintained that God would declare righteous
only sinners who had actually managed to become righteous, and
that he would not overlook even the sins of them. In Chapter 4 he is
to maintain that Abraham, who did not know Jesus Christ, was
righteous because he trusted and believed.

I do not think Paul could possibly have written vv. 25b and 26 if
they really do contain the sort of attempt to vindicate God's own

righteousness which he implicitly and explicitly rejects in 3.1–8 and in Chapter 4. Fortunately, we have substantial textual evidence that a scribe was responsible for adding one of the arguments in defence of God's own righteousness. Some manuscripts read, 'This was to show God's righteousness in the present time' instead of *This was to show God's righteousness, because in his divine forbearance he had passed over former sins; it was to prove at the present time* . . . Besides this one addition in defence of God, I am inclined to see further signs of similar additions at the end of v. 26, and to conjecture that Paul's original text was concerned not with God's righteousness, which he could assume, but with the way for men to become righteous, which was the whole issue at stake in his attempt to win the Roman Christians to support him in his approach to the Gentiles.

Verses 25b and 26 cannot be separated from vv. 21–25a; from the last sentence in v. 22, *For there is no distinction*, to the end of v. 26 is actually one sentence in the Greek, so that any shift in our understanding of the last part must be taken into account when we try to state the argument in the first part. Here the text is much less disturbed, but ever since the earliest commentators began to expound St Paul there has been a great deal of discussion about the meaning of the phrases and their connection with one another.

In 1948 Bultmann made the interesting suggestion that the complicated overloading was due to the fact that Paul was citing an older credal formula (*Theology of the N.T.*, Vol. I, p. 46; Ernst Käsemann, *Z.N.W.* 43 (1950–1), pp. 150–4, reprinted in Vol. I of *Exegetische Versuche und Besinnungen*). The creed consisted of vv. 24 and 25, except for two phrases, *by his grace as a gift* and *to be received by faith*, which were Paul's own additions to the formula. Charles H. Talbert has accepted the idea that there is a self-contained formula embedded in Paul's text (in his case, vv. 25 and 26 rather than vv. 24 and 25), but has argued that *this was added* (*by a later editor*) to what Paul wrote, not incorporated by Paul himself (*Journal of Biblical Literature*, LXXXV (1966), pp. 287–96).

Certainly, our present text contains more ideas to the verse than we should expect to find in a straightforward piece of argument, but there are not enough stylistic and linguistic indications of a set formula to make either Bultmann's or Talbert's case convincing.

The truth seems to be that Paul's text has been added to here and there by a number of hands, and that no one simple theory will explain what has happened.

I have attempted to justify my conclusion in detail in the notes, but here, to begin the discussion, is a translation of my reconstruction of Paul's original text.

21. But now the righteousness acceptable to God has been manifested separately from the Law, although witnessed to by the Law and the Prophets, (22) righteousness of God through faith, for all, yes, for all who trust and believe. For there is no distinction, (23) for all have sinned and come short of (reflecting) the glory of God, (24) but they will be freely vindicated by his grace by virtue of the redemption (from death) of Jesus Christ, (25) whom God set before (men) in blood as a means of expiation, to show in this present age the righteousness he requires, (26b) that the man who lives by faith is righteous.

On this reconstruction of the text, Paul argues that God has shown how men may actually be righteous, even though they all fall short of reflecting God's glory in their living. God will graciously declare them righteous at the end by virtue of their adopting Jesus Christ as their means of expiation. God raised him from the dead and so set him before men in blood as the sacrifice they could adopt and offer for themselves. The righteousness God requires consists in faithfully trusting oneself to Christ, and relying on him for cleansing from sin's defilement.

Verses 27-31 draw the conclusion for Jewish Christians. Although they have the immeasurable privilege of having been entrusted with the oracles of God, they have no ground for recommending themselves to God as successful keepers of the things there commanded. They are in exactly the same position as Gentiles who have believed and trusted: Jews will be declared righteous for the same reason as Gentiles, that they have trusted God and adopted as their own the sacrifice he provided.

Paul concludes by affirming that, far from destroying the authority of the Law, he is confirming its authority. He means that the righteousness made known in the death and resurrection of Jesus Christ was already recommended in the Old Testament; that will be his theme in Chapter 4.

Notes

21

has been manifested: a Greek perfect, meaning the righteousness was manifested and continues manifest. The tense suggests that it is information which is available, is manifest; one more small sign that the *righteousness of God* is the righteousness God requires rather than a deed or gift of God himself. It could, of course, refer to a quality of God himself, but that meaning is excluded by v. 22.

apart from law: separately from the Old Testament rather than lawlessly, as the RSV's over-literal rendering might suggest.

22

through faith in Jesus Christ for all who believe: Chrysostom cites this verse in the form, 'the righteousness of God through faith to all and for all who believe', and this text was probably the original. There is added support for the supposition that a scribe added *in Jesus Christ* in the fact that, while most manuscripts read, literally, 'of Jesus Christ', B and Marcion have 'of Christ', and A has 'in Christ Jesus'. Here I prefer the shorter reading, but at the end of the verse I prefer the longer reading, 'to all and for all who believe', with a great deal of manuscript support, including D, F, G, K, 33 and, of course, Chrysostom. The second expression could easily have slipped out when the scribe's eye jumped from one 'all' to the next, and the ancient editors of our text would be inclined to follow the rule about accepting the shorter reading when nothing of doctrinal importance would be lost. No ancient editor is likely to have left out the name Jesus Christ if offered a variety of possibilities, including some evidence for omission.

The faith or trust is not itself the righteousness. The righteousness God accepts is discovered by those who trust; it is there for all who trust. The double expression, to all and for all, is a rhetorical doubling, and we can hardly distinguish in English between the two prepositions.

23

fall short of the glory of God: probably means lack the glory of God which men, as creatures made in God's image, should reflect (cf. 2 Cor. 3.18).

24

they are justified: a participle in the Greek. The reference is to the future (as shown by v. 30), the day of judgement when those who have discovered the righteousness (justice) of God will be declared to be righteous or vindicated (will be justified) (cf. 1 Kings 8.32).

by his grace as a gift: literally, 'freely by his grace'. The righteous man is the man who knows he has sinned and falls short of reflecting God's glory and knows he needs to have his sin blotted out. He goes 'from faith to faith', trusting God to show him what to do, and to accept him, despite his imperfection, when he is raised from the dead to be judged. God will justify him freely by his grace.

through the redemption which is in Christ Jesus: as they stand, these words suggest that Christ Jesus was the price God had to pay before he could freely forgive sinners; men could not be united with God, that is, atonement (at-one-ment) could not be accomplished, until payment had been made. Theories of the atonement start from that basis, and then tend to divide into theories which hold that God himself needs satisfaction to be made to himself, and those which hold that the great enemy of God, the Devil, has some rights over man that have to be satisfied. The first of these theories seems to fit our context better, since here we have no mention of the Devil.

The difficulty of accepting this general reading of the verse is that Paul has just emphasized that God vindicates the righteous man who lives by faith *freely by his grace.* Of course the answer might well be, freely as far as the sinner is concerned, but at a great cost as far as God is concerned. This answer seems indeed to be confirmed by the rest of the paragraph, vv. 25 f., in which the justice of God's giving something away free is vindicated. But I have argued that this reading of vv. 25 f. is a later distortion of what Paul was writing about, which was how a sinner, who comes short of reflecting God's glory, can live as a righteous man. The subject is not how God can be just, but how man can be just.

It follows that the switch in v. 24 from God who freely vindicates by his grace men who lack his glory to the idea that this is possible through the payment of a price in the person of Christ Jesus may be part of the same distortion.

There is textual evidence for this. One minuscule, 1836, reads 'through the redemption of Jesus Christ', and I conjecture that this seemingly ambiguous expression was interpreted by a glossator in words which have swallowed up the simpler original form in all other manuscripts. (It is unlikely that the form found in 1836 was a modification of the usual reading, or a slip made by a scribe who was following a master manuscript that contained the usual reading.)

The natural meaning of 'through the redemption of Jesus Christ' would be 'by virtue of the redemption from death of Jesus Christ' (cf. 8.23), a reference to the resurrection. The first word, *through*, is not, as our glossator would have thought, a reference to the means by which God could forgive sinners and remain just, but a reference to that operation of God's grace in the first place which set in train the revelation of the righteousness he would graciously vindicate at the end. God accepts the sacrifice of those who make Jesus Christ their sacrifice, as he showed when he raised him from the dead.

25

whom God put forward as an expiation: God himself provided the sacrifice, as in fact he had always done. The repudiation of child sacrifice in Israel and the adoption of animal sacrifice was specifically said to be a provision whereby God gave a substitute for what men were forbidden to offer, their own male offspring. (See the story of Abraham's sacrifice of Isaac, Gen. 22.)

The word translated *expiation* probably means 'atoning sacrifice', although Origen, Luther, and others since have preferred another possible translation, 'mercy seat', referring to the covering of the Ark of the Covenant in the Temple, which was sometimes referred to by this one word in the LXX translation. Then Paul would have been referring to the place where God shows his mercy to his people, which was sprinkled with blood once a year (cf. Schlatter). The translation 'mercy seat' is scarcely possible because that would require some positive indication that the word was short for 'expiatory covering of the ark'. It must be short for 'means of atonement'.

The sacrifice is set before men by God to be offered back by them to him. This raises the old difficulty that God might seem to be bound to require some payment from some source in order to compensate him for being gracious to sinners. That can hardly be an adequate reading of the situation, because God himself has provided the compensation he is supposed to need. A true statement of the case is rather that men are required to acknowledge that they have defiled and stained themselves in misusing the freedom given to them by their Creator. They must take actual steps to purify themselves. The only way to do that is to offer a sacrifice to God.

It is not God who needs the sacrifice, but man. In giving man

freedom God gave him the possibility of freely obeying and worshipping his Creator and of freely disobeying and ignoring his Creator. By
disobeying and turning away from his Creator, man is doing something
that irrevocably affects himself, his society, and his environment,
which no amount of making good, however praiseworthy that may
be, can blot out. Men who are at all sensitive to their situation, however
unaware of God they may be, know this; it is the basis of tragedy, and
a constant element in our dealings with other men. In the supreme and
key relationship with God we need to find a sacrifice. The news
entrusted to the apostles is that God has put Jesus Christ before us as
a sacrifice. We are able to offer him.

by his blood: the word 'his' is doubtful. Mss. B, 1908 and 1913 have 'his
own', and 69 reads 'his' after 'blood' instead of before. I cannot see
how *his* fits the sense of the sentence – of course the blood was Jesus's
blood. The word 'his' looks like a pedantic addition to an original text
which said simply 'in the blood'. The phrase goes with the verb
(Lipsius): 'whom God set (before men) in blood as means of atonement'. The primary reference is to the cross, although every subsequent preaching or celebration of the eucharist, particularly the
latter, is a setting-forth in blood of Jesus Christ as means of atonement.
'Setting forth in blood' means God's provision of a sacrifice which
men may claim as their own sacrifice.

to be received by faith: in the Greek these words stand before *by his blood*,
and the combination would be translated most naturally as 'through
faith in his blood'. Most commentators prefer to take 'through faith'
with *expiation* and this produces the sense given by the RSV. Certainly,
the RSV reading fits in best with Paul's thought elsewhere, but the
Greek does not really allow it. The words 'through faith' are omitted
in A, 2127 and are probably a marginal note designed either to make
the point about how the expiation is to be received or to refer to the
sacramental reception of Christ's blood.

25b, 26

This was to show God's righteousness ... at the present time: as I have
said in the essay on the passage as a whole, I accept the shorter reading
in F, G, 33, 216*, 326, 336, 440, 1852 as the original. Further support
comes from 1898, which reads *at the present time* after *to show God's
righteousness* in v. 25. *God's righteousness* could be taken to mean God's
characteristic of justice, and *to show* could mean *to prove*. On this
reading, a commentator could easily feel called on to explain how
God's justice was vindicated by the atoning sacrifice, and accordingly

added the words I shall discuss in the next note. But *to show God's righteousness at the present time* in the context of Paul's argument, which is about how a man can find the righteousness acceptable to God, may equally well mean, 'to show the righteousness he requires in the present age'. In this present age God asks men to trust him by adopting Jesus Christ's death as their means of atonement with him. In a previous age, like the age of Abraham, which is to be discussed in Chapter 4, God still required faith or trust as the mainspring of righteousness, together with the same lack of trust in one's own righteousness, but in this present age God has shown his faithfulness completely by redeeming Jesus Christ from death and setting him before men in blood as their means of atonement.

because in his divine forbearance he had passed over former sins; it was to prove: two words, *passed over* and *former*, occur nowhere else in Paul, and *forbearance* only in 2.4, which I have argued is not by Paul. The meaning of this passage is much disputed when it is regarded as an integral part of Paul's text, but when we see that it is an insertion of an original marginal comment, many of the difficulties resolve themselves.

A literal translation will show what I mean, when the words are arranged as follows:

for demonstration of his
righteousness

because of the passing over of
the sins of old
in the forbearing (time) of
God;
for the demonstration of his
righteousness

in the present time
so that he is righteous in
justifying the man who has
faith in Jesus.

The glossator took the atoning sacrifice of Christ as justifying God's righteousness in two respects: in the time before the sacrifice he was righteously able to pass over sins because he would eventually see that an appropriate sacrifice was offered; and in the time since the sacrifice he is able righteously to forgive the man who has faith because he has provided the sacrifice by which his justice is satisfied.

Paul's argument, on the contrary, is that God requires his righteousness in men, and has always done so, as is clear from the example of Abraham, Chapter 4. His justice is not at all impugned when he vindicates unrighteous men, because they have learnt by faith to live righteously (1.17; 3.1–8). Jesus Christ has been set forth in blood as means of atonement to enable men to live righteously, not to allow God to receive satisfaction from one quarter sufficient to enable him to waive punishment in another quarter.

26b

that he himself is righteous and that he justifies him who has faith in Jesus: the words *in Jesus* are to be omitted, with G and the Old Latin manuscripts e, f, g. Only one word is involved in the Greek, and strictly speaking this one word would mean that the faith was like Jesus's (cf. 4.16, *those who share the faith of Abraham*). The origin of the gloss was an attempt by a glossator to define the (surprising) single man who has faith; hence the reading of 'Jesus' in the accusative to be found in some manuscripts (D, Ψ, 33, 326, etc.): the one who has faith is Jesus.

The word *and* should also be omitted, with F and G.

The clause is overloaded and awkward, and I conjecture, without support in the manuscripts, that a glossator added the pronoun *himself* and the participle represented by (*and*) *that he justifies* in the RSV. When these two words are omitted, *him who has faith* becomes the subject of the verb 'to be', and *righteous* becomes the object: 'namely, that the man who lives by faith is righteous'. (For 'that' as indicating that the content of a previous expression – here, the righteousness of God – is being given, cf. 1 Thess. 4.9.)

27

On what principle? On the principle of works? No, but on the principle of faith: the word translated *principle* is the word Law. The translation is in itself possible, but hardly in this context, where Law means the Old Testament (or, perhaps, the requirements of the Old Testament). It is hard to see why a reader would suppose that any sort of law had the power to exclude boasting. Boasting is obviously excluded by the fact that all men are sinners for whom Christ died. The question Through what (is boasting excluded)? must be rhetorically designed to elicit an answer concerning the way of life that would steadily exclude boasting. The obvious answer is that a boasting way of life is best excluded when a man lives every day by trusting and believing rather than by attempting to achieve. I conjecture that the repeated 'of law' has come in from v. 28. Paul originally wrote: 'Where then is boasting? It is excluded. Through what? Through works? No, but through faith.' 'Law' was inserted by a glossator who used the word in the sense it has in 7.23 and 9.31, the sense *principle*.

28

For we hold that a man is justified by faith apart from works of law: The word translated *works* means service (Ex. 35.21 etc.) or duties (Nu. 3.7 f. etc.). Paul is not saying that service should not be rendered or duties done, but that no man will be vindicated by them; he has already proved from the Law that a man cannot be vindicated by performing the Law's duties (citing words from Psalm 14, and Psalm 143 in support of his argument). Paul is following the teaching of Jesus; see, for example, the story of the Pharisee and the tax-collector praying in the Temple, or the saying about how a master treats his servant (Luke 18.9–14; 17.7–10). Duties are duties, but they are of no account when God comes to judge a man. Hence the joy in heaven over one sinner who repents, and the cases that seem so unfair, as when a notorious sinner repents just before death, and is promised a place in Paradise (Luke 23.39–43).

30

he will justify: A genuine future, pointing to the day of judgement, not a future of consequence.

on the ground of their faith . . . through their faith: The two prepositions are purely rhetorical and there is no real difference between them (cf. Gal. 2.16.)

4.1–25

4 *What then shall we say about*[e] *Abraham, our forefather according to the flesh?* [2]*For if Abraham was justified by works, he has something to boast about, but not before God.* [3]*For what does the scripture say? 'Abraham believed God, and it was reckoned to him as righteousness.'* [4]*Now to one who works, his wages are not reckoned as a gift but as his due.* [5]*And to one who does not work but trusts him who justifies the ungodly, his faith is reckoned as righteousness.* [6]*So also David pronounces a blessing upon the man to whom God reckons righteousness apart from works:*

[7]*'Blessed are those whose iniquities are forgiven, and whose sins are covered;*

[8]*blessed is the man against whom the Lord will not reckon his sin.'*

[9]*Is this blessing pronounced only upon the circumcised, or also upon the uncircumcised? We say that faith was reckoned to Abraham as righteousness.* [10]*How then was it reckoned to him? Was it before or after he had been*

circumcised? It was not after, but before he was circumcised. 11*He received circumcision as a sign or seal of the righteousness which he had by faith while he was still uncircumcised. The purpose was to make him the father of all who believe without being circumcised and who thus have righteousness reckoned to them,* 12*and likewise the father of the circumcised who are not merely circumcised but also follow the example of the faith which our father Abraham had before he was circumcised.*

13*The promise to Abraham and his descendants, that they should inherit the world, did not come through the law but through the righteousness of faith.* 14*If it is the adherents of the law who are to be the heirs, faith is null and the promise is void.* 15*For the law brings wrath, but where there is no law there is no transgression.*

16*That is why it depends on faith, in order that the promise may rest on grace and be guaranteed to all his descendants – not only to the adherents of the law but also to those who share the faith of Abraham, for he is the father of us all,* 17*as it is written, 'I have made you the father of many nations' – in the presence of the God in whom he believed, who gives life to the dead and calls into existence the things that do not exist.* 18*In hope he believed against hope, that he should become the father of many nations; as he had been told, 'So shall your descendants be.'* 19*He did not weaken in faith when he considered his own body, which was as good as dead because he was about a hundred years old, or when he considered the barrenness of Sarah's womb.* 20*No distrust made him waver concerning the promise of God, but he grew strong in his faith as he gave glory to God,* 21*fully convinced that God was able to do what he had promised.* 22*That is why his faith was 'reckoned to him as righteousness.'* 23*But the words, 'it was reckoned to him,' were written not for his sake alone,* 24*but for ours also. It will be reckoned to us who believe in him that raised from the dead Jesus our Lord,* 25*who was put to death for our trespasses and raised̦ for our justification.*

e Other ancient authorities read *was gained by.*

Paul has already used a number of quotations from the Bible, above all the saying in Habakkuk 2.4, 'The righteous man shall live by faith' (Rom. 1.17), to support his thesis that God will vindicate those who believe and trust him rather than those who claim to be able to serve him perfectly. The righteousness God looks for is righteousness that consists in having faith and trusting him.

Paul now turns to Abraham, who to him and to all Jewish theologians is the key figure in the Old Testament. If he can show that Abraham was righteous because of his faith and trust and not because of the service he performed, he will be able to win the wholehearted support of the Jewish Christian community in Rome for his mission to the Gentiles.

The support he wants from the Christian synagogues in Rome is not that they should dissolve themselves in order to merge into one church of Jews and Gentiles. Paul does not wish to destroy the particularism of Judaism and replace it by an undifferentiated universalism. Rather he wishes to set up Gentile congregations alongside and separate from the Jewish congregations that believed in Jesus Christ, and he is writing to the existing Jewish congregations to win their wholehearted support for his work.

The argument in Chapter 4 is not that Abraham's faith made circumcision and the Law unnecessary, but that circumcision and the Law are sign and seal of the righteousness that consists of faith and trust (v. 11). That is, circumcision is assumed to continue for Jewish Christians (cf. 3.1), although it is also assumed that Gentile Christians will not be circumcised, because the faith of Abraham, which God counted as righteousness, was exercised before he was circumcised. Abraham is 'father of uncircumcision' as well as 'father of circumcision' (see notes on vv. 11 and 12).

When we read this chapter today, we tend to extract from it the lesson that faith or trust is a supremely commendable value. For example, Dodd says, 'Perhaps the chief positive truth which emerges is that when Paul speaks of faith he is referring to something which did not begin with Christianity, but is an original and permanent element of all genuinely religious life.' Or, if these words, first published in 1932, sound a little old-fashioned, we can appeal to Ernst Käsemann, who, although professing to scorn Dodd, gives a reading of Chapter 4 that makes the same sharp division between the situation of the believer standing frozen and entirely without God, listening eternally to the sanctifying and justifying word of God, on the one hand, and the ordinary events and occurrences of life on the other hand.

Käsemann insists that the 'world remains faith's battleground', but nevertheless for him faith can learn nothing from seeing events. 'We are separated from the world and history by the cross.' Paul's whole argument assumes that faith is trust in God who has done and will do what he has promised, and what he has promised is not some mysterious religious experience for individuals or some wholly unobservable new creation of humanity that alters nothing, but a whole series of historical events. Abraham, an ordinary guilty man, was chosen by God to be the founder of a new people. Although he had no direct heir, he trusted God to do what he said he would do, and God counted this trust righteousness. God did give him a direct heir, although he and his wife were old, and Sarah barren. Paul is writing as a Jew to his fellow Jews who trace their existence back to Isaac, and he argues that their whole duty is to walk in Abraham's steps and to trust God the way he did. They are Christians now because they have continued to trust the same God, who has lately raised Jesus from the grave.

It is logically impossible to make an absolute distinction between faith and God on the one hand, and events in time on the other hand (see Willard Van Orman Quine, 'Two Dogmas of Empiricism' in *From a Logical Point of View*, second edition, Cambridge, Massachusetts, 1961), so that all attempts to commend the Christian faith by driving a wedge between God and such things as deeds, events, consequences, change, birth and death are doomed from the start. If Paul was commending Abraham as the type of the man who lived by a bare faith that expected nothing to happen in the world as a result, we should have to reject his position as untenable. If Paul was reducing the history of the Jewish people to a tribal saga with no more significance than the history of any other people, except that it happened to contain the story of a figure who symbolizes true human existence, then we should have to relegate Romans to the category of 'ancient literature', and deem all Paul's claims to be bearing news about God as illusion. The features Dodd and Käsemann and our whole general 'modern' understanding of the world try to get rid of from Paul's argument – the events that are supposed to be done by God or done at the command of God – are logically necessary to make his talk about faith coherent.

It may seem obvious from the way I have already summarized Paul's assumptions in Chapter 4 that no one could possibly imagine that Paul did drive a wedge between faith and the things promised to and provided for Abraham who had faith. Yet Paul's Epistle to the Romans has in the history of thought provided the text for just this division. Faith, instead of being a daily disposition of one's life in reliance on God and expectation of his providential leading, has been reduced to the mathematical point of bare belief; righteousness or goodness, instead of being a real and possible quality of life approved by God, has been defined as the arbitrary decree of God declaring some bad men good; and all Christian conversation with Jews has been ruled out unless the Jews renounce their people and their history. All these perversions of Paul's thought have contributed to the driving of a wedge between God and the world of things and events.

Unfortunately, our present text of *Romans* does provide a foothold for these ideas. In Chapter 4, for example, we have two verses which make a most sweeping condemnation of Judaism and the Old Testament, and imply that no Jew who follows the Old Testament requirements can possibly be a Christian. If Paul said that, he was condemning the Old Testament as a complete mistake, and the idea that God commanded his people to circumcise their male children, for example, as untrue. If he said that, he was making an antithesis between God and certain quite crucial events, and so contributing to a general tendency to separate God and all events. Yet he also says, in v. 11, that Abraham *received* circumcision, and he must mean received from God. Therefore I conclude that vv. 14 and 15 were written by a later glossator, who interpreted Paul's insistence on faith as a rejection of every special privilege of the Jews. The glossator, even in those early days, thought that the universalism of faith freed a man from seeing that particular events of the world are part of God's providential ordering of men and events towards his promised end. The glossator recoiled from the teaching that the Jews had been chosen by God and entrusted with his revelation in order to be a blessing for all the other nations on earth; and his recoil from this teaching, although perhaps fed by antisemitism and the Church's dismay that official Judaism had eventually forbidden Jews to follow Jesus Christ, sprang ultimately from a philosophical distaste for believing that the eternal and almighty God should take hold of particular events in order to draw all men to himself.

I think the plain man's reading of Romans 4 is proof against the sophistry of all interpretations that try to divorce faith from the promises and events that faith is given to take hold of and to live in. 'Following in the steps of Abraham' (v. 12) is no mysterious business to the man who believes that God will give an heir when he promises an heir, or to the man who believes that God has raised Jesus our Lord from the dead. But there is enough actually present in the chapter, on a close reading, to provide a toehold to the sophistries (particularly if the interpreters who argue on these lines have previously decided that God cannot promise or give things), and so to make necessary the rather detailed notes that follow.

Notes

1

What then shall we say about Abraham, our forefather according to the flesh?
The verb 'to say' can hardly have two simple objects in the accusative, 'what' and 'Abraham'. Consequently, many ancient authorities, whose reading is given in the RSV note, have supplied another verb to which 'Abraham' can be the subject: 'What then shall we say that Abraham gained (or, rather) discovered?' This reading has rightly been rejected by the RSV (following B, Origen cf. Chrysostom), but what is left is scarcely satisfactory. In one manuscript, 206, the connecting word *then* comes third in the sentence, not second, an impossible position. This leads me to guess that the first word, *What?* was originally an addition by a scribe who wanted to bring the sentence into line with the common expression in Paul, What then shall we say? (see 6.1; 7.7; 8.31; 9.14, 30). If we put the first word, *What?*, to one side, and read 'then' after the verb, we recover a sentence which provides rather a good transition from the objection with which Chapter 3 closed to the argument which dominates Chapter 4: 'We shall speak, then, about Abraham our forefather according to the flesh.' To the objection that he is destroying the authority of the Old Testament (the Law, in 3.31), Paul announces that he will consider the case of the Old Testament Jew *par excellence*, 'Abraham our ancestor'. He is clearly addressing an audience of fellow Jews.

2, 3

For if Abraham was justified by works, he has something to boast about, but not before God. For what does the scripture say? 'Abraham believed God, and it was reckoned to him as righteousness': the opening words, *For if Abraham was justified by works, he has something to boast about,* follow on beautifully from v. 1 as reconstructed above. Paul's conclusion would be: and then my argument (in 3.27 ff.) that boasting was precluded would fail. He has to speak about Abraham, because Abraham is a test case.

But, on this reading, the words that actually come next, *but not before God,* are following a different tack altogether. This objection implies that it is quite out of the question to suppose that anyone could be justified by works before God (whatever may be the case in the eyes of their fellow men). If we stop before these words, we get the strong impression that Paul takes the possibility that Abraham could have had cause to boast very seriously indeed, and that he wishes to argue the case with great care. The brusque *but not before God* looks like the remark of a theologian who has already surveyed the whole argument and then put a note against the passage at the point where he takes the crux of the matter to lie. And, strictly speaking, his remark is not true. A man who was justified before God because of his works would have reason to boast. The glossator argues from a definition of God, and that, perhaps, is the force of the citation from Gen. 15.6 that follows, which I should also ascribe to the glossator: 'Abraham believed in God' (and that implies *grace* must be the essence of the relationship), 'and this was accounted to him as righteousness'.

The glossator was making a profound theological point, but he is breathing a different atmosphere from Paul, who wishes to argue, and argue in a way that gives full force to the possibility that the position he is attacking could be right.

The citation is taken word for word from the LXX, in contrast to v. 9, which is a free rendering of the passage.

4

The argument in this verse implies that Abraham did nothing to lead to the reward he received; the reward was a pure gift. We should expect the continuation of the argument in v. 5 to say just this: 'But to the man who does not work, the reward is not reckoned as his due but as a gift.' However, in v. 5 the contrast is drawn, not between two ways in which rewards could be handed out (as gifts or as of right), but between two actions on the side of the recipient that could be counted as righteousness. Verse 4, therefore, looks very much like a continuation of the note by the glossator who is arguing from the nature of God. He is commenting on v. 5 from his point of view. God's rewards, he argues, are intrinsically gifts, and therefore the recipient of God's rewards cannot have earned them. Paul, however, is concerned to discover from scripture the way Abraham was reckoned righteous by God, in order to see whether in his theology he was remaining true to the Old Testament in saying that a man is justified by faith. He is arguing against the proposition that God only rewards those who work the works of the Lord, and he admits the possibility that if anyone did work the works of the Lord he would be rewarded. This possibility is denied by the glossator, on his view of the nature of God.

5

but trusts him who justifies the ungodly: the words *justifies the ungodly* mean 'acquits the wicked or guilty'. Abraham's godliness or ungodliness is not in question; indeed his willingness to listen to God argues for a certain godliness. His trust in God to acquit the guilty must mean his trust in God to acquit the guilty who trust in him. Paul is not contradicting the assumption that God cannot acquit the guilty, as expressed, for instance in Exodus 23.7 (Hebrew text), 'do not slay the innocent and righteous for *I will not acquit the wicked*'. He has already strenuously denied that God is unjust to inflict wrath (3.5), and God would be unjust if he punished some guilty men and acquitted others. Consequently, Paul means exactly what he says at the end of this verse: the *faith* of the man who does not work the works of the Lord *is reckoned as righteousness.* God counts faith to be righteousness. (The same verbal expression is used when it is said that Eli saw Hannah moving her lips without speaking and 'reckoned she was a drunken women' (1 Sam. 1.13). Eli was wrong about Hannah in taking silent prayer for drunkenness, but God was not wrong about Abraham, for God knows all the circumstances accurately and judges justly.) The lesson Paul wishes to teach is that the guilty man may become righteous not by trying to work the works of the Lord but by continually believing and trusting him who acquits the guilty.

6, 7, 8

The two opening verses of Psalm 32 are cited in the LXX translation (31.1 f.). The Psalmist uses three parallel expressions, which differ little in meaning: *iniquities* are removed, *sins* are covered, and *sin* is not charged to his account. God has forgiven the penitent sinner. So far there is little difficulty in seeing how the citation could fit into Paul's argument. The difficulty arises from the interpretation of the last clause of the citation that is put forward in v. 6. The positive of 'not reckon sin' in v. 8 is not 'reckon righteousness' but 'reckon as righteous', 'acquit'. The writer of v. 6 is either playing with words, or he thinks sin is like a black ball which can be cast into the urn against a man, and righteousness like a white ball which the happy man has cast in his favour. His words give rise to the theory that righteousness is imputed; a large sum is credited to the account of the man who really is in debt. The Psalmist did not mean this, nor did Paul mean this. Righteousness in *Romans* always elsewhere means the goodness which Israel was seeking, that is, a goodness men should try to show in their lives. This meaning is already assumed in v. 5, but will scarcely fit in v. 6. Accordingly, I conclude that vv. 6–8 were written by a later commentator who anticipated and prompted Luther's doctrine of imputation. This conjecture is supported by the fact that the Old Testament citation comes straight from the LXX.

9a

The first sentence in this verse comes from the hand of the same commentator. It assumes the question yet to be posed about Abraham in v. 10. The original comment was not a question but a statement: 'This blessing is for the circumcision and for the uncircumcision' (following 337 and 1874 in omitting *or*). The whole comment (vv. 6–9a) was meant to illuminate the passage (vv. 1, 2ab, 5, 9b, 10) against which it originally stood. Eventually the commentary was copied into the text, where it has given rise either to theories that righteousness is imputed (the Lutheran interpretation which seems closest to the meaning) or to theories that righteousness is given or infused (the older interpretation, which perhaps does less injustice to Paul's own argument).

9b

We say that: that is, the sentence from scripture we rely on for our argument is that in Gen. 15.6. Paul has paraphrased the Hebrew.

11, 12

Paul argues that the law about circumcision both confirms that the uncircumcised can become righteous and confirms that the circumcised should see circumcision as a reminder to follow in the footsteps of Abraham's faith. The Greek of these verses raises a number of problems. I should reconstruct the text here and there, usually with manuscript support, and the reconstructed text could be translated like this: 'And he received the sign of circumcision as seal of the righteousness he had while uncircumcised, which is of faith, so that he is *father . . . of uncircumcision*, that (faith) may be reckoned as righteousness (= A 1319) also to them, (12) and *father of circumcision*, (that faith may be reckoned as righteousness) not to those of circumcision alone, but even to those (of circumcision) who walk in the footsteps of the faith ... of our father Abraham.' The true Jew is not every Jew who is circumcised, but the circumcised Jew who also walks in the footsteps of the faith of his father Abraham (cf. 9.6 ff.). Notice Paul identifies himself with his fellow Jews in this last clause, and gives us one more indication that he is writing to fellow Jews.

13
The RSV begins a new paragraph, but I think Paul is continuing to talk about circumcision. *The law* here means the law concerning circumcision. The inheritance of *the world* is extraordinarily difficult. The actual promise in Genesis was that Abraham and his seed (RSV: descendants) would inherit the land. I think the word *world* was a scribe's pious attempt to supply the right word – he had in mind the idea that Christians were spiritually to inherit the world. The original text was 'that he should (be) heir', and this text is preserved in one Latin manuscript now at Oxford (Laud. Lat. 108).

14, 15
These verses clearly exclude Jews from the possibility of being heirs with Abraham. The Law brings God's wrath, and only those Jews who give up the Law will not be able to transgress God's will. If this is the meaning of the verses – and I have tried in vain to discover a meaning that will be less antisemitic – Paul cannot possibly have written them, for he consistently argues that practising Jews may also be heirs of the promises. Weisse omits these two verses, and I agree. The author belonged to the same school as the writer of the 'Epistle of Barnabas' (cf. Chapter 13), and those Christians at the time of Justin Martyr who would not have any social contact with Jewish Christians (cf. *Dialogue with Trypho*, Chapter 47).

16
That is why: these words refer back to v. 13, another indication that vv. 14 f. were an interpolation into the original text.

The whole verse in the RSV seems to refer to Jews on the one hand (*the adherents of the law*) and to Gentile Christians on the other hand (*those who share the faith of Abraham*). But this reading cannot be right, because Paul is arguing that only Jews who follow in the footsteps of Abraham's faith are his true heirs. Paul of course also holds that Gentiles who follow in the footsteps of Abraham's faith are also Abraham's true heirs (he is also 'father of uncircumcision', v. 11), but that is not the centre of his argument at the moment, for he is trying to show Jews that their ancient destiny is to live by faith and not by works.

The RSV is hardly to be blamed for offering this translation, since the quotation from Gen. 17.5 in the LXX version which follows in v. 17 suggests that v. 16 is about Gentiles. But if the LXX citation is a gloss, we are left free to translate v. 16 more fittingly. It is built on exactly the same grammatical lines as v. 12, and reads as follows: 'For this reason (the inheritance is) of faith so that it might be according to grace, that the promise should be sure to all the seed, not the seed that keeps the law (of circumcision) alone but even the seed that lives by the faith of Abraham, who is father of us all.'

17

in the presence of the God in whom he believed, who gives life to the dead and calls into existence the things that do not exist: it is very difficult to see how this statement fits with anything that goes before. Most commentators relate it to the words *he is the father of us all* at the end of v. 16, but it is no easier to see why Paul should want to emphasize that Abraham's fatherhood is *in the presence of . . . God* than to see why God's promise *I have made you the father of many nations* should be *in the presence of . . . God.* The solution to the difficulty seems to be that the statement was originally a gloss against the statement that now follows in v. 18, *in hope he believed against hope.* The glossator noted in the margin that it was entirely reasonable to believe hopefully, even against what a man could naturally hope, because this belief was belief in the presence of God *who gives life to the dead and calls into existence the things that do not exist.* This is an admirable theological sentiment, but not by Paul, and certainly not a licence to think that belief is a static passive pose by which a man expects to be created from nothing every day by the call of God (Käsemann).

18

of many nations: I suspect that this is another universalistic gloss. It certainly distracts from the main argument, by directing attention to Gen. 17.5, when the context is all about Gen. 15.5, the moment when Abraham and Sarah were promised a son in their old age.

19

This verse contains a famous textual variant. A great number of manuscripts, although not those usually considered most reliable, read 'he did *not* consider' instead of 'he did consider'. (The negative is read by D, G, Ψ, 33, 1984, etc., and omitted by א, A, B, C, 81, etc.). The reading without the negative has been translated by the RSV in a way that makes the best of a bad job; it really means, 'Although he did not weaken in faith, he (really) considered his own body dead . . .' This was probably a brilliant (but wrong) emendation of the text, by omitting the negative, in order to allow for a gloss, *which was as good as dead* (one word in the Greek), that had been inserted earlier. We can see that *which was as good as dead* is a gloss when we observe that it forces us to read the verb *he considered* in one way with regard to Abraham himself, and in another way with regard to Sarah. With Abraham the verb means, 'he considered X as Y', and with Sarah it means, 'he considered he fixed his eyes upon Z'. Omit the gloss, and we can take the verb in the second sense alone, and we do not need to omit the negative: 'And not weakening in faith, he did not fix his attention on his own body . . . and the barrenness of Sarah his wife'.

22

This is an unnecessary and distracting citation of Gen. 15.6 from the LXX, added in order to give in full the verse alluded to in v. 23.

25

for our trespasses . . . for our justification: there is a little difficulty in coordinating these two phrases; the identical preposition *for* is literally *because of*, and we probably have to understand, 'he was handed over to be crucified because of our sins (in order to atone for them), and he was raised because of our justification (in order to achieve it)'. The word here translated *justification* is very rare, and only occurs in one other place in the New Testament (Rom. 5.18). Lipsius is quite right to draw attention to the fact that Paul does not normally link the resurrection with our justification, and I rather suspect that the last clause, *and raised for our justification*, was the work of a glossator who wanted to round off the original text in a fitting way. He only succeeded in blurring the picture, for the clause *who was put to death for our trespasses* by itself is a free summary of Is. 53.5, 'But he was wounded for our transgressions, he was bruised for our iniquities'; which continues, 'the chastisement of our peace was upon him, and with his stripes we are healed'.

The thought of vv. 24 f. is this. Jewish Christians of Paul's day may take what was said about Abraham, that his faith and trust was reckoned to him as righteousness, as applying to them also, for they too believe and trust God who raised Jesus their Lord from the dead. God will vindicate them on the day of judgement because they have offered for themselves the sacrifice of Jesus' death.

5.1–11

5 Therefore, *since we are justified by faith, we^f have peace with God through our Lord Jesus Christ. ²Through him we have obtained access^g to this grace in which we stand, and we^h rejoice in our hope of sharing the glory of God. ³More than that, we^h rejoice in our sufferings, knowing that suffering produces endurance, ⁴and endurance produces character, and character produces hope, ⁵and hope does not disappoint us, because God's love has been poured into our hearts through the Holy Spirit which has been given to us.*

⁶While we were yet helpless, at the right time Christ died for the ungodly. ⁷Why, one will hardly die for a righteous man – though perhaps for a good man one will dare even to die. ⁸But God shows his love for us in that while we were yet sinners Christ died for us. ⁹Since, therefore, we are now justified by his blood, much more shall we be saved by him from the wrath of God. ¹⁰For if while we were enemies we were reconciled to God by the death of his Son, much more, now that we are reconciled, shall we be saved by his life. ¹¹Not only so, but we also rejoice in God through our Lord Jesus Christ, through whom we have now received our reconciliation.

^f Other ancient authorities read *let us.* *^g* Other ancient authorities add *by faith.* *^h* Or *let us.*

The sad consequence of trying to be righteous before God on the basis of what a man could do to please him was anxiety and lack of peace. However, it was revealed in the gospel that a man could become righteous and please God on the basis of faith. The righteous man therefore had peace with God, knew God's favour, and could face the future with confidence. He knew that he would see God's glory at the Day of Judgement, and he could go through difficulties and persecutions in this life because he was confident that God loved him. God himself inspired this confidence (v. 5).

In v. 6 Paul formulates the deep wish of those who are trying to perform the Law's requirements, who want to be counted among the

Messiah's followers, but who despair of their own attainments: 'If only Christ had died for the guilty! Why, one would hardly die for a righteous man, much less a guilty man.'

Paul answers by reaffirming that the sacrifice appointed by God's love is for sinners to take hold on. By faith, by accepting the blood of Christ, they become righteous. If that is so, they have no reason to fear the Day of Wrath when God judges men. They have already been reconciled to God, and therefore, to return to the theme of v. 2, their life can be a life of confidence and rejoicing in God, through Jesus Christ their mediator.

Notes

1

Therefore, since we are justified by faith: the man who lives by faith is righteous in God's eyes: not that righteousness is imputed to him even though he is actually unrighteous, nor that righteousness is infused into him to displace his unrighteousness, but that, as a man who believes and trusts God, he is actually righteous, for God says that that is the righteousness he requires. Translate rather, 'Therefore, since we are found righteous because of our faith ...' The verb has this meaning in 3.20 (echoing Psalm 143.2).

we have peace with God: the manuscripts we should normally prefer, including the excellent ℵ and B before correction, read 'let us have peace with God', a difference of one letter in the Greek. This can hardly be right; Paul is clearly drawing conclusions rather than mounting an exhortation. The reading adopted by the RSV has plenty of support, and its rival only got into our best manuscripts because of their editors' praiseworthy efforts to preserve difficult readings whenever possible – but this difficult reading is wrong, and arose probably as a scribe's slip when writing from dictation, since the two forms would sound the same.

2

Through him we have obtained access to this grace in which we stand: 'grace' is God's favour, the *peace with God* referred to in v. 1. The RSV is probably right to follow B, D, G, 0220, etc. and relegate the phrase *by faith* to the margin; it was an early gloss.

we rejoice in our hope of sharing the glory of God: Paul probably means not only that we shall see God in his glory and become citizens of the kingdom, but also that we shall be ourselves changed and become glorious (2 Cor. 3.18). The verb translated *rejoice* here and in v. 3 has the same stem as the noun translated *boasting* in 3.27. Bragging about one's own achievements is ruled out by the nature of the case; any confidence expressed in the face of *sufferings* is based on knowledge of God's love and the hope of glory. '*Let him who boasts, boast in the Lord*' (1 Cor. 1.31; 2 Cor. 10.17 = Jeremiah 9.24).

3 ff.
knowing that suffering produces endurance,
and endurance produces character,
and character produces hope,
and hope does not disappoint us:
This little aside about the good effects on a man's character of suffering patiently endured is really irrelevant to Paul's argument, which is concerned with the ground *in God* of confidence. A marginal reflection has been copied into the body of the text by a later scribe.

5
because God's love has been poured into our hearts through the Holy Spirit which has been given to us: v. 8, which speaks about God's *love for us*, makes it unlikely that *God's love* here means our love for God. But then the sentence looks a little odd: the Holy Spirit would not pour God's love for us into our hearts. I think the oddness is easily overcome when we see that *God's love* is short for 'the knowledge of God's love for us'. The Holy Spirit itself is 'poured out' on those who believe (Joel 2.28 f.), and with God's Spirit comes knowledge of his love. The *heart* of man is regarded as the part that receives comfort, knowledge, and assurance (Isaiah 40.2, *speak tenderly to Jerusalem* is literally, 'speak to the heart of Jerusalem').

6
While we were yet helpless, at the right time Christ died for the ungodly: this cannot be what Paul meant, for, as many commentators point out, the word *helpless* or 'weak' is far too mild as a description of those called *ungodly* (or 'guilty'), *sinners* (v. 8), and *enemies* (v. 10). The text is in great disarray. (1) The text here translated is literally, 'For still Christ, while we were weak (K, P, Ψ, 33, etc.). (2) The better manuscripts read, 'For still Christ, while we were *still* weak' (ℵ, A, C, D, 81, etc.). (3) The most intelligent attempt to get sense out of the difficult conjunction of words is the Latin rendering, '*For why* did Christ, while we were *still* weak' (G, many Old Latin Mss., and the Vulgate). (4) The hardest reading is '*For if* Christ, while we were *still* weak' (201,

syr^(pal), bo). (5) This hardest reading has been slightly modified to make v. 6 follow on from v. 5, 'because the love of God has been poured out into our hearts . . . *if indeed* Christ, while we were *still* weak' (B, sa). The hardest reading (4) itself incorporates a gloss, *still*, which someone put in the margin as a suggestion, derived from v. 8, in place of the awkward opening 'for if', so that the original was probably (6): 'for if Christ, while we were weak' (Isidore, with plenty of support for omitting *still* in its second place). But what can this mean? Our starting point is the observation already made, that 'weak' is far too mild a word to represent the state of those for whom Christ died. I take the adjective to refer rather to the state of mind of Christians ('we') who cannot bring themselves to believe that Christ died for the guilty. The words translated by the R S V *at the right time* do not refer to the moment in history of Christ's death, but refer to the occasional doubts of Christians; the phrase naturally means 'at times'. The opening words, literally 'for if', are not followed by an apodosis, and they probably represent the idiomatic way of expressing an impossible wish. Paul is putting into words the feelings of Christians who are only too aware of their moral failings and unworthiness. I should translate vv. 6 and 7 as follows: 'If only Christ – (we say) sometimes when we are weak in understanding – had died for the guilty! For it is rare even to find someone who will die for a righteous man (much less for someone guilty like me).' The great answer to these longings is given in v. 8: *But God shows his love for us in that while we were yet sinners Christ died for us.*

7

though perhaps for a good man one will dare even to die: this repeats the idea of the first half of the verse, but puts a slightly higher estimate on the willingness of men to die for others. Jülicher rightly sees that this is probably a gloss; he suggests that the gloss was made in order to take account of Christian martyrs, who are willing to die for their Lord, 'the good man'.

9

we are now justified by his blood: we are 'justified' by *God*, so that it would be better if some other English preposition than 'by' could be found for the phrase *by his blood*. The Greek is literally 'in his blood'. Barrett suggests 'at the cost of his blood', but this is not an obvious rendering, and will not fit the parallel phrase at the end of v. 10, 'in his life' (translated in the R S V as *by his life*). We are found righteous on the basis of faith (v. 1), and that same assumption would seem to apply here as well. Perhaps we could translate, 'we are found righteous now in (receiving) his blood', and v. 10, 'we shall be saved in (receiving) his life' (i.e. the resurrection life). Our present passage would then refer to our reception of Holy Communion (1 Cor. 10.16), or to our adopting Christ's death as our sacrifice.

much more shall we be saved by him from the wrath of God: the words *of God* do not appear in the Greek, but are probably rightly understood. 'The wrath to come' (1 Thess. 1.10) is either the Day of Judgement when God will judge men for what they have done, or the period of war and suffering which was to precede the eventual triumph of God. *By him* is again misleading; God will save us 'through him', the literal meaning of the Greek.

10

For if while we were enemies we were reconciled to God by the death of his Son: we were enemies of God, being unrighteous, and God knew that we were his enemies. We were reconciled to God not *by* the death of his Son, if this implies that God needed something to make him change his mind, as it were, but 'through' the death of his Son, who became accursed in order to bear the curse of the world's sin (Gal. 3.10–14; 2 Cor. 5.18–21, and see Rom. 8.3 below). The sacrifice was made and publicly set forth (Rom. 3.25; Gal. 3.1) so that men might have something to offer to God for their sins. We who were enemies have gladly recognized that God has given a way for us to be righteous, that is, by believing and trusting him, above all by accepting the sacrifice of his Son as our sacrifice.

much more, now that we are reconciled, shall we be saved by his life: reconciled now, we shall in the future be raised from the dead and given eternal life. This occurs in our receiving his risen life.

11

Not only so etc.: not only what? Most commentators say, Not only are we reconciled, but also we rejoice. This interpretation is strained. I prefer to go back to v. 8: God has recommended his love to us by giving Christ to die for us while still sinners, so reconciling us to himself and assuring us of salvation and eternal life. *Not only* do we accept this recommendation of his love, but we also *sing aloud for joy* because of him (cf. Psalm 149.5) *through our Lord Jesus Christ,* the mediator in whose name we approach God in prayer and worship (1.8). Christ our sacrifice is also Christ the bearer of our praise to God the Father. The word translated *rejoice* is the word meaning to boast or to glory or to speak out loud discussed in the note on v. 2.

¹²*Therefore as sin came into the world through one man and death through sin, and so death spread to all men because all men sinned –* ¹³*sin indeed was in the world before the law was given, but sin is not counted where there is no law.* ¹⁴*Yet death reigned from Adam to Moses, even over those whose sins were not like the transgression of Adam, who was a type of the one who was to come.*

¹⁵*But the free gift is not like the trespass. For if many died through one man's trespass, much more have the grace of God and the free gift in the grace of that one man Jesus Christ abounded for many.* ¹⁶*And the free gift is not like the effect of that one man's sin. For the judgment following one trespass brought condemnation, but the free gift following many trespasses brings justification.* ¹⁷*If, because of one man's trespass, death reigned through that one man, much more will those who receive the abundance of grace and the free gift of righteousness reign in life through the one man Jesus Christ.*

¹⁸*Then as one man's trespass led to condemnation for all men, so one man's act of righteousness leads to acquittal and life for all men.* ¹⁹*For as by one man's disobedience many were made sinners, so by one man's obedience many will be made righteous.* ²⁰*Law came in, to increase the trespass; but where sin increased, grace abounded all the more,* ²¹*so that, as sin reigned in death, grace also might reign through righteousness to eternal life through Jesus Christ our Lord.*

This is a theological excursus of beauty and of importance, which differs (like its brother in 1 Cor. 15.21 f., 42–9) both in style and in thought from anything Paul himself wrote. It is the work of a great but anonymous commentator on Paul.

The argument is not entirely clear as it stands, and in the notes I shall try to show that the references to Moses and the Law are later glosses (see on vv. 13, 14, and 20), and that glossators have also added three 'nots' in vv. 14, 15, and 16, which further muddy the stream, although they seemed theologically important to the glossators at the time.

The recovered excursus is written in a very striking style. First the argument is stated in vv. 12–14. In vv. 15a a short rubric serves to introduce the pattern of each of the remaining assertions:

> 'but as was the transgression
> so also was the grace (literally: charism)'.

These assertions all contain a contrast between Adam and Christ (vv. 15–19). In 20b another rubric,

> 'where sin flowed
> grace overflowed',

introduces the final great contrast, v. 21. Each assertion is of roughly similar length, and they each come at the same thought from slightly different points of view, rather than carry forward a connected argument. The Greek is rhetorical rather than personal, and abounds in nouns and indicative verbs rather than adjectives and participles.

The assumption behind the whole passage is succinctly stated in v. 12. The misuse of the freedom granted to the very first man by his Creator allowed the force of sin to enter the world. With sin came mortality. Mortality passed to all men because all sinned, that is, because sin passed from Adam to all men. The author means that all men cannot help sinning at one time or another, because they inherit Adam's corrupt nature (Cranfield, *Scottish Journal of Theology* 22, 1969, pp. 324–41 at p. 331). The author is not, however, advocating that men must replace their Adamic nature by Christ's nature, as the most extreme supporters of the doctrine of original sin argue. If he meant that all hinges on which nature men have, Adam's or Christ's, he would have to be taken to mean that the struggle is over, and that all men, whether they know it or not, have been given Christ's nature: *Then as one man's trespass led to condemnation for all men, so one man's act of righteousness leads to acquittal and life for all men* (v. 18). Such an assumption lies at the basis of the theology of 'universalists' like Karl Barth, but it cannot be what our author meant, for he speaks clearly in the previous verse of those who *receive* the abundance of grace and the free gift of righteousness. This shows that the condemnation of all men and their acquittal are alternatives open to all, not twin destinies which are somehow both worked out in every man. There is still room for choice in men, however ingrained sin may be as a result of Adam's disobedience. The author cannot mean that a nature totally corrupted has to be replaced by a new nature given from above.

Adam's disobedience made it inevitable that all men were to die. The issue that remains is whether or not death is to *rule* all men. If death rules, the man dies and remains dead. If death is conquered, the man still dies, because sin did pass to him from Adam, but he will be released from eternal death to live eternally because of that victory. Death is very likely to rule, because men are terribly prone to sin after the pattern of Adam's sin, that is by outright disobedience to God's commands. But fortunately another man, whom Adam foreshadowed, has come, and he by his obedience has brought a new power to the human situation which enables those who accept it to conquer sin rather than let sin conquer them. The awful consequence of Adam's disobedience has been that masses of men have become confirmed sinners. The glorious possibility now is that by Jesus Christ's obedience masses of men may receive the rich power of God's grace to live for ever through him.

This is a grand vision of the essential predicament of mankind, which cannot be ignored simply because it assumed that the whole trouble with the human race hung on the behaviour of one man (and his wife) in the Garden of Eden. The writer certainly assumed that all men are descended from Adam, a man who was created by God and refused to obey God one day in the Garden. We now think it possible that men appeared in different parts of the world, and are not descended from one man. However, we do also assume that what distinguishes men from the animals is that men hold themselves responsible for their actions. The writer assumes that death came with sin. We take it that death is a natural phenomenon (as Paul himself seems to have held, 1 Cor. 15.50). However, we do seem to have an ingrained hunch that man may somehow survive death. In other words, we are still able to grapple with the issues he was grappling with, although we have a better knowledge of the actual biological development of mankind.

But perhaps there is one contrast between his assumptions and ours that scuppers all our attempts to follow his argument. If we do not believe that one man was individually responsible for the salient features of the human condition, how can we accept that one man, Jesus Christ, was responsible for the reversal we wish so much to rely upon? I don't think this objection is as great as at first sight appears. The parallel between Adam and Christ is not so close that our loss of belief in the drastic consequences of one man's actions at the Fall need remove grounds for belief in the glorious consequences of one man's actions on the Cross. If Adam was supposed to be the mechanical origin of all our troubles, and Christ the mechanical origin of all our hopes, we could well draw the conclusion that the literal falsity of the first proposition undermined the likelihood of the second proposition's being true. But Adam is pictured here not simply as the one who brought mortality on mankind, but as the typical sinner by following whose example we put ourselves under the rule of sin and condemn ourselves to death for ever. We have no need to believe in a historic Adam to see imaginatively that this is our human possibility. But if we are to escape this fate, we need to see that death can be conquered and we need to have a way of righteousness pointed out to us. We can look in many directions for such knowledge, but there is nothing intrinsically unlikely in God's granting such a boon to mankind in one man. The resurrection of Jesus Christ shows that God will overcome eternal death for men, and the death of Jesus Christ is a seal on the sort of obedience men should emulate.

The imaginative correspondence between Adam and Christ is scarcely touched by these rather literal difficulties, and I see no reason to be ashamed of surrendering oneself to the poetic power of the vision. The difficulties raised by a fuller knowledge of the way mankind has developed do not prevent the system of correspondence between Adam and Christ from working in practice.

We do not know precisely what are the origins of this sort of argument about human nature and destiny. Late Jewish theology, as preserved in the apocryphal and pseudepigraphal Old Testament writings or in the records of the rabbis, says a great deal about Adam and the Fall. 'O Adam, what hast thou done to all those who are born from thee?' (*Syriac Apocalypse of Baruch* 48.42) is a common complaint. But, so far, we have failed to discover any mention in these works of an explicit comparison between Adam and the Messiah. It may be that our author was himself responsible for this daring connection, but it is more likely that some less known Jewish groups, which were greatly interested in cosmic speculations about man's plight and salvation, had already connected the first man with a figure yet to come who would be sent by God to redeem his own. Certainly both ideas – the cosmic first man, and the redeemer who descends into the cosmos and ascends again to God – are present in these writings, and their connection by way of comparison and contrast is not hard to imagine. We must suspend judgement on the question of the precise origin of the ideas and themes, noting simply that the atmosphere is more speculative, more interested in a cosmic scheme, than we are used to in Paul. The affinities of this passage lie with *Ephesians*, *Colossians*, and the *Epistle to the Hebrews*, rather than with *Galatians* and 1 *Thessalonians*.

Notes

12

Therefore: the Greek phrase means 'for this reason', and indicates that what has been asserted previously in vv. 1–11 is to be explained in other terms in what follows.

as sin came into the world . . .: we should expect a clause beginning *as* would be completed by a clause beginning '*so also*'. One manuscript, and a number of commentators, reverse the Greek words *and so* in the clause *and so death spread* to produce the expected construction '*so also*', but it is extremely unlikely that the original author meant to compare the mode of entry of sin into the world with the mode of sin's spread.

We are left with a broken construction. Günther Bornkamm ('Paulinische Anakoluthe im Römerbrief' in *Das Ende des Gesetzes: Paulusstudien*, Munich, 1952, pp. 76–92 at pp. 80–90) has argued that the failure to follow arose because Paul had to correct and modify the thought that the original comparison on which he had embarked would have introduced. I find this explanation highly unlikely. A failure of this sort is more likely to arise through a scribal slip or 'correction' than through a lapse on the part of the author and his amanuensis. I conjecture that one slip, the writing of the common 'so also' instead of the correct *and so* at the end of v. 12, led to the insertion of an *as* at the beginning of the sentence. The excellent ancient editors who prepared our best texts preserved the now awkward *and so*, but were not bold enough to remove the well-established *as* at the beginning. The original sentence ran, 'The reason is this: through one man sin came into the world, and through sin death; and so death passed to all men, because all sinned'. (On my conjecture the sentence starts with two phrases each beginning with the same preposition, once with the accusative and once with the genitive. This is awkward, and would count against my theory, did not the author do exactly the same thing in verse 14b.)

and so death spread to all men because all men sinned: the words translated *because* could just possibly mean 'in him whom'. This latter interpretation was known to the early Greek commentators, and was usually followed by the early Latin commentators. Augustine is the most famous of these Latin commentators, and he held, against Pelagius who followed the translation *because*, that all sinned in the first man, because all were present in him when he sinned, and from that moment sin was transmitted through birth. He was relying on the view that a descendant can be said to be 'in the loins' of his forefather, as Levi was said to be in the loins of Abraham (Heb. 7.9 f.).

The same theology can be built on a recognition that the Greek almost certainly should be translated *because* (2 Cor. 5.4; Phil. 3.12); 'and so death passed to all men because (in Adam) all sinned'. Against this, one would have expected such an important assumption to be stated explicitly if it really was in the author's mind; we should even expect to read, 'and so death passed to all men because *Adam* sinned'.

However, the sentence does not allow us to go to the other extreme and interpret the writer in the entirely opposite sense, to mean 'and so death passed to all men because all men in fact also choose to sin'. For this meaning we should expect a present tense rather than the aorist (past completed) tense of the verb 'to sin', 'because all men sin'.

The logic of the sentence as a whole is built on the following scheme:

Because of A, S;
Because of S, D;
Why D to M?
Because MS.

The first part speaks of the entry of Sin, and the consequent entry of Death. The second part raises the problem of the transmission of Death to all Men, and promises an answer (that is the force of *and so*). The aorist tense of the verb in the last clause makes it likely that the promised answer is basically, 'because sin passed to all men'. If I am right, the author was not pointing to an empirical fact, that all men choose to sin and so died, but to an inevitable consequence of belonging to the genus of human being, which had such a disastrous beginning in Adam, the one who first admitted sin and death to the race of men. The author is stating that death and sin are inevitable infections that follow from the first disobedience. He goes on to say that many men conquer death and that death will not reign over all, but he does not seem to mean that they will be bodily assumed without dying. He states, on the contrary, that all will die, but that some of those who died will conquer death and enjoy eternal life. All men die because they are inevitably tainted with sin, even though they should avoid the ultimate sin, the sin of Adam, who plainly rebelled against God's commandment. All men inherit a nature tainted with sin and so die; the question is whether or not death will conquer them completely.

I hold, then, that this verse does provide evidence for a modified doctrine of 'original sin', provided it is not interpreted in a way that excludes man's cooperation in grasping the divine aid offered him to enable him to escape final conquest by Death. (Note that some men 'take' or *receive* grace in v. 17.) The author did not write, 'and so death passed to all men because *Adam* sinned'; nor did he write, 'and so death passed to all men because all men *sin*'. He wrote, 'and so death passed to all men because all men sinned', meaning that all men, being descendants of Adam, inevitably sinned, and so, inevitably, die.

13 f.

sin indeed was in the world before the law was given, but sin is not counted where there is no law. Yet death reigned from Adam to Moses, even over those whose sins were not like the transgression of Adam: the not reckoning or not counting of sin to which this refers must be at the coming judgement of men by God, since all men suffer the 'reckoning' of death. (Bultmann objects that it is hard to see how sin was not counted when, after all, it resulted in death. The suggestion that the reference is to the last judgement was made by my student, the Rev. Francis Cattermole.) Consequently, we must understand the reign of death as the permanent victory of death, the final rejection of the sinner at the last judgement; and as a further consequence, we must omit the word *not* in v. 14 with 385, 424[mg], the Latin side of d, and Origen. Death finally conquered those who sinned after the likeness of Adam's transgression, that is, those who sinned against a clear commandment of God. Those who lived from Adam to Moses generally had no such clear commandment, and so escaped rejection at the end; if they did sin like Adam, death conquered them, and they will not inherit eternal life.

The word *not* was added by a scribe who missed the distinction between physical death and eternal death, and had to assume that Paul was asserting that men died from Adam to Moses, even though they had no explicit command to sin against.

I believe the understanding of the passage I have given is possible and clear, and yet it is hard to imagine the original writer's having devoted so much attention to the rather speculative question of what would happen to men who died after Adam but before Moses, when his primary intention must have been to establish the distinction between physical death and permanent spiritual death. He establishes this distinction by the key word *reigned*: death is the mortal lot, but there must be the possibility that death will not finally reign.

I conclude that the whole of v. 13 and the words *to Moses* in v. 14 are a scholastic gloss by a theologian who recognized that the existence of the Law as a series of explicit commands on a par with the explicit command given to Adam raised some interesting problems which he set out to solve. (See further on v. 20.)

Without this gloss, we have a clear transition to the vital question about the reign of Death. All men die because all sinned (v. 12), 'but death *reigned* from Adam onwards, even over those who sinned after the likeness of Adam's transgression'.

14

who was a type of the one who was to come: This is a mistaken translation. The Greek says Adam 'is' the type of him who is to come; Adam is now a figure whom men can look at to see the significance of Christ. The *type* was originally the opposite impression left in something like wax or clay by an object, and that literal meaning fits rather well in our context, because each of the following comparisons between Adam and Christ is a contrast.

15

But the free gift is not like the trespass: a pious scribe has added the word *not*, because he felt sure that Paul could not have written, 'But as the trespass, so also the gift'. That the original did say just this is clear from what follows, as well as from the word 'also' (significantly enough, not translated by the RSV and omitted as awkward by B, given the presence of *not*). Adam's trespass against God's clear command may lead to eternal death, but so also can Christ's gift lead to eternal life.

many: the word *many* in vv. 15 and 19 has caused difficulty to commentators from the time of the Fathers onwards. Origen and the Greek Fathers generally took *many* to be different from *all*, but Didymus of

Alexandria, Theodore of Mopsuestia, Chrysostom, and Augustine understood *many* to mean all. In the present verse the meaning 'all' might seem to be required by v. 12, where the writer said that all died. But three things count against this interpretation. First, it is unlikely that a writer would use 'many' in a context where he also uses 'all' if he believed them to be interchangeable terms. 'Many' may possibly not exclude the possibility that all are included, in a context where 'many' is contrasted with 'one' or 'some', but hardly in a context where 'all' is also used. Second, it is unlikely that the last part of this verse is meant to teach that all men will in fact receive the grace of God and inherit eternal life. Finally, the aorist tense of the verbs *died* and *abounded* suggest an observable contrast; the present tense would be more natural if the author had wished to state that although all die grace abounds for all. I conclude that the death of many here referred to is the rule of death, eternal death, which is contrasted with the eternal life graciously given to many by the grace of the one man Jesus Christ. The many who died and the many to whom grace has abounded are different people.

the grace of God and the free gift in the grace of that one man Jesus Christ: the Greek is not straightforward, and the text in disorder. I suspect that the words *in the grace* should be set aside. The one man Jesus Christ is God's gracious gift to the race to enable many to attain eternal life. The grace of God is expressed in a free gift, that of the one man, Jesus Christ.

16

And the free gift is not like the effect of that one man's sin: the Greek is literally, 'And not as through the sinning of one (is) the gift', or, to adopt the text of D, G, it, syᴾ, which better fits the context, 'And not as through one transgression (is) the gift'. The RSV has made a valiant effort to extract sense from this, by introducing the notion of *effect*, but this will not do, because although *judgment* may be the effect of *one trespass, justification* can hardly be the effect of many trespasses. The point is that judgement followed one trespass, and vindication followed many trespasses. The author is not pointing to a law but to a fact. Once again, a pious scribe has spoilt his point by inserting a *not*. The word 'as' means 'as if', to warn us that a paradox is coming. The original said: 'And as if through one transgression came the free gift.' This is meant to be a startling paradox, and the paradox is resolved in the rest of the verse: although the verdict passed on one transgression led to doom, God's gracious gift of his Son in face of the many transgressions men since Adam have committed has led to acquittal. Therefore one could almost say that one fateful transgression led to grace! *O felix culpa.*

17

If, because of one man's trespass, death reigned through that one man: the text here followed (ℵ, B, C, etc.) has been 'mechanically conformed' (B. Weiss) to the text of v. 15. The original was, 'For if by one transgression death reigned through one (man) ...' (A, F, G; cf. D). The reign of death is death's power not only to take all men in the end, but also its power to deprive them of eternal life.

much more will those who receive the abundance of grace and the free gift of righteousness reign in life through the one man Jesus Christ: the RSV is following an inferior text, because the best texts seem impossibly clumsy. The best texts read, 'the abundance of grace and of the free gift of righteousness' (P46, ℵ, A, D, G, K, P, etc.). Origen gives two forms, one omitting 'of the free gift' (with B) and the other omitting 'of righteousness' (with C). Probably one of these expressions was originally a gloss in the margin to explain the other. The question is, Which? Obviously 'of righteousness' was put in by a glossator to explain the seemingly redundant 'of the free gift'. Therefore we should read, 'those who receive the abundance of the grace and of the free gift', meaning 'the abundance of the free gift of grace'.

Although this contrast assumes that men are in a parlous state and need grace, it also assumes that they are free to cooperate or to refuse to cooperate with that grace. Death reigns when men, who are already tainted with sin, give themselves over completely to the open disobedience of Adam. But men may reign with God in eternal life if they receive the abundance of the gift of grace. Death reigns over men who sin after the likeness of Adam's transgression (v. 14) so that one transgression led to the triumph of death's rule; men may escape death's rule who receive the abundance of the gift of grace which was given embodied in Jesus Christ. The choice before men is either to repeat the one great trespass of disobedience or to receive the abundant gift of grace, to belong to one man or to belong to the other man, to choose Adam or Christ.

18

one man's trespass ... one man's act of righteousness: the Greek may mean this, but more probably should be translated, 'one trespass ... one vindication'. The vindication referred to is the resurrection; the RSV has translated this word 'vindication' as *act of righteousness* in order to get a strict parallel with *trespass*, but the word has already occurred in v. 16, as here, in close proximity to *condemnation*, and there it means vindication (RSV: *justification*). We must therefore keep the same meaning here too.

condemnation for all men ... acquittal and life for all men: the previous verse, which speaks of men's receiving grace, makes it highly unlikely that the author means that all men are both condemned and acquitted. He means that condemnation and acquittal are possibilities for all men; Adam's sin and Christ's resurrection are the two events that open up eternal death or eternal life for all men.

19

many were made sinners ... many will be made righteous: the RSV translation of the verb as *made* is nicely indeterminate, as when we say 'made mad' or 'made happy'. Perhaps we can be a little more precise, and avoid a possible ambiguity, if we note that the verb in the active means 'to appoint', usually to an office. In the context of the rule of death and the possibility of men's ruling with God in life, we could even retain that strict meaning here and take the author to mean that 'as through (adopting) the disobedience of one man many were appointed to office in death's kingdom as sinners, so through (adopting) the obedience of one man many will be appointed to office in God's kingdom as doers of right'.

20

Law came in, to increase the trespass: The verb *increase* is here used transitively, meaning 'to aggravate', whereas it is used intransitively in the second half of the verse, meaning 'to abound'. The one author is very unlikely to make such a pointless pun and, when we observe that the second half of the verse is by itself a perfect contrast in full accord with all the other contrasts (compare particularly v. 15a), we must conclude that the first half of v. 20 is a gloss. The theologian who was responsible for the note in vv. 13 and 14 (the note concerning the interesting effect the giving of the Law through Moses had on the possibility of men's being able to sin, like Adam, against an explicit command of God) was responsible for this addition too.

21

so that, as sin reigned in death, grace also might reign through righteousness to eternal life through Jesus Christ our Lord: the parallelism between the two halves of the contrast is as follows:

As	sin	so	grace through righteousness
	reigned		may reign
	in death		leading to eternal life
	(through Adam)		through Jesus Christ our Lord

It is clear from this parallelism that the reign of sin in death must refer to spiritual as well as physical death because the contrast is the eternal life which follows after physical death but does not avoid physical death. 'Grace through righteousness' could possibly refer to a gift of righteousness, as in v. 17 (but see my note); the more likely meaning is recovered if one takes the righteousness as referring to the behaviour of the men who receive grace, since this phrase follows so closely on v. 19, which speaks of the many who will be appointed to be doers of right. God's grace produces righteousness in men, just as, in the first half of the contrast, sin produces sin in men.

Romans 6

6 *What shall we say then? Are we to continue in sin that grace may abound?* ²*By no means! How can we who died to sin still live in it?* ³*Do you not know that all of us who have been baptized into Christ Jesus were baptized into his death?* ⁴*We were buried therefore with him by baptism into death, so that as Christ was raised from the dead by the glory of the Father, we too might walk in newness of life.*

⁵*For if we have been united with him in a death like his, we shall certainly be united with him in a resurrection like his.* ⁶*We know that our old self was crucified with him so that the sinful body might be destroyed, and we might no longer be enslaved to sin.* ⁷*For he who has died is freed from sin.* ⁸*But if we have died with Christ, we believe that we shall also live with him.* ⁹*For we know that Christ being raised from the dead will never die again; death no longer has dominion over him.* ¹⁰*The death he died he died to sin, once for all, but the life he lives he lives to God.* ¹¹*So you also must consider yourselves dead to sin and alive to God in Christ Jesus.*

¹²*Let not sin therefore reign in your mortal bodies, to make you obey their passions.* ¹³*Do not yield your members to sin as instruments of wickedness, but yield yourselves to God as men who have been brought from death to life, and your members to God as instruments of righteousness.* ¹⁴*For sin will have no dominion over you, since you are not under law but under grace.*

15*What then? Are we to sin because we are not under law but under grace? By no means!* 16*Do you not know that if you yield yourselves to any one as obedient slaves, you are slaves of the one whom you obey, either of sin, which leads to death, or of obedience, which leads to righteousness?* 17*But thanks be to God, that you who were once slaves of sin have become obedient from the heart to the standard of teaching to which you were committed,* 18*and, having been set free from sin, have become slaves of righteousness.* 19*I am speaking in human terms, because of your natural limitations. For just as you once yielded your members to impurity and to greater and greater iniquity, so now yield your members to righteousness for sanctification.*

20*When you were slaves of sin, you were free in regard to righteousness.* 21*But then what return did you get from the things of which you are now ashamed? The end of those things is death.* 22*But now that you have been set free from sin and have become slaves of God, the return you get is sanctification and its end, eternal life.* 23*For the wages of sin is death, but the free gift of God is eternal life in Christ Jesus our Lord.*

Paul's assertion that sinners can become righteous by God's grace has suggested to his detractors that he was, wittingly or unwittingly, encouraging men to sin. If sinners can be forgiven and righteous, why should not even men who have believed go on sinning so that the grace of God, when it is again and again invoked, may have all the more scope for its marvellous operation?

In answer, Paul speaks both of baptism and of moral endeavour, and he speaks both of Christ's death and resurrection and of Christians' death and resurrection. Consequently, this chapter has become a battleground, fought over by Christians of all theological schools, each claiming that his interpretation is the right one and trying to refute the claims of his opponents.

The 'plain issue', as Albert Schweitzer puts it in his masterly history of *Paul and His Interpreters* (English translation, London, 1912, p. 164), is 'whether baptism and the Supper effect redemption or only represent it'. Both views find some support in Romans 6: v. 6, which says, *We know that our old self was crucified with him*, seems to imply that baptism effects redemption, but v. 11, *you also must consider yourselves dead to sin and alive to God in Christ Jesus*, seems to imply that the baptized could think otherwise, and that baptism simply represents redemption.

The doctrinal disputes have become entangled in historical disputes about whether or not Romans 6 has been vitally affected by the rites of initiation practised by some of the Mystery Religions that were flourishing at this time which involved ritual washing or immersion in water, intimately connected with myths of the death and rebirth of the gods. These myths all go back to nature religions which identified the death and rebirth of the year at winter and spring with the death and rebirth of a god.

The question in Romans 6 is whether there is any connection at all between Paul's understanding of baptism and these Mystery Religions and, if there is a connection, whether it is one of opposition, of harmless borrowing of terms, of deliberate reinterpretation of the Mysteries, or of complete submission to the assumptions of the Mysteries.

There has long been a deep suspicion that at this point Paul has stepped out of the sphere of Judaism and has entered the realm of Hellenistic ideas, has left behind 'justification' and 'faith' and has adopted 'rebirth' and 'baptism'. Albert Schweitzer, by a *tour de force*, accepted the theory that rebirth and baptism and mystic identification with Christ were the central teachings of Paul, and then argued that such ideas were thoroughly Jewish. The doctrine of righteousness by faith, previously regarded as the really Jewish part of Paul's teaching, is taken to be simply 'a subsidiary crater, which has formed within the rim of the main crater – the mystical doctrine of redemption through the being-in-Christ' (*The Mysticism of Paul the Apostle*, English translation, London, 1931, p. 225).

But Schweitzer's *tour de force* has merely suspended the debate for seventy years. The questions still remain. Did Paul succeed in combining his views on faith with his views on baptism? Is there any clear connection between his sacramental teaching and his teaching about ethics? Does baptism effect redemption or simply represent it? How far did Paul adopt the language of the Mysteries, and to what extent, if any, has he adopted their ideas?

My own solution to these problems is that Paul's original argument has been overlaid with commentary that boldly adopted the language of the Mysteries. The diverse interpretations that have arisen all have

their roots in the words of Chapter 6 itself. All can claim some justification, but no one interpretation has succeeded in providing a
convincing explanation of every feature of the chapter: one or two
verses, at the very least, have had to be forced or distorted to fit in
with the overall pattern.

In broad outline, I hold that Paul wrote most of the chapter, and
that one commentator, or one school of commentators, has added vv.
4a and 5–7.

The commentator was able to base his theology of baptism on
Paul's words because one crucial verse, v. 3 in Paul's original letter,
was capable of his sort of interpretation, and because another crucial
verse, v. 8, offered an idea that he was able to take up and use.

Let us take v. 8 first: *But if we have died with Christ, we believe that
we shall also live with him.* Paul is referring to the promise that all who
acknowledge the Messiah will be received into the Father's Kingdom
at the general resurrection when the Messiah returns to earth in glory.
The principle of identification, whereby Christ acknowledges those
who have confessed him before men, is firmly anchored in the teaching of Jesus (Mark 8.38 and parallels; Luke 12.8 f.; Matt. 10.32 f.;
2 Tim. 2.12; Rev. 3.5), and Paul is able to assume that the Christians
at Rome understand what he means and are able to draw the proper
ethical conclusions. The commentator, who probably shared the same
belief, saw here the principle that played so great a part in the Mystery
Religions with which he was surrounded, the principle that an initiate
is enabled here and now to share the death and rebirth of the god of
the religion. Death and rebirth are present experience.

Verse 3, the other important starting point in Paul for the commentator, was capable of interpretation in this sense. The words are
literally, *Do you not know that all of us who have been baptized into
Christ Jesus were baptized into his death?* The two prepositions *into*
can be taken to imply that both *Christ Jesus* and *his death* are metaphysical
states or substances into which the initiate is plunged at baptism; he
enters Christ and enters death, as it were, in baptism.

However, it is possible that Paul's words are not rightly taken in
this sense (see the notes). What at first sight appears to be a very close
parallel, in Gal. 3.27, suggests, on the contrary, that the preposition
into means something different. Gal. 3.27 is literally, *as many of you as*

were baptized into Christ have put on Christ, but if *into* implied that Christ was the spiritual substance into which the believer was plunged Paul could hardly draw the conclusion that the baptized had *put on Christ* as one puts on clothes. To be baptized *into* Christ probably means to be baptized 'because of' Christ. The preposition *into* simply expresses reference or relation, a point well taken by the Latin versions, which translate our verse in *Romans* with *in*: in Christo Jesu; in morte ipsius. The commentator could understand v. 3 as implying mystical identification of the initiate with Christ just as the initiates of the Mysteries were identified with the dying and rising god, but in so doing, the commentator is probably misunderstanding the original force of the preposition, and the true nature of the relation to which the preposition was referring.

What, then, according to Paul, is the relation between us and Christ, and between us and his death? The relation is, from the believers' side, the relation of faith. We commit ourselves to Christ and trust our future to him, hoping that by so doing we shall rise from the dead and share his glorious reign for ever. But that faith, says Paul, involves trust in his death as the great sacrifice for our sins and the gateway to a new righteous life. We have to live like those who will rise and live for ever with Christ. We shall no doubt sin again, and therefore constantly plead his sacrifice by taking part in the Eucharist (Romans 5.9), but we cannot deliberately sin, since our baptism was the moment when we first claimed his death for ourselves.

Under the Law everything was hopeless because we failed to do what was required. Now there is hope, because a new way to be righteous has been shown, witnessed to in the Old Testament already. By faith we can find God's grace, in claiming Christ's death as our sacrifice. But naturally we cannot presume on the grace of God who freely forgives us our sins. Therefore we must behave in accordance with our profession and our destiny.

Does baptism, then, represent our redemption or effect our redemption, to return to Schweitzer's question? I should say that the death and resurrection of Jesus Christ is what effects our redemption, if only we will take them for our own. The way to take them is to accept baptism. Baptism is not just a sign that a man acknowledges his sin and his need of grace; baptism is the only way we clearly know (God may have his other ways) by which redemption is to be claimed, and when baptism is received, the benefits of Christ's death are really received. We can repudiate baptism and lose our final reward (1 Cor. 9.27), but baptism is nevertheless the event by which our salvation is both represented to us and made effectual in us.

Paul's words were addressed to men and women who had been baptized as adults, but it is worth noticing that they would apply equally well to those who had been baptized as infants; as infants they, too, would have been baptized because of Christ and therefore because of his death. The commentator's words, on the other hand, would not apply nearly so well to people who had been baptized as infants because the commentator is speaking in terms of adult initiation where, if magic is at all to be avoided, the rite of washing with its mystic consequences must be the free choice of mature men and women.

Notes

2

How can we who died to sin still live in it? The phrase 'to die to sin' is probably not peculiar to Paul. Death is used figuratively in Rev. 3.1 as well as in 2 Cor. 6.9, and the phrase in 1 Peter 2.24 ('who himself bore our sins in his body on the tree, so that we who have died to sins might live for righteousness') is probably not dependent on Paul, since 'sin' is in the plural, and a quite different word is used for 'to die'. I suspect the idea was present in the call to repentance of John the Baptist. Repentance implied that a man no longer wished to live as a sinner.

3

Do you know that all of us who have been baptized into Christ Jesus were baptized into his death? A number of manuscripts, including B, omit *Jesus*, and the shorter reading is probably the original.

The meaning of the preposition *into* has already been discussed in general in the introductory section. *Into* can mean 'in the medium of' (cf. Mark 1.9), but the normal preposition with that force is 'in' (1 Cor. 10.2). I have argued above that Gal. 3.27 excludes the sense 'in the medium of' for 'into', and have suggested the sense 'because of' (cf. Acts 2.38; Matt. 10.41). This fits the context in 1 Cor. 1.13, 15;

10.2, where Paul also speaks of being baptized *into* the name of Paul or *into* Moses. The possibility of taking *into* in a metaphorically spatial sense has given scope for the commentator to add his glosses in vv. 4a and 5–7.

4a

We were buried therefore with him by baptism into death: the word *baptism* is not found outside Christian writings and occurs nowhere else in Paul (apart from writings I take to be the work of followers of Paul: Eph. 4.5; Col. 2.12). The whole clause does not seem to be known to Irenaeus, and is probably an early gloss, very similar in substance to Col. 2.12. The idea of baptism as burial is not inextricably bound up with the primitive ceremony itself, where the primary significance was probably that of washing. In the Mystery Religions where such rituals were employed, however, the primary symbolic force did lie in the burial of the initiate with the dying god in order to be reborn with him. The gloss makes a very natural connection between Christian baptism and the Mystery initiation. The identification is, however, secondary in the history of baptism, and the commentator who made the identification would have been well aware that the Mysteries were proclaiming false myths, and that Christian baptism was burial with a man who had really died and been placed in a grave.

4b

so that as Christ was raised from the dead . . . we too might walk in newness of life: this clause originally followed directly on v. 3. The logic is not that of v. 4a, by which a man who had been buried with Christ would naturally rise with him, but the logic of v. 3, by which a man who had been baptized because of Christ (and therefore because of his death) would wish to live a new life in order eventually to share the glorified life of his redeemer.

by the glory of the Father: glory here means power (cf. John 2.11; Eph. 3.16). The phrase used to cause dogmatic difficulties, as though the Son lacked the power to raise himself. The words are omitted in citing this verse by Irenaeus and Tertullian, and perhaps we have here another early explanatory gloss.

5

For if we have been united with him in a death like his, we shall certainly be united with him in a resurrection like his: the words *with him* in the RSV do not occur in the Greek. The AV gives the Greek more closely: 'For if we have been planted together in the likeness of his death, we shall be also in the likeness of his resurrection.' I take the phrase 'in the likeness of his death' as referring to the moment in baptism when the person baptized goes down into the water; the Greek dative is instrumental. In the second part of the sentence the verb is not expressed, and I should understand 'we shall be flourishing', rather than a simple repetition of the first verb, 'we shall be planted together'. I take 'the likeness of his resurrection' to refer to emergence from the baptismal waters. My translation would be, 'For if we were planted by the representation of his death, we shall certainly flourish by the representation of his resurrection'.

6

The image of the death of the seed in order that the crop might grow and flourish is continued in v. 6. *Our old self* is literally 'our old man', a phrase found elsewhere in the Pauline corpus only in Eph. 4.22; Col. 3.9. *The sinful body* assumes the picture of the world where the body is the prison that prevents the true inner self from rising to God. *Sin* is the personified force that holds the *body* captive. Escape is possible only when the *body* is killed – not literally, of course, but spiritually. Baptism effects this death, because the baptized is identified with the Crucified One. Compare the rather different view of man in v. 12.

7

This is tomb-stone wisdom: Lietzmann cites an inscription on a grave that reads, 'Resting-place of those who are free from sins'. The tomb-stone wisdom is applied to this present life. Those who have achieved the death of their 'old man' by participation in the rite of baptism are now freed from the grip of sin, because that part of their nature which formerly provided a foothold for sin has now been *destroyed*, having been crucified with Christ.

8

In vv. 4a and 5–7, death and resurrection lie in the past for the baptized. Verse 8, on the other hand, refers to death as past and resurrection as the object of faith, and in the future. Lagrange has attempted to interpret the verse as referring only to the new life of the Christian. He takes *we believe that* to mean 'we have confidence that', and the future, *we shall also live*, as logical rather than temporal. Lagrange's interpretation would keep v. 8 much closer to vv. 4a, 5–7, but at the cost of distorting the plain meaning of the words. While v. 8 provides a basis for the sort of meditation put forward in 4a and 5–7, the thought of v. 8 cannot be entirely subsumed to the thought the commentator proposes.

To *have died with Christ* meant, for Paul, to have *died to sin* (v. 2), but these words immediately suggested to the commentator the rich resources of language in the Mystery Religions. To live with Christ meant for Paul to be raised from the dead in order to share in the life of the Kingdom of God which was to come, but Paul's words suggested to the commentator mystical rebirth. The other possibility is to regard the words *we believe that* as a gloss. Then the verse clearly makes baptism initiation into a mystery, and I begin to wonder whether any of Chapter 6 can be rescued for Paul.

9–11

There is a strange feature in the argument. Why should Christ be said to have *died to sin* (v. 10)? *His* dying to sin would have to be different from ours. This statement would be much more appropriate as a statement about us. Perhaps we should, therefore, omit *Christ* in v. 9 and read 'he who has been raised from the dead' (cf. 242, 489, 1311). The *too* in v. 11 should then be put at the beginning of the sentence, with 1245, where it would mean 'and' and the verb *consider* becomes an imperative: 'And so consider yourselves to be dead to sin. . .'

11

in Christ Jesus: means simply 'through Christ Jesus'. There is no need to suppose that Paul had any doctrine of mystical incorporation in mind.

12

Let not sin therefore reign in your mortal bodies: literally, 'in your mortal body'. The mortal body is simply the life we lead before we die, and there is no suggestion that the body stands for the prison that keeps us from God as we saw it did in vv. 5–7. Mortal men who recognize their sin and accept Christ's death by baptism, with the revelation of the righteousness God requires, should refuse to allow sin to go on ruling in their lives.

to make you obey their passions: this implies that the body is the seat of the passions. The shorter reading, 'to obey it (sin)', given by P46, D, G, is probably the original.

13

as men who have been brought from death to life: literally, 'as alive from the dead'. Paul probably meant first of all that they should present themselves to God as those who would rise from the dead at the glorious resurrection. They should now, therefore, live as those who would live eternally, and *consider* themselves *dead to sin and alive to God* (v. 11). Paul did not think that the resurrection was already past for believers although his words gave scope for the commentator to introduce his own interpretation of baptism as the rite of mystical identification with Christ in death and resurrection.

14

For sin will have no dominion over you, since you are not under law but under grace: the future *will have no dominion* is probably an imperatival future, like the 'Thou shalt not' of the Ten Commandments: 'Sin shall not have dominion over you.' Under the Law obedience to all the commandments seemed to be the only way to live in God's sight. Since no man seemed capable of this without sin, sin could be said to have the upper hand. But now that God's grace and forgiveness are clearly revealed in Christ, the way through sin to righteousness has been opened up. When we commit sins, all is not lost, but it would be absurd to go on sinning and so allow sin to exert the old domination it once exercised when we were under the Law. There is no need to go on serving a master to whom we no longer owe any service.

16

either of sin, which leads to death, or of obedience, which leads to righteousness: the logic of this seems to have gone wrong. Men can be servants of sin, but scarcely servants of obedience. The idea that serving obedience is the way to righteousness implies that disobedience is the permanent condition of man and that 'obedience' must imply 'obedience to God'. This assumption, however, cuts across the metaphor in v. 16a, which implies that a man can choose whom to obey, sin or God. I conjecture that the word *obedience* was originally a gloss by a scribe who assumed that obedience could be only obedience to God. There is some evidence for this conjecture in the fact that 33 substitutes 'obedience' for 'righteousness', a possible indication that 'obedience' once stood in the margin, where it could have been taken to be a correction. The words *which leads to death* are not in D, 1739*, and the Old Latin versions, and should be omitted as a gloss from v. 21. The clause originally read, 'whether of sin or for righteousness' implying 'whether as servants of sin or as servants of God living righteously'. *Righteousness* is, of course, the righteous way of living, not imputed righteousness, a point well made by Lipsius.

17

who ... have become obedient from the heart to the standard of teaching to which you were committed: from the heart and *the standard of teaching* are foreign to Paul's usual way of speaking. The whole clause disturbs the flow of argument from v. 17a to v. 18, and implies that the point at issue is whether the Roman Christians adhere to orthodox teaching or not. The real issue is of their allegiance to God and its moral consequences. The gloss has been recognized by Weisse, Michelsen, and Bultmann. Paul's original statement was, 'Thanks be to God because you were once slaves of sin', an open invitation for a glossator!

18-20

This is a self-contained meditation on the two masters, Sin and Righteousness, and play is made with the concepts of slavery and freedom. Freedom from Sin implies slavery to Righteousness, just as slavery to Sin implied freedom from Righteousness. Verse 19 is probably a justification of this fanciful way of speaking: 'I speak humanly because of the frailty of your flesh (and consequent inability to understand divine things except allegorically).' Paul himself could hardly have written this section. He does not personify righteousness, although he comes close to personifying sin. The opposite of slavery to sin is for Paul the service of God. (v. 22). Righteousness and holiness are for him the aim of the Christian, but here Righteousness is the Master and *sanctification* or 'holiness' the aim. More seriously, 'lawlessness' (translated *iniquity* by the RSV in v. 19b) is the end of servitude to sin, implying that lawfulness is the end of servitude to Righteousness. Paul did think that the life of a believer was meant to be holy and righteous, but he could hardly have used the word 'lawless' to describe the opposite, without giving some explanation of how that previous 'lawless' life was also life 'under the Law'. This meditation was probably directed to an audience of converts from paganism. It breaks the connection between 17a and 20: 'But thanks be to God because you were servants of sin. What fruit did you then have from the things of which you are now ashamed? For the end of them is death.'

22

the return you get is sanctification: literally, 'you have your fruit in holiness'. The result of obeying God is growth in goodness. The end of such a life is eternal life after resurrection from the dead.

23

Sin pays wages in the shape of death. 'Death' here and in v. 21 stands for eternal punishment. The free gift of God is eternal life with Christ Jesus our Lord, when he comes at the resurrection to claim his own. The preposition *in* means 'with', and does not imply incorporation of the believer into Christ.

7 Do you not know, brethren – for I am speaking to those who know the law – that the law is binding on a person only during his life? ²Thus a married woman is bound by law to her husband as long as he lives; but if her husband dies she is discharged from the law concerning the husband. ³Accordingly, she will be called an adulteress if she lives with another man while her husband is alive. But if her husband dies she is free from that law, and if she marries another man she is not an adulteress.

⁴Likewise, my brethren, you have died to the law through the body of Christ, so that you may belong to another, to him who has been raised from the dead in order that we may bear fruit for God. ⁵While we were living in the flesh, our sinful passions, aroused by the law, were at work in our members to bear fruit for death. ⁶But now we are discharged from the law, dead to that which held us captive, so that we serve not under the old written code but in the new life of the Spirit.

⁷What then shall we say? That the law is sin? By no means! Yet, if it had not been for the law, I should not have known sin. I should not have known what it is to covet if the law had not said, 'You shall not covet.' ⁸But sin, finding opportunity in the commandment, wrought in me all kinds of covetousness. Apart from the law sin lies dead. ⁹I was once alive apart from the law, but when the commandment came, sin revived and I died; ¹⁰the very commandment which promised life proved to be death to me. ¹¹For sin, finding opportunity in the commandment, deceived me and by it killed me. ¹²So the law is holy, and the commandment is holy and just and good.

¹³Did that which is good, then, bring death to me? By no means! It was sin, working death in me through what is good, in order that sin might be shown to be sin, and through the commandment might become sinful beyond measure.

In the previous chapter Paul has begun an argument that demands to be taken to its conclusion. He is writing to *Jewish* Christians, that is to people whose whole history had been sustained by obedience to the Law, and to them he has said, *you are not under law but under grace. What then? Are we to sin because we are not under law but under grace? By no means!* (6.14b, 15). He has met the charge that to be under grace rather than the Law leads to sin, but he has not yet explained why Christians are not under the Law, and what part the Law played (and plays) in God's economy. This is to be the subject of Chapter 7.

The previous argument in 6.1–13 in outline is reasonably clear. Christians have come to see that they are sinners in dire need of grace from God. They have laid hold on Christ's death as their sacrifice and live in trust and expectation that he who raised Christ will also raise them and welcome them into his kingdom. By faith they discover the righteousness God requires, and this righteousness is not the old righteousness which tried without success to keep the Law. They may be said, therefore, to have *died to the Law* when they began to rely on the death of Christ in partaking of *the body of Christ*.

Does this mean that the Law is sin, because Christians are supposed also to have *died to sin* (6.2)? No, because the Law is the only way a man can know the full seriousness of sin. The Law is God's chosen instrument for revealing to a man his true plight. Paul picks on the last of the Ten Commandments, *You shall not covet*, to illustrate what he means, for this commandment shows clearly that nothing less than total obedience, reaching even to the inward motives, is demanded by God. Faced with this commandment, every man must confess that he is a sinner, and ask how he can become righteous.

I think that this way of paraphrasing Paul's argument is coherent and fits in with his main line of thought in the previous six chapters. However, when we come to the details of 7.1–13, we are faced with two great difficulties. The first concerns the picture of the woman whose husband must die before she can marry another, and here Paul has been charged with being 'confused': 'He lacks the gift for sustained illustration of ideas through concrete images . . . It is probably a defect of imagination' (C. H. Dodd). The second difficulty concerns the logic of the defence of the Law's goodness. If a man is alive before the Law comes, how can it be said to be a good thing that the Law should kill him (v. 9)? Why not leave him in peace?

I wish to adopt a double line of defence to each of these attacks on Paul, the attack on his imagination and the attack on his logic. My first defence, in each case, is that when the arguments are properly understood they will stand up to criticism; the illustration about the woman is coherent and imaginatively sound, and the argument about the goodness of a Law that kills is perfectly valid. But where there is smoke there is fire, and there are good reasons why commentators, from the very beginning of commentaries, have found these difficulties in the text. My second defence, then, is to deny that Paul was responsible for the arguments in question. In fact, the coherence of the arguments cannot be clearly recognized until they are seen to be later meditations upon Paul's original text by commentators who did not entirely share his view of things and his particular history.

My argument is that Paul wrote vv. 4a, 6, 7, 12, and 13, and that two major additions were made by later commentators; the first consisting of vv. 1, 2, 3, 4b and 5, and the second of vv. 8–11.

The heart of the first commentary is vv. 1 to 3, the illustration concerning the woman whose husband had to die before she could marry another man.

Most modern writers find the illustration confused because vv. 1 and 4 assume that Christians have died in order to escape the Law, whereas in the illustration the one who escapes the Law is the woman, but she is the one who remains alive. If we follow this line of reasoning, we come up against yet another difficulty: the woman who marries a second husband after her first husband's death does not remain free from the law concerning adultery, since on remarriage she immediately becomes subject to it again.

The mistake the modern writers make, I think, is to regard the illustration as a parable. We have been so impressed by the demonstration that Jesus' stories are parables rather than allegories that we have forgotten that allegory existed at that time and was a well-established literary form. The patristic writers who took this story as an allegory could have been on the right track, however misleading may have been their attempts to allegorize the parables of Jesus.

Most patristic commentators took the woman in the story to be the soul, the husband to be the law, and the other to be Christ. Origen, for example, translates v. 1 as though it meant *the law is binding on a person only during* its *life*. The difficulty of this interpretation is that the law is both an actor in the story (the first husband) and the regulation concerning adultery that governs the whole situation.

Gifford, followed by Sanday and Headlam, suggests an ingenious way out. He identifies the woman with 'that inmost self, or personality, which survives all changes, moral or physical, and retains its identity under all conditions of existence', 'the very self'. The first husband is then 'our old man' (6.6), whose death represents 'the crucifixion of "our old man" with Christ'. The second husband is Christ.

This interpretation seems to be on the right lines, but it lacks the naturalness that is essential for a good allegory. Would anyone at the time have supposed that a wife should stand for 'the very self' and the first husband for 'the old man', if there were not available some common images to suggest the imaginative and intellectual leap? The illustration was meant to support the argument, not the argument the illustration.

My own suggestion is that the first husband and wife in the story stand for body and soul. Everyone would understand this illustration immediately, and everyone would know that the body had to die before the soul could depart and be with God. The allegory is quite straightforward. In the hands of this writer the allegory is adapted to its spiritual purpose with great skill. He draws attention to the fact that law, with its regulations about adultery, keeps a wife from living with another man, but that death ends the law's power. Of course the death of a husband does not end the law's power over a wife in real life, but in the allegory the death of the husband is the death of the body, and law only applies to bodies and not to souls.

The spiritual purpose of the allegory is to persuade men now, before they die, to put to death their fleshly natures and to live only for Christ. The first husband in the story is allegorically the body, but spiritually the whole human nature in opposition to God; the wife in the story is allegorically the soul, but spiritually the essential self which was made for communion with God.

This spiritual message was the great theme of the Hellenistic religions of the day, and had permeated Hellenistic Judaism, the theme of 'dying as to the life of the body in order to obtain a share in incorporeal and imperishable life with the Unbegotten and Imperishable One' (Philo, *On the Giants*, 14). The theme is often illustrated allegorically with the picture of marriage; examples can be found in the Mystery Religions, in Hellenistic Judaism, and in heretical and orthodox Christian writings. Philo, for example, draws a contrast between the union of men and women and the union of God and the soul to make just this point. 'The intercourse of men for the begetting of children makes virgins lose their virginity; but when God begins to have intercourse with the soul he first makes the soul that was not virgin into a virgin again' (*On the Cherubim*, 50).

Paul could easily have been familiar with this sort of allegory and this sort of spiritual theme. He could possibly have employed the illustration of the woman and her two husbands in this context, although there would still remain a certain tension between this way of talking about the body as symbolizing what has to be put to death and the perfectly neutral use of phrases like 'in the flesh' in other contexts. However, there is positive evidence in this passage itself that the illustration is a foreign element that has been added later to Paul's argument, and that Paul himself did not write the allegory. In v. 4 the argument states that Christians died to the Law *through the body of Christ*. The allegory illustrates only the first half of the argument, the dying to the law, and does nothing to help the second part, the dying through Christ's body. The second half, by introducing Christ's body, indeed rather spoils the allegory, for there the second husband is Christ and the only body is the body allegorically represented by the first husband. Now a commentator is at perfect liberty to use the common images that belong to his own spirituality to illustrate half a verse or one particular theme that he sees sticking out from the text on which he is commenting, but an author is much more likely to keep his thought consistent and coherent. If we set aside vv. 1 to 3, 4b, and 5, we are left in vv. 4a and 6 with a terse and packed argument that carries forward the line of thought started in Chapter 6: 'So, my brothers, you too have died to the Law by taking the body of Christ. For we have now been discharged from the Law, having died to what held us captive, so that we may serve in newness of the Spirit and not in the old way of the letter.'

The second difficulty lies in vv. 7-13. If the Law kills a man who was previously alive, how can it still be accounted *holy and just and good*?

This objection is easily met, once we recognize the hidden assumption. The argument assumes that the soul without God is living a meaningless life, a life that can only be compared to sleep, to drunkenness, or even to death. When the commandment came, sin sprang to life and killed me. This death, however, can be salutary, because it brings out into the open my true condition. Sin is able to cheat and deceive the drunken soul and use the commandment actually to kill the soul.

The starting point of the argument is that the soul is drunk, asleep, empty, and this assumption is so taken for granted that it does not need to be stated. Consequently the author does not need to raise the question of God's justice and wisdom in giving a Law that had the capacity to be used by sin to kill a man's soul. The soul was lost in any case, and the attack of sin and the death of the soul may prove to be the way to life. A saying of Jesus in the Coptic *Gospel of Thomas* expresses this assumption very neatly.

> Jesus said:
> I stood in the midst of the world,
> And I appeared to them in flesh.
> I found all of them drunken;
> I found none among them athirst.
> And my soul was afflicted for the sons of men,
> For they are blind in their heart, and do not see
> That they have come into the world empty,
> Seeking to go out of the world empty again.
> But now they are drunken.
> When they shake off the effects of their wine, then
> they will repent.
>
> (*Logion* 28, tr. B. M. Metzger,
> arranged after B. Gärtner)

In the Egyptian *Corpus Hermeticum* we find the same assumption about the soul's natural drunkenness and imprisonment, and the necessity to divest oneself of 'the living death, the corpse with five senses, the grave you carry with you' (*Poimandres* vii, 1–2).

Similarly, the idea in *Romans* that the imprisoned soul is liable to attack by the hostile force of sin is paralleled in contemporary Gnostic literature. The soul is the food or prey of heavenly powers and needs desperately to find a password to escape their clutches (Epiphanius 40.2).

All these themes are allegorical readings of the story of Adam and

Eve in the garden, and of how they were deceived by the serpent. But that story is now set against the assumption, not that Adam and Eve before the Fall were innocent and blessed, but against the assumption that they were living only a life of stupor from which they needed to be freed in order to enjoy full life with God. The deception achieved by the serpent was a terrible thing, but it could turn out for the best if properly understood.

Again, it is perfectly possible that Paul could have used these images and shared these assumptions, although it must be admitted that he does not generally seem to regard the human condition as one of imprisonment in the body. But again there are positive indications in the text before us that Paul did not write the section which expresses this point of view. The section that runs from v. 8 to v. 11 is clearly based on the story of the Fall, whereas the surrounding verses, which I ascribe to Paul, just as clearly refer to the Mosaic Tenth Commandment. Verses 8 to 11 alone carry with them the whole apparatus of gnostic speculation about the human condition I have outlined and illustrated above, whereas vv. 7, 12, and 13 are a simple statement of the devastating knowledge of his own sinfulness which a man achieves when he really pays attention to God's Law. Verses 8 to 11 are written in justification of preaching the Law to Gentiles, for thereby they may be stabbed dead to be stabbed awake from their drunken sleep, and the voice that speaks is a Gentile voice: *I was once alive apart from the law, but when the commandment came, sin revived* (or better, sprang to life) *and I died* (v. 9). Verses 7, 12, and 13, on the other hand, are written by a Jew speaking to his fellow-Jews in order to show them the true effect of God's holy Law which they have always had.

The whole section of Romans 7.1-13 is a perfect example in miniature of the history of the epistle. Paul's own words have been expounded in another milieu to another audience, and the assumptions of rather different religious systems have been introduced into Paul's theology. When Paul was accepted as the leading teacher of the Church, her first theologian, in the second half of the second century, the Church was committed to a long struggle to see that this rich but ultimately alien cosmology it got along with Paul's writings did not engulf the truth. Gnostic ways of thought remained an imaginatively fruitful part of the Church's life, and have helped to produce great art and literature and much helpful speculation about the human condition, but gnosticism unchecked could have destroyed the sober realism of the gospel. The gospel sees men whole, and sees them as sinners; these men are addressed by God in specific laws, and offered resurrection and eternal life with the specific man who was crucified under Pontius Pilate and rose from the dead. That gospel allowed all sorts of speculations to gather round it, but it stands apart from the speculations because of its persistent attention to this one corner of history and this one man Jesus Christ.

Notes

1
for I am speaking to those who know the law: the law must be the Christian law, because the argument requires that the wife who wishes to live with another man cannot escape the charge of adultery except by the death of her first husband, and both Roman and Jewish law allow the possibility of divorce. It could be objected that Jewish law does not allow the wife to divorce the husband, but that objection does not alter the fact that Jewish law itself provides a regulation by which a wife is free to marry another, although her first husband is still alive.

4
Likewise, my brethren: the word translated *likewise* simply means 'therefore' or 'so'. I have argued above that vv. 1–3 were added later to Paul's words, which begin here. The later allegory was added to provide a buttress for the 'therefore', but originally the 'therefore' was a conclusion from the argument in 6.14–17a, 21–23. Those who are not under the Law but under grace may be said to have died to the Law.

you have died to the law: the Greek says 'you too', with particular emphasis. Paul means, even you Jews, who might have expected always to live with the Law, whatever else happened.

through the body of Christ: if Paul had said 'to the body of Christ' we might have been able to fit this remark to the allegory: we died in order to be united in marriage with Christ's body. Most modern commentators take the reference to be to the mystical union of Christians with Christ in his body, the Church, which union involves death with him.

This idea would more likely have been expressed by, 'you have died to the Law *in* the body of Christ'. The preposition *through* indicates the means of death adopted by the brethren, and the words *the body of Christ* could refer to the eucharist, in which the participants receive Christ's body (1 Cor. 10.16; 11.24, 27, 29). Or perhaps the words *of Christ* are a gloss; then the meaning is 'through the death of your body', and the verse fits the allegory after all.

4b, 5
so that you may belong to another etc.: this is the spiritual interpretation of the allegory in vv. 1–3. The purpose of the spiritual death is, on the one hand, to marry Christ and to bear fruit for God and, on the other hand, to get rid of the body. The body with its *members* is the natural prey of sins. When we were *in the flesh* we could be attacked by *sinful passions* (or perhaps sufferings inflicted because of sins). Then Death was our master to whom we bore fruit; now it is God to whom we bear fruit. Note that *living in the flesh* is a pejorative expression, and contrast this with Paul's use of the phrase simply to denote our life before we die (Gal. 2.20: 'the life I now live in the flesh . . .').

6
This is Paul's continuation of the argument begun in v. 4a. He is contrasting two different ways of serving God, not two different masters, God and Death, as the allegorist has done. *That which held us captive* was the Law (Lietzmann; not the flesh, as Lipsius would argue). Under the Law we thought God was to be served by meticulously keeping his commandments, but the service he has always required has been for men to live by faith. This is the way of service now confirmed in the new covenant promised in Jeremiah 31. We no longer pay anxious attention to the old written code, but serve God the new way by spontaneously welcoming every prompting of his Spirit.

7
Yet, if it had not been for the law, I should not have known sin. I should not have known what it is to covet if the law had not said, 'You shall not covet': Paul is not asserting, as the RSV rather suggests by the translation *I should not have known what it is to covet*, that all his moral knowledge was completely dependent on the explicit formulations given in the Law. The Greek of the clause reads simply, 'I should not have known covetousness'. Paul obviously could have known the meaning of the word 'covetousness' and even the meaning of the word 'sin' (though this latter is more doubtful) without the Law to instruct him. With the Law to instruct him he would be quite clear about the meaning of

covetousness and sin, but the knowledge he is speaking of is more than that. The Law is essential for him to know the full enormity of sin and covetousness as offences against the holy love of God for men. Paul is not, however, suggesting what the same RSV translation makes him say, that the activity of coveting or the activity of sinning came about only through the Law. That would be an absurd suggestion, although the glossator in vv. 8–11 gives a little support to such an interpretation by his argument that the Law was the means used by sin to aggravate covetousness. In v. 7 Paul simply says that the Law made clear to him that he was a sinner against God.

9

I was once alive: Greek verbs show their person in the ending, so that normally the pronoun subject, which is necessary in English, is not expressed. 'I – was – alive' could be one word in Greek. Here, and in 7.14, 17, 20, 24, and 25, the pronoun *ego* has been added. This must have been done for particular emphasis. It is clear from parallels in other Greek literature contemporary with *Romans* that there is no particular reference to the speaker's private experience (W. G. Kümmel, *Römer 7 und die Bekehrung des Paulus*, Leipzig, 1929, pp. 126–32). I have argued above that vv. 8–11 in fact have in mind man in his natural state, a prisoner in the world, alienated from his true life with God.

sin revived: the verb does not necessarily mean 'came to life again'. Here it must mean just 'came to life', for there is no suggestion that sin had once long ago been alive, had then died, and now has come alive again.

10

the very commandment which promised life: the author of this comment on Paul is thinking of the commandment given by God to Adam and Eve not to eat of the tree of the knowledge of good and evil lest they die (Gen. 2.16 f.). This interpretation is confirmed by the mention of deception in v. 11, a reference to the activity of the serpent. Paul, of course, was thinking of the Mosaic Law, as his citation of the Tenth Commandment shows.

13

The knowledge that covetousness is forbidden by God condemns the covetous man who knows this to eternal death. The argument implies that God would be merciful on a sinner who did not know he was sinning against God, in other words, that those who have the Law are judged by higher requirements than those who do not. Nevertheless the Law is good, because it reveals the true sinfulness of sin. Paul's personification of sin provided the starting point for the meditation in vv. 8–11.

7.14–25

14*We know that the law is spiritual; but I am carnal, sold under sin.* 15*I do not understand my own actions. For I do not do what I want, but I do the very thing I hate.* 16*Now if I do what I do not want, I agree that the law is good.* 17*So then it is no longer I that do it, but sin which dwells within me.* 18*For I know that nothing good dwells within me, that is, in my flesh. I can will what is right, but I cannot do it.* 19*For I do not do the good I want, but the evil I do not want is what I do.* 20*Now if I do what I do not want, it is no longer I that do it, but sin which dwells within me.*

21*So I find it to be a law that when I want to do right, evil lies close at hand.* 22*For I delight in the law of God, in my inmost self,* 23*but I see in my members another law at war with the law of my mind and making me captive to the law of sin which dwells in my members.* 24*Wretched man that I am! Who will deliver me from this body of death?* 25*Thanks be to God through Jesus Christ our Lord! So then, I of myself serve the law of God with my mind, but with my flesh I serve the law of sin.*

Verse 14 switches from the past tenses of vv. 1–13 to the present tense. Does this mean that the subject changes from past experience of the working of the Law to present experience, from the drama of a man's conversion to Christ in the past to the present drama of the Christian life?

The earliest commentators in the Church took this section as a description of weak man, whether or not he was a Christian; Paul wrote as though he himself were weak in order to help the weak to find relief. The earliest commentators left open the question whether Paul was talking about man before or after conversion, but very soon opinion hardened in favour of the view that Paul was talking about man *before* his conversion. Nevertheless, some of the Latin Fathers held to the opposite position, and eventually Augustine made that view triumph in his controversy with the British monk, Pelagius. Pelagius argued that men are created able to do what God commands, and he bitterly attacked the passive Christian life that expected to go on sinning and waited for God to give what he willed men to do. Pelagius interpreted Romans 7 as the story of man still under the Law and not yet a Christian. Augustine saw this as the tip of the iceberg of a great system that would end by sinking the whole of Christian theology; Pelagius's ideal that every Christian should be a monk would turn the Church into a group of small enthusiastic cells, full of intensely self-conscious individuals bearing full responsibility for their sins. Augustine opposed to Pelagius the view of man in solidarity with other men, burdened by the past, an invalid needing constant help in order to be healed. Romans 7 was the picture of the Christian in his daily struggle, crying out for deliverance. (See Peter Brown, *Augustine of Hippo*, London, 1967, Chapters 29-31.)

Luther followed the Augustinian line, with the difference that, although he held that Christians continued to struggle against sin, he also held that they were at the same time completely righteous because of the grace of God by which they were completely and fully reckoned justified before God (Luther's *Introductory Discourse to St Paul's Epistle to the Romans*, 1522 (revised 1546) on Romans 8.10 ff.).

The older view, which Pelagius had followed, was revived by the pietist movement of the eighteenth century and has become the dominant modern position.

As our text stands, there is little doubt that Augustine has the better of the argument. At the beginning of 7.25 Paul gives thanks to God for his deliverance through Christ, and then goes on to conclude with substantially the same picture of his inner division as he had painted before in vv. 13-24. Although he is delivered, he is still torn in two.

Modern commentators who follow the Pelagian interpretation usually deal with this difficulty – to them a minor difficulty, affecting only one or two verses – either by supposing that v. 25b is a summarizing gloss (Weisse, Bultmann, Kuss), or by supposing that the great cry of thanksgiving for deliverance has been displaced from its true position after v. 25b (Venema, Lachmann, Moffatt). Neither of these theories seems likely, and I have argued in the notes for the view that the words *Thanks be to God through Jesus Christ our Lord!* represent an amendment of what was originally a gloss.

If the great thanksgiving for deliverance is set aside, the whole debate between Pelagians and Augustinians becomes altered. Without these words, our passage no longer contains a specifically Christian message at all. It is simply the cry for deliverance of a man who realizes that he is imprisoned by the human situation itself.

The picture is this. The sensitive man who can understand his plight is aware that he is deeply divided. He acknowledges that there is a spiritual law he should follow; he agrees fully with its requirements, yet there seems to be another law holding him in its grip which makes him do evil instead of the good he knows he should do. In his inner being he agrees with the spiritual law, but in his flesh, in his members, sin has taken up residence. In the struggle between his inner being and the law at work in his members *the law of sin* triumphs, and he knows himself powerless. He can only cry to God to be delivered from the flesh that holds him captive.

This statement of the human predicament appears elsewhere in literature contemporary with *Romans*. Epictetus (c. A.D. 60–140) comes close to the same idea in his advice to the moralist to adopt the Socratic method for helping a man who is in error to see the contradiction in which he is involved. The moralist should prove to him that 'what he wants he does not do; and what he does, he does not want to do' (II. xxvi. 4). Epictetus, however, assumes that knowledge of the contradiction will bring power to resolve the dilemma, whereas Romans 7.14–25 argues that knowledge of the dilemma is precisely knowledge that one is powerless to escape by oneself.

The man in Romans 7 is much more like Medea in *The Metamorphoses* of Ovid (43 B.C.–A.D. 18). Medea fell in love with Jason. Because she was under the power of Cupid, she was compelled to act against reason and even against her own interest to save Jason from her father's plot to kill him. Her cry of despair (vii. 20 f.) is very like the cry of despair in Romans 7.24: 'I see the better course and approve it, but I follow the worse.'

The view of man expressed in Romans 7.14–25 sees him as made up of mind, the inner being that agrees with the law, and flesh, the outer nature which has been invaded and subdued by sin. What was taken to be the process of death, the destruction of the body so that the soul could rejoin its source, was interpreted spiritually and applied to this present life: a way must be found of destroying the outer nature in order that the inner nature might be free for union with God. (See for example, Philo, *On the Allegories of the Sacred Laws*, i.105–8.)

If this is the picture of man in Romans 7, Augustine is in the end more faithful to Romans than Pelagius. Man really only finally escapes at death, and until death comes he is constantly in need of spiritual mortification and deliverance from the power that resides in him so long as he is alive. Yet Pelagius has taken seriously the setting of this passage in *Romans* as a whole. Deliverance has been achieved in the death of Jesus Christ, and surely nothing can be the same again for the man who has once grasped that. Pelagius can appeal to the great change wrought by baptism. *He who has died is freed from sin* (6.7). If the nature of a man who has become a Christian is so transformed, surely God can expect from him the deeds he requires.

I think a resolution of this old and still continuing controversy lies in a patient disentanglement of the separate elements that make up *Romans*. Paul himself emphasized both the newness of the life of a man who once takes hold of Christ, and the constant need for moral struggle thereafter. The righteous man must constantly live by faith, serving as best he can in the new life of the Spirit, but always claiming the forgiving grace of God for his sins. Paul's basic picture, however, was glossed and commented upon by later thinkers, who introduced various new assumptions and new perspectives. Some of these additions emphasized the complete change of nature undergone by the new initiate into the Christian faith. This was the view taken up and exploited by Pelagius. Another of these additions, the passage we are discussing, emphasized the basic incompatibility of the human situation with the claims of divine law. This was the view taken up and exploited by Augustine.

For I hold that 7.14–25 was not written by Paul. There are two main reasons for doubting that Paul was the author. First, the word *law* is used in an entirely general way, with no reference to the crucial problem, which dominated Paul's thinking, of the Law of Moses. *Law* in this passage is the universal divine moral law which corresponds to the inner judgement of the conscience. Or *law* is the necessity of things, arising from their very nature. It is hard to imagine that Paul would have switched over so completely into another realm of discourse without giving an explanation of what he was doing.

Second, the dualism between flesh and spirit does not fit naturally into Paul's usual neutral way of talking about life in the flesh meaning simply human life before death. Again we should expect more explanation if Paul was really switching from one realm of discourse to another.

The best explanation I can offer for the insertion of such a long passage into Paul's original letter is that an editor thought it proper to incorporate, at what he took to be the right point, an old statement of the inescapable human predicament. I conjecture that this powerful and moving picture was composed by a Hellenistic Jew, perhaps before the coming of Christ, to help persuade his non-Jewish neighbours of their need of deliverance if they were to live up to the high ideals they knew they should follow.

Notes

15
I do not understand my own actions: man knows that he should keep the moral law, but he examines his actions and finds to his dismay that he does not do what he really wants. His actions turn out bad; he does what he hates. Bultmann, in a famous essay, 'Romans 7 and the Anthropology of Paul' (1932) (translated in *Existence and Faith*, New York, 1960, pp. 147–57), tried to avoid the idea that obedience to the moral law is the end of the deliverance here being sought. He suggests that these words really mean, 'I do not know what I am bringing about', and that what he is bringing about is the death that results from trying to bring about anything at all. Man can find life only if he surrenders all attempts to will to be himself and surrenders himself to the claim of God. This interpretation manages to sound very religious at the expense of cutting the connection between religion and morality. Certainly the author of 7.14–25 wishes men to accept the deliverance given by God, but this deliverance is the freeing of the inner man from bondage to sin in his members so that he may begin to do what he wants to do and keep the moral law. To agree that the law is good (v. 16) does not mean, as Bultmann says, to affirm that the law's fundamental intention is to lead to life, but to agree that its concrete demands are right and should be followed. Failure to do what he knows to be right leads a man to turn to God for help. He needs concrete specific help, not simply the discovery of how to discover his own 'authenticity'.

22

in my inmost self: literally 'according to the inner man'. Cf. Rom. 6.6; 2 Cor. 4.16; Eph. 3.16; Col. 3.9; 1 Peter 3.4.

24

this body of death: literally 'the body of this death', meaning the outer nature which has been invaded by sin, which fights against 'the inner man', and which, unless I can be freed from it, will drag me down to death.

25a

Thanks be to God through Jesus Christ our Lord! This is the reading supported by אª, B and the Coptic versions. The Western reading, found in D, G, and the Old Latin versions is 'The grace of God through Jesus Christ our Lord', with variations. א*, A and the Syriac versions have 'I thank God through Jesus Christ our Lord'. The second reading, 'The grace of God . . .', is so abrupt an answer to the question that it has a good claim to be considered the original reading, for it is hard to imagine a scribe's altering 'Thanks be to God' or 'I thank God' in such a difficult way. But if 'The grace of God' is original, it would almost certainly have first been a gloss to the original text rather than a part of the original. When we put these words aside, we see that v. 24 was meant to be a rhetorical question, and v. 25b a restatement of the predicament out of which man cries for help. ('The grace of God' could be a glossator's note to the question 'Who?' in Greek, because the interrogative can mean 'What masculine or feminine thing?' as well as 'Who?' 'Grace' is feminine in Greek.)

25b

I of myself: this is an over-translation first suggested by J. C. K. von Hofman in an attempt to make this verse refer even to the man who is a Christian, because he is serving the law of sin when he forgets to depend on God and tries to live on his own. The emphatic construction hardly bears this meaning (Kümmel, 66 f.). The statement is simply a summary of the whole section. Translate 'I myself'.

Romans 8

8 There is therefore now no condemnation for those who are in Christ Jesus. ²For the law of the Spirit of life in Christ Jesus has set me free from the law of sin and death. ³For God has done what the law, weakened by the

flesh, could not do: sending his own Son in the likeness of sinful flesh and for sin,¹ he condemned sin in the flesh, ⁴in order that the just requirement of the law might be fulfilled in us, who walk not according to the flesh but according to the Spirit. ⁵For those who live according to the flesh set their minds on the things of the flesh, but those who live according to the Spirit set their minds on the things of the Spirit. ⁶To set the mind on the flesh is death, but to set the mind on the Spirit is life and peace. ⁷For the mind that is set on the flesh is hostile to God; it does not submit to God's law, indeed it cannot; ⁸and those who are in the flesh cannot please God.

⁹But you are not in the flesh, you are in the Spirit, if the Spirit of God really dwells in you. Any one who does not have the Spirit of Christ does not belong to him. ¹⁰But if Christ is in you, although your bodies are dead because of sin, your spirits are alive because of righteousness. ¹¹If the Spirit of him who raised Jesus from the dead dwells in you, he who raised Christ Jesus from the dead will give life to your mortal bodies also through his Spirit which dwells in you.

¹²So then, brethren, we are debtors, not to the flesh, to live according to the flesh – ¹³for if you live according to the flesh you will die, but if by the Spirit you put to death the deeds of the body you will live. ¹⁴For all who are led by the Spirit of God are sons of God. ¹⁵For you did not receive the spirit of slavery to fall back into fear, but you have received the spirit of sonship. When we cry, 'Abba! Father!' ¹⁶it is the Spirit himself bearing witness with our spirit that we are children of God, ¹⁷and if children, then heirs, heirs of God and fellow heirs with Christ, provided we suffer with him in order that we may also be glorified with him.

¹⁸I consider that the sufferings of this present time are not worth comparing with the glory that is to be revealed to us. ¹⁹For the creation waits with eager longing for the revealing of the sons of God; ²⁰for the creation was subjected to futility, not of its own will but by the will of him who subjected it in hope; ²¹because the creation itself will be set free from its bondage to decay and obtain the glorious liberty of the children of God. ²²We know that the whole creation has been groaning in travail together until now; ²³and not only the creation, but we ourselves, who have the first fruits of the Spirit, groan inwardly as we wait for adoption as sons, the redemption of our bodies. ²⁴For in this hope we were saved. Now hope that is seen is not hope. For who hopes for what he sees? ²⁵But if we hope for what we do not see, we wait for it with patience.

²⁶*Likewise the Spirit helps us in our weakness; for we do not know how to pray as we ought, but the Spirit himself intercedes for us with sighs too deep for words.* ²⁷*And he who searches the hearts of men knows what is the mind of the Spirit, because*ʲ *the Spirit intercedes for the saints according to the will of God.*

²⁸*We know that in everything God works for good*ᵏ *with those who love him,*ˡ *who are called according to his purpose.* ²⁹*For those whom he fore-knew he also predestined to be conformed to the image of his Son, in order that he might be the first-born among many brethren.* ³⁰*And those whom he predestined he also called; and those whom he called he also justified; and those whom he justified he also glorified.*

³¹*What then shall we say to this? If God is for us, who is against us?* ³²*He who did not spare his own Son but gave him up for us all, will he not also give us all things with him?* ³³*Who shall bring any charge against God's elect? It is God who justifies;* ³⁴*who is to condemn? Is it Christ Jesus, who died, yes, who was raised from the dead, who is at the right hand of God, who indeed intercedes for us?*ᵐ ³⁵*Who shall separate us from the love of Christ? Shall tribulation, or distress, or persecution, or famine, or nakedness, or peril, or sword?* ³⁶*As it is written,*

'*For thy sake we are being killed all the day long;*
we are regarded as sheep to be slaughtered.'

³⁷*No, in all these things we are more than conquerors through him who loved us.* ³⁸*For I am sure that neither death, nor life, nor angels, nor princi-palities, nor things present, nor things to come, nor powers,* ³⁹*nor height, nor depth, nor anything else in all creation, will be able to separate us from the love of God in Christ Jesus our Lord.*

ⁱ Or *and as a sin offering.*
ʲ Or *that.*
ᵏ Other ancient authorities read *in everything he works for good,* or *everything works for good.*
ˡ Greek *God.*   ᵐ Or *It is Christ Jesus . . . for us.*

This is a very long chapter, which seems to offer a welter of themes, and yet it should not be divided up into sections. One theme domi-nates the whole. Those who love God and rely on the intercession of Jesus Christ have nothing to fear while they are alive, whatever happens to them, and nothing to fear on the day of judgement when the kingdom of God comes. Their bodies will be raised from the dead and made incorruptible and they will receive the inheritance promised to the sons of God. The rest of creation will also be transformed at the same time. The sufferings that have to be endured now are nothing compared to that glory. Even these sufferings are under God's providential ordering, however hard that is to believe, and he answers the prayers which Christians are enabled to make because the Spirit helps them.

Paul's original argument has attracted a number of comments from glossators and editors. Two of these are particularly important, the comment that identifies Christians as those who walk 'according to the Spirit' and not 'according to the flesh' (vv. 4b-10; 11c-14; and see note on v. 3), and the comment that says Christians are predestined from the beginning (vv. 28c-30; 33). The first of these is easily identifiable, because its insistence that 'the body is dead because of sin' (v. 10) does not fit very easily with the dominant theme that 'your mortal bodies' will be given life by him who raised Jesus from the dead (v. 11). The second also separates off fairly clearly from the rest of the chapter, because the chapter assumes that men may choose whether or not they will receive the Spirit by faith (cf. Gal. 3.1-5), and that those the Apostle is addressing have so chosen. Nevertheless, Paul's emphasis on the certainty of the Spirit's witness that they are in fact children of God (v. 16) has provided the commentator with some grounds for introducing the doctrine of predestination, which leaves no room for genuine human choice.

Paul's argument is the culmination of his plea to the Roman Christians not to live under the Law. The Law is unable to condemn sin, but only able to show sin up for what it is. The death of Jesus Christ alone is able to condemn sin, and by relying on him whom God raised from the dead they may live without fear, in perfect hope and confidence. God loves them; he cares for them now, and will give them resurrection and eternal life as his children. Nothing can separate them from that love.

Notes

1

now: omitted by D*, 1908^margin, syr^p, and placed after *condemnation* in Ψ, 1827; therefore probably a gloss (Zahn). Paul meant, there will be no condemnation. He works back from the crucial day of judgement.

for those who are in Christ Jesus: the Greek article, translated *those*, is omitted by 1739 and g. If that is right, translate, 'There will be no condemnation with Christ Jesus'. Zahn translates as a question: 'Is there then no condemnation for Christians?'

2

has set me free: me is read by A, C, D, and the Latin Vulgate; the better text we usually rely on reads *thee* (ℵ, B, G, 1739, Old Latin); other good witnesses have *us* (Ψ, Marcion); and there is a little support for no pronoun at all. I think *thee* is the harder and better reading. This verse is, then, an answer to the cry of despair in 7.24, *Who will deliver me from this body of death?*

the law of the Spirit of life in Christ Jesus . . . the law of sin and death: the word *law* cannot mean the Mosaic Law but must mean something like the word *mind* in vv. 6, 7. The required contrast is already present in 7.23, between the *law of my mind*, which agrees with the *law of God*, and *the law of sin which dwells in my members*. This verse fits in with the argument at the end of Chapter 7, and is part of the commentary on Paul. Paul's problem is the Law of Moses.

3

For God has done what the law, weakened by the flesh, could not do: v. 1 has stated that Christians need fear no condemnation. That happy state of affairs has not, however, come about because they have succeeded in keeping the Law. The Law has proved weak and God has had to give another means to free men from sin.

The words *by the flesh* are suspicious. Paul's argument has been that the Law cannot help a man when he transgresses; the trouble is in the Law's basic nature, not in the fact that the men to whom the Law applies happen to be alive, that is, in the flesh. The words 'through the flesh' here of course imply a quite different reason for the Law's weakness, namely that the fleshly part of man is the place sin has occupied and only if a man can get rid of his fleshly part can he obey the Law as he knows he should. I suspect, therefore, that the words *by the flesh* were added to Paul's original text by the commentator responsible for vv. 4b–10 and 11c–14, who sees the moral struggle as a fight between two opposed ways of life, life according to the Spirit and life according to the flesh. The words are omitted by Hippolytus, *Against Noetus* 15. Translate: 'As for the powerlessness of the Law in which it was weak, God sending his own Son etc.'

in the likeness of sinful flesh: literally 'in the likeness of flesh of sin'. Does *likeness* mean 'appearance' (cf. Rev. 9.7) or 'form' (Phil. 2.7)? There is no doubt that Paul thought of Christ as a man who could actually die, so that we should probably prefer 'form'. Yet, even on this translation, the word implies some reservation about the identification, and the reservation must spring from the presence of the word *sinful* (literally, 'of sin'). My own difficulty with the phrase lies in the implication that flesh is, by nature, sinful, because Paul generally gives a neutral sense to 'flesh' (1.3; 4.1; 9.3, 5; Gal. 2.20). God sent his Son because of sin, not because of the fact that men are alive in the flesh. The word 'of flesh' is omitted in two Latin manuscripts, and transposed in a third (T*, V*; Z*), and I conjecture that 'of flesh' was a gloss by a commentator who took flesh to be the decisive reason for the existence of sin. God sent his Son in the likeness of sin and for sin. Cf. 2 Cor. 5.21, *For our sake he made him to be sin who knew no sin, so that in him we might become the righteousness of God*; Gal. 3.13; *Christ redeemed us from the curse of the law, having become a curse for us*. Christ suffered as a sinner for sinners, and so made it possible for sinners to become righteous. The reference is to his sacrificial death, without its being necessary to translate the words *and for sin* as *and as a sin offering* with the RSV footnote.

he condemned sin in the flesh: in the flesh goes with the verb and indicates the place where this condemnation occurred. Here is Paul's decisive statement of the incarnation, without any pejorative overtones about flesh. The commentator, however, was able to take *in the flesh* with *sin* and to draw the conclusions which followed from his view of man as an essentially good spirit trapped in the flesh.

4

in order that the just requirement of the law might be fulfilled in us: not by some legal fiction where righteousness is imputed to sinners, but by the sinners' having found a sacrifice to offer for their sins and a way of life, witnessed to by the Law and the Prophets, that is actually righteous, the way of faith.

4b–10

who walk not according to the flesh but according to the Spirit: this is the beginning of the commentary, which consists of vv. 4b–10 and 11c–14. According to the commentator, man consists figuratively of two parts, flesh and spirit. Man's aim should be to free himself from the flesh, which would eventually destroy him, and to live according to his spirit. He cannot do this by himself, since flesh already holds him captive. The Spirit, which is Christ, comes to his rescue and dwells in him, enabling him to walk according to the spirit, and to please God, and to live. The theology based on this view is consonant with Paul's theology, particularly with his view of the Christian life as a battle or a race that could be lost through lack of perseverance, but it presupposes a view of man's nature that Paul did not hold, and it could lead to a denial of the goodness of creation and to a denial of the resurrection of our mortal bodies. Paul's own theology stands out very clearly in v. 11ab (see next note).

11ab

If the Spirit of him who raised Jesus from the dead dwells in you, he who raised Christ Jesus from the dead will give life to your mortal bodies also: the second reference to Jesus, in the words *he who raised Christ Jesus,* is textually very uncertain, and I suggest that Paul originally said, 'he who raised from the dead', and scribes added 'Christ', 'Jesus', 'Christ Jesus', or 'Jesus Christ' where they saw fit. The word *also* is omitted by ℵ and should be omitted as an accommodation of Paul's words to the words of the commentator, who would think of the raising of the body as a most surprising work of supererogation on the part of God. The resurrection to life is the reward for those who have found God's remedy for sin and have become righteous according to the gospel (vv. 3, 4a).

11c–14

through his Spirit which dwells in you: this is the reading of ℵ, A, C; B, D, G, Ψ, 33, Origen, Irenaeus, and Tertullian read 'because of his Spirit's dwelling in you'. The second reading looks like a correction to guard against the idea that God works in nature by means of a spiritual substance. The first reading, adopted by the RSV, probably does imply this thought, and is to my mind one more reason for ascribing these words to the glossator responsible for vv. 12–14. His message is that the flesh or the body must be 'put to death' by an ascetic life in order that the spirit, infused by God's Spirit, might triumph, and eventually achieve the eternal life of God's sons.

15

For you did not receive the spirit of slavery to fall back into fear, but you *have received the spirit of sonship:* the words *to fall back* are an imaginative rendering of the Greek word 'again'. But this word is a gloss, being omitted by Ψ, 326, 491, 623*. The gloss has forced on our translation the idea that two human spirits are in question, the spirit of slavery and the spirit of sonship. That was the conception held by the glossator, who assumed that the new converts had come out of a state dominated by the spirit of fear. Paul, however, is talking about the gift of the Holy Spirit, as is clear from v. 16, where the human spirit is a unified entity, leaving no room for two spirits (cf. Gal. 3.1–5). Translate, 'For you have not received a Spirit binding you in fear, but you have received a Spirit making you sons'.

When we cry, 'Abba! Father!' Abba is an Aramaic word meaning 'Father'. It was particularly used by small children addressing their fathers or addressing loved and respected older men. Jesus, with one exception, began his prayers with this address to God, and he taught his disciples to follow his example: the Lord's Prayer probably began originally 'Father' (Luke 11.2), rather than 'Our Father in heaven'. It is possible that Greek-speaking Christians at Rome would retain the Aramaic word, just as we retain the Hebrew word Amen. Paul is not referring specifically to the use of the Lord's Prayer, but to the way Christians customarily began every prayer, in accordance with Jesus' habit and teaching. The intimacy with which they could address God was a sign of the nature of God's Spirit that they had received, a Spirit making them sons and not a Spirit binding them in fear.

16, 17

God's Spirit speaks with our spirit in prayer, and the nature of the prayer itself and the hearing the prayer receives assure us that we are God's children. Children will be heirs provided they persevere in the suffering which probably will be the lot of God's children before the coming of the glorious kingdom.

18

this present time: this present age, before the kingdom of God comes.

19

the creation: the whole non-human universe. Paul is referring to the Old Testament vision of a new heaven and a new earth (Isaiah 65.17; 66.22; Rev. 21; 2 Peter 3.13). The open acknowledgement of God's children by God himself will be accompanied by a renewal of creation.

20

for the creation was subjected to futility, not of its own will but by the will of him who subjected it in hope: this translation implies that God subjected creation to futility against its will but in order to give it something to hope for, a strange idea. The phrase *by the will of him who subjected it* is literally 'because of him who subjected (it)' and probably refers rather to Adam, who by his sin involved the whole of creation. The words *in hope* hardly belong here at all, but go with the verb *waits* in v. 19: creation waits in hope for the revelation of God's sons. I conclude, with Weisse, Michelsen, and van Manen, that the whole of v. 20, apart from the last two words *in hope,* was originally a gloss on Paul's argument. The glossator wished to explain that, since creation was subjected to futility by Adam's fall, it was appropriate that creation's restoration should follow the restoration of mankind on the day when the saints were openly revealed.

21–23

Eternal life depends on *the redemption of our bodies,* and redeemed bodies will need an incorruptible world to live in. Paul probably did believe in the continued existence of 'separated souls' between death and resurrection, and he compares this state to sleep, but his primary message of hope is the message of *the redemption of our bodies.* In this he was faithfully repeating the teaching of Jesus and the other apostles.

24

For in this hope we were saved: meaning, for this hoped-for outcome we have been saved. God's sending his Son to save us was in order to give us eternal life in his kingdom.

26

Likewise: as the Spirit launches us on the way to perseverance, so the Spirit gives us strength in our weakness along the way, until the hope is realized. The strength consists of help in making useful and sensible prayers.

26b, 27

but the Spirit himself intercedes for us with sighs too deep for words. And he who searches the hearts of men knows what is the mind of the Spirit because (or *that*) *the Spirit intercedes for the saints according to the will of God:* the last clause betrays the real purpose of this section. The true translation is *that* (RSV footnote) rather than *because,* for God who knows men's hearts can hardly be said to know the mind of the Spirit only because it intercedes according to his will: God can see disobedience as clearly as he can see obedience. But the statement *that the Spirit intercedes for the saints according to the will of God* is obviously designed to reassure those who doubted whether inarticulate groanings were to be trusted; the argument is, If God can trust these inarticulate sounds to be according to his will, so can you. The whole note is, therefore, a defence of inarticulate prayer in Christian worship. Paul was ready to tolerate such prayer, provided a translation was given then and there, but we can hardly imagine his putting in a full-scale justification of the practice, without qualification, in the middle of another argument. Paul, in any case, wishes to emphasize that Christ intercedes for us, v. 34. Verses 26c and 27 are a gloss designed to defend the practice of offering inarticulate prayers in public worship. Paul's actual argument in v. 26ab is that by ourselves we do not know how to pray as we ought (or as our needs require), but that the Spirit comes to our aid and helps us to formulate better prayers. Verse 28 goes on to assure the Romans that God will answer their prayers.

28

We know that in everything God works for good with those who love him: this is probably right, and preferable to the other possible translation, 'And we know that all things work together for good to them that love God' (AV). The verb 'to work' probably needs an object, which must be 'all things', and this holds, whether or not the subject of the verb is expressed. (א, C, D, G, and the text upon which the Authorized Version was based omit the subject 'God', while P46, A, B, and the Sahidic version add the subject.) God does govern the events of the universe in order to further the good of those who love him, however difficult it is to understand this when confronted by tribulation, distress, persecution, famine, nakedness, peril, or sword (v. 35) .

who are called according to his purpose: this is a definition of those who love God from God's point of view, as it were. It is the beginning of the second of the main commentaries I suggested in the introductory note as having been added to Paul's original argument. The comment extends to the end of v. 30, and the same commentator was also responsible for v. 33. There is a logical contradiction between the first part of v. 28 and this comment in vv. 28c-30 that is so great that we can scarcely believe that the one man was responsible for both. To love God implies a free choice of God that could have gone the other way, but the election of some men and not others by God implies that they had no choice. It is no defence against this argument to say, 'Love knows itself to be altogether the gift and operation of God, altogether the calling which is grounded upon the purpose comprehended in God before all time and before every moment of time' (Barth, *The Epistle* to the Romans, 2nd ed.). Love knows it is called by God and is unworthy of God, but if love knows that it had no choice it could not go on being love. The predestinarian comment is the work of a theologian so imbued with the assumptions of gnosticism that he could not believe in a created world's having the necessary independence of God so that men would have the ultimate freedom to reject, as well as to accept, their Creator's love. The commentator got a foothold in Paul's argument because Paul is emphasizing the great hope of which Christians can be assured. The commentator took this certainty for his sort of certainty, the certainty of what could never possibly have been otherwise.

32

The ground of Christian hope is the love of God who gave men his Son to die for them. The gift of *all things with him* is the gift of *the redemption of our bodies* and eternal life in the company of Christ in the kingdom.

33

An addition of the predestinarian commentator responsible for vv. 28c–30. Verse 34 is clearly the original rhetorical question, because it takes up v. 1, with which the argument began.

34

I prefer to take the second sentence as a statement, with the RSV footnote. No one would suppose that Jesus Christ would condemn him. Their real fear was that God would condemn them for not keeping the Law. But Christ has died for men; the sacrifice has been made. And Christ has been raised from the dead, so that his sacrifice can be offered for their sins, in confidence that he is alive to bring it before the throne of grace and to intercede for them day by day, until the last day comes and they are redeemed.

35

the love of Christ: one manuscript, ℵ, has 'the love of God', and B has 'the love of God which is in Christ Jesus' (cf. v. 39). Perhaps 'the love of God' is the original reading (Lipsius). Paul means God's love for us (cf. v. 37).

36

The emphasis implied by this citation from Psalm 44.22 (LXX 43.23) is on our love for God. Since this contradicts the emphasis in vv. 35 and 37 on God's love for us, and since the citation is word-for-word from the Greek Old Testament and Paul made his own translations from the Hebrew, we may suspect a gloss.

38-39
Paul's list of ordinary perils of this world seems to have been supplemented by a list of cosmic perils. The gnostic systems were all designed to give initiates the secret of how to escape from the perils put in the path of the soul to God by the astral powers. The powers were called *angels*, *principalities*, and *powers*, and they had to be placated, or tricked, or mastered before the soul could pass through them and approach God. (Compare the system under attack in the pseudo-Pauline *Epistle to the Colossians*.) Paul has already assured the Romans of God's help for them in the midst of peril through the presence of the Spirit to formulate their prayers, through God's providential protection of them, and through Christ's continual intercession for their sins; he has also assured them that their bodies will be raised to incorruptible life with Christ. The idea that anything more is needed belongs to a different world of thought, which thinks more of the soul's journey out of creation through the realm of cosmic enemies than of the redemption of creation itself.

Chapters 9–11 at first sight interrupt the flow of Paul's argument. Van Manen (in the article 'Romans (Epistle)' in the *Encyclopaedia Biblica*, 1899–1903) has argued that this part of *Romans* 'betrays tokens of an originally different source' from Romans 1–8, and that neither part was written by Paul. Dodd suggests that Paul could have been incorporating an earlier piece of work, perhaps a sermon, 'to save a busy man's time and trouble in writing on the subject afresh'.

According to this sort of view, Romans 9–11 is at best a digression to develop hints given elsewhere in *Romans*, and at worst a completely alien interpolation.

Such views assume that *Romans* is basically a doctrinal treatise for all Christians everywhere. I have been arguing, however, that *Romans* was first written by the apostle to a specific audience in Rome for a specific purpose. His audience was the members of the synagogues in Rome that had come to believe in Jesus Christ, and his purpose was to win their support for his special mission to the Gentiles, by which he hoped to persuade Gentiles in Rome to come together in their own congregations alongside the already existing congregations of mostly Jewish Christians.

Here I am following the main features of an argument first put forward by Ferdinand Christian Baur. He finds in these three chapters of *Romans* 'the germ and centre of the whole, from which the other parts sprang; . . . we should take our stand on these three chapters in order to enter into the Apostle's original conception, from which the whole organism of the Epistle was developed, as we have it especially in the first eight chapters' (*Paul the Apostle of Jesus Christ, His Life and Work, His Epistles and his Doctrine*, English translation, Vol. 1, 1876, p. 315).

If we can understand Romans 9–11 correctly, we shall be better able to understand the rest of the letter.

The very specificness of this section, which has led to its comparative neglect by later generations of Christians not troubled by the problem of Israel, is what recommends it. Our quest is for the specific situation to which Paul's letter was first directed, for I suspect that many of the more general doctrinal reflections are secondary meditations on what the apostle first said to meet the questions and fears of his original audience. I have already isolated remarks and small sections in Chapters 1–8 that show signs of being just such additions, but even our present section, Chapters 9–11, is not free from this sort of enlargement. For the question of the Jewish people and their place in God's plan of salvation was a burning issue not only for Paul and his generation but also for the second-century Church. Jewish Christian congregations still existed, the question of whether or not Christians had also to become Jews was still alive, and a powerful popular movement has arisen in the Church, under the leadership of Marcion, to remove as much of the Old Testament religion as possible from the Christian faith.

These questions are still questions today, not only the pure theological questions of the nature of the Christian faith, but also the theological questions that are more closely connected with a Christian's relations to his fellow men, questions about the Church and the Jewish people. Our generation has lived through a period when the Third German Reich attempted systematically to exterminate Jews in the territory under its control and Christians had to ask themselves where their theology had got them if genocide could be seriously considered as a possible national policy, and where their theology had got them if antisemitism could have become a possible part of their thinking.

For all these reasons, Romans 9–11 needs very close attention, and promises rich rewards to our attention.

9.1–29

9 *I am speaking the truth in Christ, I am not lying; my conscience bears me witness in the Holy Spirit, ²that I have great sorrow and unceasing anguish in my heart. ³For I could wish that I myself were accursed and cut off from Christ for the sake of my brethren, my kinsmen by race. ⁴They are*

Israelites, and to them belong the sonship, the glory, the covenants, the giving of the law, the worship, and the promises; ⁵to them belong the patriarchs, and of their race, according to the flesh, is the Christ. God who is over all be blessed for ever." Amen.

⁶But it is not as though the word of God had failed. For not all who are descended from Israel belong to Israel, ⁷and not all are children of Abraham because they are his descendants; but 'Through Isaac shall your descendants be named.' ⁸This means that it is not the children of the flesh who are the children of God, but the children of the promise are reckoned as descendants. ⁹For this is what the promise said, 'About this time I will return and Sarah shall have a son.' ¹⁰And not only so, but also when Rebecca had conceived children by one man, our forefather Isaac, ¹¹though they were not yet born and had done nothing either good or bad, in order that God's purpose of election might continue, not because of works but because of his call, ¹²she was told, 'The elder will serve the younger.' ¹³As it is written, 'Jacob I loved, but Esau I hated.'

¹⁴What shall we say then? Is there injustice on God's part? By no means! ¹⁵For he says to Moses, 'I will have mercy on whom I have mercy, and I will have compassion on whom I have compassion.' ¹⁶So it depends not upon man's will or exertion, but upon God's mercy. ¹⁷For the scripture says to Pharaoh, 'I have raised you up for the very purpose of showing my power in you, so that my name may be proclaimed in all the earth.' ¹⁸So then he has mercy upon whomever he wills, and he hardens the heart of whomever he wills.

¹⁹You will say to me then, 'Why does he still find fault? For who can resist his will'? ²⁰But who are you, a man, to answer back to God? Will what is moulded say to its moulder, 'Why have you made me thus?' ²¹Has the potter no right over the clay, to make out of the same lump one vessel for beauty and another for menial use? ²²What if God, desiring to show his wrath and to make known his power, has endured with much patience the vessels of wrath made for destruction, ²³in order to make known the riches of his glory for the vessels of mercy, which he has prepared beforehand for glory, ²⁴even us whom he has called, not from the Jews only but also from the Gentiles? ²⁵As indeed he says in Hose'a,

'Those who were not my people
I will call "my people,"
and her who was not beloved

I will call "my beloved".'

²⁶'*And in the very place where it was said to them, "You are not my people,"
they will be called "sons of the living God".'*

²⁷*And Isaiah cries out concerning Israel: 'Though the number of the sons
of Israel be as the sand of the sea, only a remnant of them will be saved;*
²⁸*for the Lord will execute his sentence upon the earth with rigour and
despatch.'* ²⁹*And as Isaiah predicted,*
*'If the Lord of hosts had not left us children,
we would have fared like Sodom and been made like Gomor'rah.'*

ⁿ *Or Christ, who is God over all, blessed for ever.*

Paul's success among the Gentiles must have intensified the problem
of Jewish Christians. Their basic problem was that Israel, the people
prepared by God to be the cradle of the Messiah, had largely rejected
him when he came, and was slow to turn to him in the time still given
them to repent. Paul's work aggravated this problem. If Gentiles
were prepared to welcome the Messiah when God's chosen people
were not, did this mean that God's promises had failed?

Paul's answer has two parts. First, he assures the Roman Jewish
Christians that his own mission to the Gentiles does not mean that he
is indifferent to the response his fellow Jews make to the gospel. If his
own damnation would help bring them to acknowledge Jesus Christ,
then he would accept damnation – much as Moses had offered to be
blotted out of the Lord's book if thereby the people's sin could be
forgiven (Ex. 32.32).

Second, Paul argues that the choice of Israel by God did not mean
that all Israel would always be faithful. The Old Testament was full
of examples of unfaithfulness and of unexpected response. God's
choice of Israel was first made known as a promise, and the true seed
of Abraham were those, like Abraham, who relied on God's promises
before the promises were fulfilled.

The assumption behind both these arguments is that unbelieving
Jews still have an open choice before them of whether or not to
believe. Paul can hardly be in great pain and sorrow over those of his
fellow Jews who have not believed if their fate is already sealed, nor
can he draw attention to the conditions upon which a Jew can be
truly a Jew if those conditions were impossible to fulfil.

Nevertheless, our section as it stands contains passages that imply that God has already decided men's fate, irrespective of the choices they have made or will make. In v. 11 God's love for Jacob and his hatred for Esau are explicitly stated to have been determined before they were even born, so that it would be perfectly clear that nothing depended on their actions, whether good or bad, and everything depended on God's election of one and rejection of the other. In vv. 14–23 there is a rhetorical attempt to justify this position, which hinges on the case of the Pharaoh who was reigning in Egypt at the time of Moses. His rejection by God was not, as one might think, an entirely inexplicable discarding of a creature God decided to have no use for. Pharaoh, although he was to be 'hardened' and rejected, was also useful to God, having been raised up to show God's power and to further God's plans for the true Israel, the *vessels of mercy, which he has prepared beforehand for glory* (v. 23). If anyone should complain that God's moral condemnation is a sham, because the reprobate have been ordained to reprobation by him, they are told that they have no more right to argue with God than a pot with its potter (vv. 19–21).

The objection this last argument is supposed to meet, *Why does* (God) *still find fault?* (v. 19), seems to me unanswerable. The system expounded in vv. 11–23 seems only tenable on a view of God which excludes moral praise or blame from his nature; we might still praise and blame ourselves and others for certain actions in a determined moral world, but the One who determined which men were to be praised and which men were to be blamed could not be said to praise or blame. The answer given in vv. 20 f. to the objection is in fact far more profound than at first sight appears, and answers the seemingly unanswerable objection by redefining the terms. The argument starts by admitting that no one can withstand God's will; God does determine who are good and who are evil, and the good will be glorified and the evil destroyed (vv. 22 f.). Praise and blame are popularly attached to men's actions, and this praise and blame are normally identified with God's praise and blame. If God were like a general who first ordered his troops to rob, murder and rape and then court-martialled them for their behaviour, he could justly be censured by the poor soldiers caught in his trap, but – and here is the rub of the argument – God is not like that. He is not part of the moral human system, but is completely above the system, like a sculptor and the figures he has made or a potter and his pots. Figures or pots may use moral terms to distinguish between themselves, but these terms do not apply to the sculptor or the potter. Shakespeare cannot be blamed for both making Lady Macbeth who she is and then seeing that she dies; he can even, in a sense, find fault with Lady Macbeth, and still see that she is destroyed.

The man who mounted this argument is no fool, and his argument has to be taken seriously, but he cannot be Paul.

It is possible to reconcile a deterministic view of the world with moral striving and with hoping and fearing for the good of others (because even this moral striving and hoping and fearing are determined). I cannot, therefore, simply put aside vv. 11-23 on the grounds that Paul could not have pleaded *great sorrow and unceasing anguish* over the fate of those whose rejection by God was already fixed. But he could scarcely have asked about the failure of *the word of God* (v. 6), which he defines as a word of promise (v. 9), if he held the deterministic view expressed in vv. 11-23. God, of course, cannot break his promise, but on the other hand he cannot make a promise unless he knows that men are free to rely on his promise or to disbelieve his promise. On the deterministic view of the universe, logically we may or may not 'trust' God, but logically we cannot speak of God's decrees as promises. I cannot promise a stone that in five minutes I shall lay it as foundation stone. I make a promise to my child because I know that the promise may or may not make a difference to the child.

Paul, however, need not have been logical, in which case he could perhaps have written the whole of Romans 9.1-29.

My answer to this argument is that it is reasonable to prefer to assume that Paul was logical rather than that he was not. Then, when we come to defend this assumption, we find that the division between the section that assumes a determined universe and the section that does not is fairly clearly defined; and that stylistically the deterministic verses look more like comments on the verses we assume Paul himself to have written than like mere continuations by the same writer of his unified train of thought. Literary incompatibility matches logical incompatibility. The literary arguments are discussed more fully in the notes; but without going into the matter in detail, we can see from a careful reading of vv. 14–23 in the RSV that here we have a distinct style and method of argument which strike a chill in the heart of anyone who has seriously felt the objections the argument is designed to refute. That author does not seem the same man as the author of the opening three verses, 9.1–3, or as the author of v. 6. Paul assumes that God is subject to the moral logic he has given the world of men to live by; we are not characters in a play written by God, but moral agents given the choice of discovering or rejecting the right way to live. God's promise of life is a conditional promise which we are free to take up or to spurn.

Notes

1

in Christ ... in the Holy Spirit: the two references to Christ and the Holy Spirit are rather awkward. The first, *in Christ*, would seem most naturally to mean 'by Christ', while the second, *in the Holy Spirit*, would seem to mean 'with the Holy Spirit' (cf. 8.16: *it is the Spirit himself bearing witness with our spirit*). The second is unnecessary here, and the first even seems superfluous. Jerome once cites this verse without either expression, and I think that may well have been what Paul originally wrote: *I am speaking the truth, I am not lying; my conscience bears me witness that ...*

3

accursed: literally 'anathema', a Greek word which has come into English. Paul would sacrifice his own salvation for the sake of his fellow Jews who had not believed, if it would do any good.

4, 5

This list of the distinctions of the Jewish people sits very strangely in a letter from a Jew to fellow Jews. It reads much more like an affirmation inserted by a commentator who wished to defend the Jews from the attack of those Christians, like Marcion, who tried to prove that Jewish religion was on a distinctly lower plane than Christianity. Cf. the similar comment added in John 4.22, *salvation is from the Jews.* Sonship means the adoption of the Jewish nation as God's son (but Paul uses the word to refer to the adoption of all Christians as God's sons; cf. Rom. 8.15, 23; Gal. 4.5; Eph. 1.5); *glory* means the glory of the presence of God with them in the great moments of their history; *the covenants* are the succession of covenants, perhaps even going back to Adam and Noah, but certainly to Abraham and Moses (P⁴⁶, B, D read the singular, 'convent', meaning that on Mount Sinai, so that the *convenant and the giving of the law* refer to the same moment); *the worship* means the Temple worship; *the promises* mean the successive messages of hope entrusted to the patriarchs and the prophets. Above all, the Messiah (*the Christ*) comes from the Jews.

5

of their race, according to the flesh, is the Christ. God who is over all be blessed for ever: the RSV text is unlikely to be correct, although it is the interpretation supported by such great scholars as Wettstein and Semler. Lagrange's objection seems to be decisive: no doxology could begin as this one would have to, and read, 'He who is over all, God, be blessed for ever'; doxologies always refer back to God who has already been mentioned (Rom. 1.25; 2 Cor. 11.31; Gal. 1.5; 2 Tim. 4.18; Rom. 11.36). In any case, if a full stop is placed after 'flesh', as the RSV text does, the subsequent words should not be translated *God who is over all be blessed for ever*, but 'He who is over all is God – blessed be he for ever' (Sanday and Headlam). But this translation, although 'correct', runs counter to all expectations (cf. the form of the doxology in 2 Cor. 11.31), and is an unnatural translation of the Greek.

A second possibility is to adopt Erasmus's expedient, and put a full stop after *over all*, and read, 'of them is Christ according to the flesh who is over all. God be blessed for ever'. But again we never find a doxology which begins simply with 'God'. (Ps. 67.19 in the LXX is no real exception.)

A third possibility is the rendering given in the RSV note: ... *of their race, according to the flesh, is the Christ, who is God over all, blessed for ever.* This is the best rendering of the Greek text as it stands and yet, leaving aside all doctrinal problems, the Greek does not really justify the rendering. The word translated *who* is not, as we should expect, the relative pronoun, but the simple article. (This objection is Erasmus's.) The article makes us expect a further adjectival description of Christ, not a new identification with someone or something named by a noun. A relative pronoun could be used either way, to introduce either a statement or an adjectival description, but the article can hardly do the full work of the relative, by leading into a full-scale relative clause containing a new assertion.

This difficulty, as well as the strangeness of finding in Paul a straight assertion that Christ is God, has led commentators to conjecture that the two words at the beginning of the last clause, 'he being above all God blessed for ever', should be reversed to give an entirely new translation, 'from whom (is) the supreme God, blessed for ever'. (This conjecture is found in the writings of Jonas Schlichting (1592–1661); Artemonius (Samuel Crell, 1660–1747); and Richard Bentley (1662–1742).) By this conjecture God becomes the last and greatest contribution of the Jews – a most unlikely way to speak, since the whole list otherwise assumes that God is the author of the gifts entrusted to the Israelites.

We are left with an assertion that defies translation; all attempts to turn the words into a reference to God in distinction to Christ fail, and yet the interpretation given in the RSV note, which says that Christ is God, is not completely satisfactory either.

I think we must suspect that a glossator has been at work, and his marginal notes have been incorporated into our text. How otherwise can we explain the fact that such a tremendous affirmation about Christ appears so casually in an ascription of praise? Some Latin manuscripts perhaps give us the clue to what has happened. The words *according to the flesh* are omitted by D; the word *God* is omitted by G; and Irenaeus gives us a text in which the words *over all* are transposed after *God*. With this evidence in mind, it seems possible that originally the text ran, 'of them is Christ, who is above all blessed for ever'. If so, it is easy to see that a glossator would be prompted to add a note to the effect that Christ received only his fleshly nature from the Israelites, while he was, at the same time, God. This note was even called for by the text, because an ascription of praise to Christ such as this was a clear sign of his divine nature (cf. 2 Cor. 11.31).

The conjectured original runs very smoothly, and is open to none of the grammatical objections to the traditional text mentioned above.

6–9

Paul begins his argument to show that not all of Israel are Israel (v. 6). As our text stands, his first argument seems to be that Abraham had two sons, Ishmael and Isaac, and his 'seed' (that is, his descendants) are only those who trace their ancestry back through Isaac, not those who trace their ancestry back through Ishmael. Such an argument, however, does nothing, in this form, to support Paul's case, because as all Jews trace their ancestry through Isaac rather than Ishmael. However, the explanatory note in v. 8, *this means that it is not the children of the flesh who are the children of God*, makes it clear that Isaac and Ishmael are to be taken allegorically, as in Gal. 4.21–31, as spiritual and fleshly men, with

153

the implication that only spiritual men can truly claim to be Abraham's seed. But the contrast between fleshly and spiritual cannot have been present in Paul's mind, because he is wanting to find a way of showing a difference within the physical descendants of Abraham and Isaac and Jacob (or 'Israel') that will explain why some Israelites have not greeted their Messiah when he came. The distinction hangs on their attitude to the promise. This point is rather obscured by the translation of the opening of v. 9 in the RSV. A more accurate rendering would be: 'For this word [referring back to the *word of God* in v. 6, which has not failed] is (a word) of promise' (and then follows the reference to Gen. 18.14, cf. 10). If God's word is a word of promise, the true Israelites will be those who rely on God's promise. The very nature of their ancestry, which goes back to Isaac born to Abraham who believed God's promise, should lead them to rely always on God's promises, that is, to live by faith. If this is the argument, I conjecture that the words which introduce a contrast between Isaac and Ishmael, and make this an allegory of the contrast between spiritual and fleshly men, are a later interpretation added to Paul's original text. The interpolation consists of the following words: '*Through Isaac shall your descendants be named*'. *This means that it is not the children of the flesh who are the children of God* (7b, 8a).

10–13

Paul's second argument for saying that those of Israel are not all Israel is that Scripture tells of divisions between descendants of Abraham, the most famous of which is the difference between Jacob and Esau. No two children could be more closely related than twins, and yet one twin, Jacob, despite his immoral behaviour in stealing Esau's birthright, in the end becomes the man who relies on God and accepts his promises.

11, 12

Verses 11 and 12 hang very awkwardly on the assertion that Rebecca *had conceived children by one man, our forefather Isaac* (v. 10). If we take these verses by themselves (omitting 'to her' with D) we get a sentence that runs, 'It was said, "The elder will serve the younger" before they had been born or had done anything good or bad in order that the electing purpose of God might abide, based not on men's works but on his call; as it is written, "Jacob I loved and Esau I hated"'. This sentence is always linked to the previous statement, 'Not only so, but also Rebecca had intercourse with one man, Isaac our father', because the verb here is a participle that seems to demand a main verb on which to depend. Yet the main verb, 'it was said', is very remote and does not in itself fit at all well with 'Rebecca having intercourse'. (In the Greek the participle is nominative feminine, not agreeing with the impersonal passive verb 'it was said'.) But we know from the papyri and from other passages in the New Testament that participles could sometimes stand alone to represent indicative or imperative verbs, and it seems likely that Paul meant his remark about Rebecca to be such a construction (cf. 2 Cor. 8.19 and the discussion of this sort of construction in James Hope Moulton, *A Grammar of New Testament Greek, Vol. I Prolegomena*, 2nd edition, Edinburgh, 1906, especially pp. 222–5). The remark was rather elliptical, yet clear enough to his fellow Jews. Even the twins born to 'our father Isaac' did not both accept God's promise; we should not therefore be surprised if only some Jews in our day respond to the fulfilment or all the promises in Christ.

Verses 11 and 12, however, work on a different assumption, the assumption that God predestined one of the twins for salvation and the other for damnation before ever they were born. I have argued above in the essay that Paul could not possibly have written these verses and remained consistent. Here I would add that these two verses (vv. 11 and 12) are quite distinct from the rest of his writings. First, the wording of the Old Testament citations from Gen. 25.23 and Mal. 1.2,3 is taken straight from the LXX, in contrast to the citation of Gen. 18.10 in v. 9 which is from the Hebrew, in Paul's own translation (which in turn has been added to or corrected from the LXX of Gen. 18.14). Second, in vocabulary, this verse contains one word not found elsewhere in Paul (*though*), and two others each found only once elsewhere (*bad* in 2 Cor. 5.10, but the text there is doubtful; *purpose* in Rom. 8.28, which I hold to be the start of another predestinarian gloss). It is easy to see how the reference to Jacob and Esau would lead a commentator whose mind was already inclined to a predestinarian view of the world to add the sort of comment to be found in vv. 11 and 12; and, on the other hand, Paul himself, with a theology of promise, could hardly have meant his argument to go in this direction, and, if he had, he would have expressed the case in a more straightforward way, using familiar words.

14–23

The section consists of a series of rhetorical questions, two Old Testament citations, and two categorical assertions. The two assertions are, *so it depends not upon man's will or exertion, but upon God's mercy* (v. 16), and *so then he has mercy upon whomever he wills, and he hardens the heart of whomever he wills* (v. 18), and these assertions are clear and un-equivocal statements of a strict predestinarian system. Those on whom God has mercy have willed nothing and done nothing antecedent to God's choice of them, and anything they will or do is the result of God's choice of them. Those whom God hardens and rejects are not simply allowed to fall into the destruction all men deserve; they are positively created for destruction in order to make known God's power.

Arguments have been put forward in the essay above to show that Paul could hardly have written this section. The style itself counts against his authorship. Although he does employ rhetorical questions (cf. 3.1-9) he never employs them so thickly: of the thirteen sentences in 9.14-23, all but five are questions.

15

The citation is from the LXX version of Ex. 33.19. The original context is Moses' request to be granted the privilege of seeing God face to face, but here the saying is twisted to support the argument that God has mercy on some men entirely arbitrarily. The original concerns a special mark of favour God withholds, while granting the lesser privilege of seeing his glory from behind, as it were, but here it is used to justify the argument that God favours some men (or withholds his favour from others) for no discernible reason.

16

The Greek is, literally, 'So then (it is) not of the one who wills, nor of the one who runs, but of the one who has mercy, God', but the RSV correctly expands this rather neat and epigrammatic saying by making explicit that the first two participles refer to man. Although there could be truth in this saying as one side of the paradox discovered by every sinner whom God restores to new life, who is told, *work out your own salvation with fear and trembling; for God is at work in you, both to will and to work for his good pleasure* (Phil. 2.12 f.), the saying cannot stand by itself without producing intolerable consequences. If God disregarded the relative moral achievements and worth of men, and chose some on whom to have mercy, he would be unjust; if all men were completely undeserving of praise, and God chose some, while allowing others to perish, he would still be unjust. Of course it is true that men would not exist for God to have mercy on them unless he had created them, but, having created them and given them freedom, he cannot then choose some and leave others except on the basis of what they have willed and achieved, without being unjust. The theologian who formulated this saying has seen that God's acceptance of those men whom he accepts is a merciful act – Paul's theology, the teaching of Jesus, and the Old Testament make that perfectly clear – but he has gone on to draw the false conclusion that God's mercy entirely excludes man's activity. God's mercy is not diminished by being sought and striven for; it is only nullified by the man who begins to claim it is a right which he believes he has deserved. The Philippian jailor who asked, What must I *do* to be saved? was not asking a silly question, and was not detracting from the power and sovereignty of God on whom alone he depended for salvation. The theologian who formulated Rom. 9.16 seemed to believe that God's 100 per cent mercy would be diminished to 95 per cent if man exerted a force 5 per cent as great as God's, and that diminution he rightly could not contemplate. But God's mercy is not reduced one particle if he shows mercy to sinners who discover his way of righteousness, which really is righteous, even though these sinners do still from time to time sin and break his commandments. The solution to this seeming contradiction – that sinners can become righteous – is not at first sight obvious, but it cannot be that God arbitrarily decides to call some (or all) evil men good. Then God would be evil, in rewarding evil men as though they were good.

17

The first part of this citation of Ex. 9.16 is different from both our Hebrew text and the LXX, but the second part, after the comma, follows the LXX. The original context concerns God's mercy in sparing Pharaoh, when he could have destroyed him and his people, presumably in order to demonstrate his power in rescuing Israel from slavery without having to destroy their captors. In the context of *Romans*, the verse is probably meant to be taken to refer to the ultimate fate of Pharaoh, who was hardened and so rejected. The argument would then be: God is not unjust to raise up a man whom he was at the same time hardening and rejecting because by so doing he caused his sovereign power to be proclaimed throughout the world.

This argument follows as little as the argument behind v. 16. However important it might be for God's power to be made known, and be seen to be absolute, the achievement of that end cannot turn unjust power into just power. We recoil from the thought of a sculptor who would make a statue just in order to smash it to assert his authority in the eyes of his friends; how much more at the thought of God's making men in order to destroy them so that others could see his absolute power.

18

A thoroughly immoral doctrine.

19–21

The objection is entirely warranted, and the reply does nothing to answer it. Or course a potter is free to make different pots for different purposes, some noble and some ignoble, but he cannot find fault with the ignoble pots for their menial purposes. Only if God is completely indifferent to the behaviour of men could the objector be silenced, and perhaps the theologian who put forward this argument was really trying to lead the objector to see that what appeared to him as God's moral disapproval of certain actions was actually the impersonal working out of God's purposes, which were inaccurately described by use of the imperfect analogy of human fault-finding. In a determined universe, men who to us seem to be the sort of men with whom God would find fault may still be necessary parts of the whole scheme. 'We are all working together to a single end', writes Marcus Aurelius, 'some consciously and with understanding, some without knowledge ... One helps in one way, one in another, and *ex abundanti* even he who finds fault and tries to resist or destroy what is coming to pass' (*Meditations* vi. 42, translated by A. S. L. Farquharson, Oxford, 1944). But this is a Stoic view of the universe which scarcely fits with the Old Testament vision of God as creator of men in his own image, who asks for freely-chosen righteousness and judges men's wickedness. God can be compared to a potter (Is. 29.16; 45.9–13; 64.8, 9; Jer. 18.1–12) but he is a potter who destroys his creation when it becomes evil, not a potter who apportions to his creation their good and evil roles. God as the potter ready to smash a spoiled pot is always hoping that the evil nation will repent and turn away from evil (Jer. 18.7 f.). He has not made some pots for mercy and others for destruction.

22f

There are several other possible translations of these two verses. The main question is whether or not to take the clause *desiring to show his wrath and to make known his power* as the reason for God's enduring *with much patience the vessels of wrath* (and not destroying them forthwith), or as the expression of what God would like to do but desists from doing for the time being *in order to make known the riches of his glory for the vessels of mercy*. The RSV adopts the former reading, regarding God's patience as designed *to show his wrath and to make known his power*, and this seems the right choice, particularly in the light of the reference to Pharoah in vv. 17 f.

Nevertheless, difficulties remain. It is hard to see why one reason for bearing with vessels of wrath is expressed by a participle (*desiring*), and another reason by a subjunctive beginning *in order to*. Perhaps more note should be taken of the textual variants of which two are important. In the second, the RSV has followed B in omitting 'and' before *in order to* at the beginning of v. 23, against ℵ, A, D, G, K, P, Ψ, 33, 1739*, 1984, etc. The omission of 'and' makes things so much easier that we are wisest to conclude that it is original (Kühl). The first variant is the omission of the main verb *has endured* by G, d (who consequently have to read a preposition before *vessels of wrath*). This omission is very surprising, and hardly accidental or deliberate, for it seemingly deprives the sentence of its most necessary word. However, it is possible, particularly in Greek of this type, to find a participle standing in place of a main verb; which means in this case that *desiring* should be translated 'desired'. If we read vv. 22 f. in this way, we recover a much more straightforward sentence as regards thought, even if a rather unusual sentence as regards grammar. I should translate like this: 'What if God wanted to show his wrath and make known his power by (his) great patience towards vessels of wrath created for destruction, even in order to show the richness of his glory on vessels of mercy which he had prepared for glory?' – implying, who are you to object?

The readers assume that they are *vessels of mercy . . . prepared beforehand for glory*, and they are advised not to question God's reasons for also creating *vessels of wrath . . . for destruction*; the reason God so acted was in order to display both his absolute power and his entirely unmerited mercy on those whom he chooses to glorify. Calvin expounds the thought of the passage very clearly, although I cannot agree with him that the thought is at all admirable. He writes, 'The elect differ from the reprobate only in the fact of their deliverance from the same gulf of destruction. This, moreover, is by no merit of their own, but by the free goodness of God. It must, therefore, be true that the infinite mercy of God towards the elect will gain our increasing praise, when we see how wretched are all those who do not escape His wrath' (translated by Ross Mackenzie, Edinburgh, 1961). It is hard to see how such a God can be described as 'good', or that worshippers who praise him for making some of his creatures undeservedly wretched are worshipping God at all.

24

This verse is usually translated as part of the long sentence before, vv. 22 f., but it is grammatically hard to attach there. It is probably a gloss to explain the composition of the *people* referred to in the citation of Hosea 2.23 in the next verse, v. 25. The glossator explains that the *people* are the members of the Church made up of both Jews and Gentiles. But Paul is, so far, talking just about Israel, and trying to get the Roman Jewish Christians (see v. 10) to understand that they must not expect all Israel to respond to Christ's coming. Some will reject God's fulfilment of his promises, but some will also accept. The passage in Hosea refers to the return of the tribes of Israel to God their father, and God hastens to welcome them back, although they had so far fallen away as to be no longer worthy of being called his people. The gloss presupposes a unified Church containing Jews and Gentiles, not the situation of Paul's day, when believing synagogues containing some Gentile proselytes or adherents were having to get used to living alongside churches of Gentile Christians, the fruit of Paul's missionary work.

25 f.

A citation of Hosea 2.23 and 1.10. The rendering of 2.23 follows neither the Hebrew nor the LXX, although it accurately represents the thought, and may point to a different Hebrew original from the one we have. The rendering of Hos. 1.10 is much closer to the LXX, although there are too many textual variants in both the LXX and *Romans* to be sure that the LXX was really the source. The original reference was to Hosea's children, the girl Lo-ruhamah (Not-pitied) and the boy Lo-ammi (Not-my-people), who symbolize the rejection of Israel for her unrighteousness. When Israel returns to God as a faithless wife to her husband in righteousness, justice, steadfast love, and mercy, then he will have pity on Not-pitied and say 'You are my people' to Not-my-people. If vv. 14–23 and v. 24 are interpolations into Paul's argument, then the reference to Hosea is not designed to show how Gentiles come into the Church, but is designed to show that the whole history of Israel has been a history of God's approach to his people in love, and of how some accepted this love, some rejected it, and some who had fallen into unrighteousness returned to God and were welcomed back.

27

Paul cites Isaiah 10.22a in his own translation, and gives us the clue to what he means by saying *Isaiah cries out*. The RSV could be right in translating the next word as *concerning*, but a possible meaning would be 'for the sake of Israel'. Isaiah is a prophet, and his cry is designed to warn Israel of the terrible consequences of their action unless they repent. He sees the awful inevitability in the evil life the people are leading, and he can see almost no hope of averting God's destruction, but nevertheless his cry is designed to avert it and to encourage as many as possible to repent. Similarly, Paul has to face the fact that only a remnant of the great number of Jews have turned to God by accepting Christ, and he has to help the Roman Jewish Christians to face that fact; but his aim remains to do anything he can, within the terms of his special mission to the Gentiles, to bring back more and more of his fellow Jews to the right way (9.1–3).

28

Verse 28 is a truncated form of Is. 10.22b, 23, following the LXX, with a variation in the last phrase. A number of manuscripts, ℵᵉ, D, G, K, P, Ψ, 33, 1984, etc., give the full LXX text, '. . . for he is completing and cutting short the affair in righteousness, because a summary affair it is the Lord will make upon the earth.' A scribe's eye could easily have jumped across the words and omitted the part that says, 'in righteousness because a summary affair'. It is much harder to imagine the words being added to the text by a scribe wanting to complete the quotation. Indeed, the completion of quotation was done at an earlier stage: Paul made his own translation of Is. 10.22a from the Hebrew, and a scribe added Is. 22b, 23 from the LXX. Then the addition was incompletely copied, and the omission was not noticed because the shorter text is rather easier to understand than the longer LXX version.

29

A scribe has added the LXX version of Is. 1.9 which intrudes a note of finality into Paul's argument that he would not feel. He does not believe that the rejection of Jesus Christ by a large part of Israel is final; he does not wish to encourage Jewish Christians to regard themselves as the *children* left (literally, the seed), but rather as men who, having found the righteousness of God, must do everything to give this discovery to their fellow Jews.

9.30–10.15

30*What shall we say, then? That Gentiles who did not pursue righteousness have attained it, that is, righteousness through faith;* 31*but that Israel who pursued the righteousness which is based on law did not succeed in fulfilling that law.* 32*Why? Because they did not pursue it through faith, but* *as if it were based on works. They have stumbled over the stumbling stone,* ³³*as it is written,*

'*Behold, I am laying in Zion a stone that will make men stumble,*
a rock that will make them fall;
and he who believes in him will not be put to shame.'

10 Brethren, my heart's desire and prayer to God for them is that they may be saved. ²I bear them witness that they have a zeal for God, but it is not enlightened. ³For, being ignorant of the righteousness that comes from God, and seeking to establish their own, they did not submit to God's righteousness. ⁴For Christ is the end of the law, that every one who has faith may be justified.

⁵Moses writes that the man who practises the righteousness which is based on the law shall live by it. ⁶But the righteousness based on faith says, Do not say in your heart, 'Who will ascend into heaven?' (that is, to bring Christ down) ⁷or 'Who will descend into the abyss?' (that is, to bring Christ up from the dead). ⁸But what does it say? The word is near you, on your lips and in your heart (that is, the word of faith which we preach); ⁹because, if you confess with your lips that Jesus is Lord and believe in your heart that God raised him from the dead, you will be saved. ¹⁰For man believes with his heart and so is justified, and he confesses with his lips and so is saved. ¹¹The scripture says, 'No one who believes in him will be put to shame.' ¹²For there is no distinction between Jew and Greek; the same Lord is Lord of all and bestows his riches upon all who call upon him. ¹³For, 'every one who calls upon the name of the Lord will be saved.'

¹⁴But how are men to call upon him in whom they have not believed? And how are they to believe in him of whom they have never heard? And how are they to hear without a preacher? ¹⁵And how can men preach unless they are sent? As it is written, 'How beautiful are the feet of those who preach good news!'

Those Jews who had embraced the gospel and had gladly accepted Jesus as the Messiah they had been waiting for were, by the time *Romans* was written, up against a problem which threatened their whole position. If Jesus was Messiah, why did not more of their fellow Jews, who held the same hope and worshipped the same God and read the same scriptures, recognize and accept him? If Jesus was Messiah, why did Gentiles accept him more readily than Jews?

Paul embodied this painful problem for them. He seemed so indifferent to their dilemma that he actually accentuated the problem by throwing himself exclusively into work among Gentiles, and seemed not to care about the effect his work was having on the struggling group of Jewish Christians.

Paul was no fool, and he could understand the bad impression his mission to the Gentiles was creating. In this section he boldly states the problem and does his best to meet it. But, in meeting the great unease that Jewish Christians felt, he refuses to admit the solution that some of them must have been tempted to provide. They must have been tempted to question the genuineness of the righteousness the Gentile Christians were practising, and they must also have been tempted to reaffirm the essential righteousness of Jews who had not yet believed.

Paul therefore states the problem in provocative terms when he asserts that Gentile Christians have actually become righteous, and that Jews, for all their zeal for God, have actually failed to attain the righteousness the Law is talking about.

Paul's argument is through and through an argument that the Law itself requires the righteousness that consists in trusting and believing. Jews who think that they can do what the Law requires by meticulously carrying out each one of the commandments are not thereby half-way to Christ; they have not even begun, because they have missed the essential message of the Law itself. Gentiles who live by faith, without becoming Jews, have actually discovered the righteousness God requires.

If we concentrate on 9.30–10.3 alone, there is a strong *prima facie* case that my reading of Paul's argument is correct. The language used seems to point in the direction of saying that righteousness is man's, something which he somehow must discover and learn to live out. He must find how to become righteous in God's sight. Thus, righteousness is to be pursued (9.30, 31, 32); righteousness can be *attained* or made one's own (9.30); righteousness can be found by those who have *zeal*, provided their zeal is well informed (10.2); and God's righteousness is something that can be submitted to or obeyed (10.3).

Yet the RSV translation makes it plain that commentators always avoid this natural interpretation of the words in favour of the interpretation that takes God's righteousness to be the righteousness he bestows. The phrase 'the righteousness of God' in 10.3 is translated *the righteousness that comes from God,* and this translation reflects the traditional interpretation of the phrase which is found in commentaries of all traditions. Catholics and Protestants may disagree about how God's righteousness is given to men, but they all agree that the righteousness is a quality or status that comes from God's side to men. The traditional Catholic interpretation has been that righteousness is infused into men; the traditional Protestant interpretation has been that righteousness is imputed to men, that they are declared righteous although they are not. There have been many attempts to combine both views: both are to be found in Augustine; the Lutheran Osiander in the sixteenth century shocked his fellow Lutherans by attempting a combination; and Anglicanism has always been hospitable to a similar solution, that 'the Righteousness which faith receives is not external only but internal, not imputed only but imparted to the believer' (Liddon). Recently, the idea of the believer's mystical incorporation into Christ has been called on to solve the problem of how a sinner could actually be said to become 'really and truly righteous' without ceasing to be a sinner, that is, by actually sharing in the risen life of Christ (J. A. Ziesler, *The Meaning of Righteousness in Paul,* Cambridge, 1972).

This unanimity in the tradition, an underlying unanimity despite the fierce battles that have been fought over the precise method by which God gives men righteousness, cannot be lightly set aside. Although I think that the natural reading of such verses as 9.30 ff. and 10.2 ff. counts against taking God's righteousness to be something he bestows, 10.10 counts strongly in favour of the traditional view. The literal rendering of 10.10 is, 'For with the heart it is believed unto righteousness, and with the mouth it is confessed unto salvation'. 'Righteousness' and 'salvation' are parallel concepts and, since salvation is obviously something God bestows, righteousness must also be something he bestows. Furthermore, the whole context of 10.10 is about the correct belief which secures salvation: those who confess *Jesus is Lord,* and believe that *God raised him from the dead* will be saved.

If salvation and righteousness depend on correct belief, then righteousness, like salvation, must be the reward God gives those who believe. Finally, righteousness is actually personified in this passage, in the introduction to 10.6. If righteousness is personified and made to speak to men, righteousness must be thought of as a divine power which men who listen to her voice will receive, just as in Proverbs 8 those who listen to Wisdom, and seek her, will be rewarded by her dwelling with them.

However, all three arguments for taking righteousness in the traditional fashion turn out, on closer examination, to be arguments for regarding the whole section, 10.6b–15, as the work of a later theologian who commented on Paul's words in a new sense.

Let us take the last argument first. The words attributed to Righteousness personified (10.6) are words from Moses; they are cited from Deut. 9.4 and 30.12. In our text we are told that Moses said one thing (10.5) whereas a higher wisdom comes from Righteousness, who says another thing (10.6). But Paul could never have been responsible for such a contrast, particularly not to an audience that would be bound to know that both references came from Moses. Obviously a later glossator has been at work, and we are lucky to have at least one manuscript that enables us to guess how the distorting additions came about.

The other two arguments for holding that the righteousness is essentially God's righteousness which he bestows are perfectly correct, but they too betray the fact that another hand than the hand of Paul has been at work. In 10.6b–15 faith is no longer the basic attitude of trusting and believing that characterized the life of Abraham, the teaching of Moses, and the message of the prophets; faith is correctly formulated belief, which alone guarantees salvation. Christ was, of course, just as central to Paul's position as he was to this commentator (although Paul preached the death and resurrection rather than the incarnation and resurrection, an interesting difference in emphasis). But Paul's immediate concern was to convince Jewish Christians that faith was the key to the Old Testament. Faith in this sense could obviously not mean belief in the incarnation and resurrection of Jesus Christ. Faith meant for him the loving and trusting way of living which believed God when he made promises and gladly accepted that

God opened up for sinners an easy and pleasant way to be righteous, free from the consuming anxiety to perform perfectly all the works of the Law.

Paul is obviously arguing from scripture, not in a strained way that finds hidden references to the incarnation and resurrection in obscure phrases, but in an easy and natural way that finds faith preached on every page.

This contention of mine is strengthened, although it does not depend on it, if we can accept two conjectural emendations. In 9.31 I have argued that the original statement of Paul's was, 'But Israel in seeking the Law did not reach the Law', and in 10.4 I have argued that the original was, 'For the end of the Law is righteousness for everyone who believes and trusts'. The case for these conjectures is argued in the notes. If I am right, it is more than ever clear that Paul was above all trying to show that the followers of Jesus Christ were those who had discovered the key to the Old Testament and the only way for sinners to become righteous.

Notes

9.30

That Gentiles who did not pursue righteousness have attained it, that is, righteousness through faith: the assumption that Gentiles in general were not looking for righteousness is perhaps a little hard on the finer spirits in the ancient world who were concerned with moral probity; and this moral earnestness was recognized by the Jewish tradition preserved in Rom. 2.14 ff., but that section is probably not by Paul. Paul's attitude slips out in his casual remark in Gal. 2.15, a report of his words to Cephas: *We ourselves, who are Jews by birth and not Gentile sinners* . . .

The words *that is* do not appear in the Greek, and they are misleading if they suggest that there is more than one sort of righteousness, or that *righteousness through faith* is different from ordinary simple righteousness. Paul means that the only way to be righteous is to trust and believe God.

31

but that Israel who pursued the righteousness which is based on law did not succeed in fulfilling that law: a literal translation of 9.31 would be, 'But Israel in seeking a law of righteousness did not approach the law'. It is very hard to make sense of this except on the assumption that 'law' means a rule or principle (Calvin), but then we are faced with the difficulty of seeing how Paul can use 'law' so casually in a quite different sense from 'the Law of Moses' in a passage that is concerned with the Law of Moses. A further difficulty is that we should expect the last phrase of the sentence to be 'unto righteousness' rather than 'unto law': 'Israel in seeking a law of righteousness did not approach (or reach) righteousness'. What we expect may be precisely what an early glossator expected, so that we may well conjecture that a glossator added 'righteousness' in the margin to balance this sentence with the previous one about the Gentiles. The marginal word came later to be copied into the text as a genitive, attached to the first occurrence of 'Law'. There is textual evidence for this conjecture. Two manuscripts (P, 623) have the two words 'Law of righteousness' in the reverse order, and one manuscript (489) reads 'righteousness' (in the accusative case) in place of 'Law of righteousness'. Both variant readings suggest the sort of disturbance for which I have been arguing.

If Paul wrote 'But Israel in seeking the Law did not reach the Law', his thought becomes clear. He means, by trying to do everything the Law commands, as though it were possible to do the Law's works perfectly, Israel failed to keep the Law and missed the Law's intention.

Israel, in pursuing the keeping of the Law, did not reach the goal for which the Law was given. They wrongly thought that men were capable of keeping all the commandments of God always: *they did not pursue it through faith, but as if it were based on works* (9.32).

32 f.

Two passages from Isaiah, Is. 28.16 and 8.14, have been freely combined by Paul, who is, as usual, rendering the Hebrew into his own Greek. Is. 28.16 is a passage in which the Lord mocks those who think they can escape impending disaster by making a covenant with death and taking refuge in lies. He has laid a stone in Zion, and those who rely on this foundation will not be moved. The stone is linked with justice and righteousness:

> *And I will make justice the line,*
> *and righteousness the plummet.*
> (Is. 28.17)

Is. 8.14, the other source of Paul's allusion, comes in a passage in which the Lord tells Isaiah not to be afraid of what the people fear. *The Lord of hosts, him you shall regard as holy; let him be your fear, and let him be your dread* (Is. 8.13). Isaiah must *wait for the Lord* and *hope in him* (Is. 8.17), and if Israel do not accept this teaching they will find the Lord 'a stone of stumbling and a rock of offence'. (The LXX translation of the Hebrew is strikingly different here; this is another clear example of Paul's use of the Hebrew original.)

Paul has skilfully isolated a key theme from the Book of the Prophet Isaiah to illustrate that righteousness is found only by those who trust in the Lord, listen to his righteous decrees, and wait hopefully for his promises to be accomplished.

10.1

Paul prays for those Jews who are stumbling, another indication that he can hardly have regarded their fate as eternally decreed by God.

3

For, being ignorant of the righteousness that comes from God, and seeking to establish their own, they did not submit to God's righteousness: the context makes it highly unlikely that the traditional translation of the ambiguous original 'the righteousness of God' by *the righteousness that comes from God* can be correct. In the previous sentence Paul has spoken about their *zeal for God*, and the construction is exactly parallel, literally 'zeal of God'. This parallel, and every other consideration of context make it best to translate 'the righteousness of God' by 'the righteousness God requires'. The NEB translation is good: 'For they ignore God's way of righteousness, and try to set up their own . . .'

God's righteousness is to be submitted to or obeyed, not in the sense of a quality which by some mysterious transaction is imputed or imparted to the man who obeys, but in the perfectly ordinary sense of a revealed way of living that men can understand and follow.

4

For Christ is the end of the law, that every one who has faith may be justified: literally, 'For the end of the law is Christ unto righteousness for every one who believes'. Most commentators take *end* to mean the finish of the law, and take *law* to be the Law of Moses. Some commentators take *end* as the aim or fulfilment, and some take *law* to be law in general. There is little doubt that *law* means Law of Moses. In view of vv. 5 and 6, where what Moses says, that the Law must be done, is set against what Righteousness says, that the faith must be believed, it seems necessary to take *end* to mean the finish. Yet doubts begin to arise. The Law of Moses does not mean simply the commandments in the Law, but comprises the whole Old Testament, or at least the first five books.

What Righteousness is supposed to say (10.6) is actually a citation from one of these books, the Book of Deuteronomy.

Can Christ be said to end the Law? This can hardly be Paul's meaning, since he has already affirmed that the Law is confirmed by Christ's coming (Rom. 3.31; 8.4). Zahn seeks to avoid this difficulty by distinguishing between a sense in which the Law is ended and a sense in which it still holds; it is ended, he says, as a method of justification. This is the force of the alternative translation offered by the NEB margin, 'Christ is the end of the law as a way of righteousness for everyone who has faith'. However, this interpretation is hardly supported by the order of words in the Greek, and should not be adopted.

As the Greek stands, Christ must be the subject of the sentence governing two complements: Christ is the end of the Law, and Christ is unto righteousness for everyone who believes. But the idea that Christ is 'unto righteousness' is very obscure (compare the clarity of 1 Cor. 1.30: Christ Jesus became righteousness for us).

The solution to all these difficulties lies in observing that a prepositional phrase using 'unto', which goes so awkwardly as complement to a name such as 'Christ', goes naturally and easily with the word 'end'. (The words in Heb. 6.8, *its end is to be burned*, are precisely parallel, being literally, 'the end of it is unto burning'.) 'The end of the Law is unto righteousness' is a perfectly idiomatic construction, which we should translate, 'the end of the Law is righteousness'. Once we see this, it becomes plain that *Christ* is an intrusion, representing a marginal gloss that offered another answer to the question, What marks the end of the Law?

I conjecture that Paul originally wrote, 'The end of the Law is righteousness for everyone who believes'. 'End' here means fulfilment or goal, and the Law is indeed the Law of Moses, which remains the Bible of Christians. In that Law they can see the righteousness that consists of faith portrayed and recommended, just as in that Law they can read about the curse which those will encounter who think they can become righteous by doing the works of the Law without faith (Gal. 3.1–14). Paul is arguing for his right to claim he is a faithful heir to Abraham and Moses; his subject is the Law, not Christ.

5, 6

As these verses stand, what Moses writes is distinguished unfavourably from what Righteousness says in Scripture. This is an unreal distinction, since the words ascribed to Righteousness are words of Moses (Deut. 9.4; 30.11 f.). Nowhere else in the New Testament is Moses set against scripture or against God. When Jesus said that Moses permitted divorce to meet their hardness of heart (Mark 10.3 f.; Matt. 19.7 f.), he did not mean Moses was wrong – Jesus did not forbid divorce, despite those sayings that seem to make him legislate in that sense – but that the hard-hearted men were wrong to want divorce. Our starting point for unravelling these difficult verses must be the content of Deuteronomy 30.11–14. This is a passage about how easy it is to do what God commands.

'For this commandment which I command you this day is not too hard for you, neither is it far off. 12It is not in heaven, that you should say, "Who will go up for us to heaven, and bring it to us, that we may hear it and do it?" 13Neither is it beyond the sea, that you should say, "Who will go over the sea for us, and bring it to us, that we may hear it and do it?" 14But the word is very near you; it is in your mouth and in your heart, so that you can do it.'

If Paul is arguing faithfully from scripture, he must be trying to show that scripture supports one way of acting rather than another. But, according to the present text of Romans 10.5–9, Paul seems to be condemning what Moses says about acting; he seems to contrast acting with believing, so as to condemn acting and praise believing: *Moses writes that the man who practises the righteousness which is based on the law shall live by it. But the righteousness based on faith says . . . if you confess . . . and believe . . . you will be saved.*

This can hardly have been Paul's argument. If it had been, no Jew who knew his Bible would have taken him seriously: fancy attempting to confute Moses by Moses, or fancy attempting to prove that belief rather than action was required by referring to a passage which was primarily about what one had to do!

Fortunately, we have evidence from the Greek manuscripts of *Romans* that Paul's original argument from Moses has been overlaid by glosses from commentators who thought that Paul was advocating a higher wisdom than Moses'. The manuscript A reads v. 5 as follows: 'For Moses writes that he who practises the righteousness which is of faith shall live by that faith.'

The first step in the corruption of this original was made by a scribe who thought that Paul was citing Lev. 18.5, as he had done in Gal. 3.12, in order to condemn the Law: *but the law does not rest on faith, for 'He who does them shall live by them.'* He consequently changed 'faith' to 'law', and thereby set in train a number of other changes, the most drastic of which was the ascription of the citation in Romans 10.6 to *the righteousness based on faith*. (One other consequence of this first change was the addition of the word *man* to the supposed citation from Leviticus in Romans 10.5, an addition which wrecked the grammar of the original, and led to jugglings with the position of *that* in vain attempts to remedy the situation.)

Paul's original argument was a straight case from the Old Testament that faith and trust were then, as now, the only way for a righteous man to live. He is referring in v. 5 not to Lev. 18.5 but to Hab. 2.4, which he has already cited in 1.17, 'The righteous man shall live by faith'. He defines the righteous man by referring to Deut. 9.4 and 30.11–14: the righteous man is the man who practises the righteousness of faith and lives in faith, that is, by trusting and believing. Paul's way of indicating the importance of Deuteronomy is by combining Deut. 9.4 and 30.12: '(Moses) speaks thus: "Do not say in your heart, Who shall go up to heaven?"' The words 'Do not say in your heart' refer to Deut. 9.4: '*Do not say in your heart, after the Lord your God has thrust them out before you, "It is because of my righteousness that the Lord has brought me in to possess this land"*'. The words 'who shall go up to heaven?' refer to Deut. 30.12, a question evocative of the whole anxious way of life condemned in Deut. 30. 11–14, already cited above in this note.

6–10

Paul of course believed that the Old Testament messianic promises had been fulfilled in the death and resurrection of Jesus Christ, but his argument here concerns the pattern of life which the man who would be righteous should adopt. He did not set the Law over against the Gospel, but rather argued that the Law itself constantly recommended the trusting and believing way of living that alone could prepare a man to live forever with Christ. He did not contrast doing with believing, but rather said that the only acceptable form of action was the action of believing, trusting, having faith.

His citation of Deut. 9.4 and 30.12, however, led a great commentator to add a midrash concerning the distinctive substance of the Christian faith. This commentator took the faithless question, 'Who shall go up to heaven?' as the question of a man who would not believe that Christ had already come down and been incarnate. This commentator added his interpretation in the words, *that is, to bring Christ down* (10.6). He then continued with a reference to the resurrection. The second question in Deut. 30.13, '*Who will go over the sea for us, and bring it to us?'*, did not suit his purpose so well, so that he turned to Psalm 107.26 to formulate a better faithless question, *'Who will descend into the abyss?'* and again added an interpretation, *that is, to bring Christ up from the dead* (10.7).

He then returned to Deut. 30.14: *But what does it [the righteousness based on faith] say? The word is near you, on your lips and in your heart,* which he interpreted by reference to the Christian creed, *that is, the word of faith which we preach* (10.8). Note that here *faith* means the creed, not the basic attitude and life of trusting and believing.

9

The great commentator referred to in the previous note now inserts the substance of an early creed. Only the confession of this creed guarantees salvation. With the lips you confess that *Jesus is Lord*, and in your heart you believe that *God raised him from the dead*.

There are three broad lines of interpretation of the confession *Jesus is Lord*. According to the first, those who confess *Jesus is Lord* are protesting against the growing Roman tendency to demand of loyal subjects the confession, 'Caesar is Lord'. According to the second, those who confess *Jesus is Lord* are pledging their cultic allegiance to Jesus in opposition to the confessions made by initiates into pagan mystery religions who say things like 'Isis is Lord'. According to the third, those who confess *Jesus is Lord* are simply affirming that Jesus is the long-expected Messiah spoken of by David in Psalm 110.1 when he said, *The LORD says to my lord: 'Sit at my right hand, till I make your enemies your footstool'.*

All three interpretations have something to be said for them, and at various times in the history of the Church all three interpretations became important to meet a particular external thread: from the cult of Caesar-worship, from the mystery religions, and from Judaism. If I had to choose between them, I should say that the third interpretation was originally more important, and that the other two were subsidiary. But the context of *Romans* demands that we consider a fourth possibility.

Romans 10.9 contains two confessions, *that Jesus is Lord* and *that God raised him from the dead*. The second confession obviously refers back to the faithless question in v. 7, *'Who will descend into the Abyss?'* (*that is, to bring Christ up from the dead*). It is likely then, that the first confession should refer to the faithless question in v. 6, *'Who will ascend into heaven?'* (*that is, to bring Christ down*). In that case, the confession *Christ is Lord* is a confession that Christ is God incarnate. Support for this interpretation comes from Rom. 10.13, where Joel 2.32, a passage originally referring to the Lord God, is applied to Christ: '*every one who calls upon the name of the Lord will be saved*'. Paul himself never makes this direct identification of Christ with God, and the Hebrew text, which contains the sacred name YHWH, would hardly allow him to identify Christ with the Father. But the Greek translation of the LXX probably contains the word *Lord*, and this could be taken by a later commentator as a hidden prophetic reference to the incarnate Son.

The double confession in Rom. 10.9 may well be an early example of the two-membered Christological confessions cited in the notes on Rom. 1.3, 4 which refer to the Incarnation and Resurrection.

10

This verse forms a perfectly regular couplet. (Moffatt saw the poetic structure, and prints the verse as poetry in his translation:

> with his heart man believes and is justified,
> with his mouth he confesses and is saved.)

The second line exactly parallels the first, both in thought and in number of syllables. The order, mouth and heart, in Deuteronomy is reversed. Note that *righteousness* and *salvation* are parallel, which means that, for this commentator, *righteousness* has already become a given entity bestowed on the believer by God, who likewise will bestow salvation. The long story of misinterpretation of what Paul means by *righteousness* has already begun at this early stage.

11

The commentator repeats the citation from Is. 28.16 which Paul has already used in 9.33, but there Paul retained the original force of Isaiah, he who trusts in the stone will not be put to shame, whereas the commentator takes the pronoun to refer to Christ: *No one who believes in him will be put to shame*. The *no one* comes not from Isaiah, but from Joel 2.32, to be cited in v. 13: '*every one who calls upon the name of the Lord will be saved.*'

12

Paul held that circumcised and uncircumcised would be acquitted for the same reason, that each had lived by trusting and believing (3.30), but he could hardly have said, in a context in which he is so strenuously insisting on the advantages possessed by the Jew, that *there is no distinction between Jew and Greek*. There is a distinction, because the Jew had Moses and the Law, and he wished to argue that the Jew should learn from his distinctive heritage that the only way to live was by faith.

The terrible problem with which he is grappling is grounded in the surprising reversal of expectation, that Gentiles who did not pursue righteousness have attained it, whereas Israel which pursued the Law did not reach the Law (9.30 f.). He grapples with the problem, but never in such a way as to deny the distinction between Israel and the Gentiles.

This comment comes from the time of one Catholic Church, made up of Jews and Gentiles, bound together in an equality based on adherence to the one creed.

14–15

The commentator lived at a time when the orthodox creed was guarded by authorized preachers. He works back from the necessity of men to hear the preaching of this creed to the necessity for preachers to be commissioned to carry this message to the ends of the earth. Verse 15, which Michelsen took to be a gloss because of the change of subject from 'they', the hearers of the message, to 'they' the preachers who are sent, is really the conclusion of the chain of rhetorical questions, as the citation of Is. 52.7 shows: *'How beautiful are the feet of those who preach good news!'*

10.16–11.36

¹⁶*But they have not all heeded the gospel; for Isaiah says, 'Lord, who has believed what he has heard from us?'* ¹⁷*So faith comes from what is heard, and what is heard comes by the preaching of Christ.*

¹⁸*But I ask, have they not heard? Indeed they have; for*
'Their voice has gone out to all the earth,
and their words to the ends of the world.'
¹⁹*Again I ask, did Israel not understand? First Moses says,*
'I will make you jealous of those who are not a nation;
with a foolish nation I will make you angry.'
²⁰*Then Isaiah is so bold as to say,*
'I have been found by those who did not seek me;
I have shown myself to those who did not ask for me.'
²¹*But of Israel he says, 'All day long I have held out my hands to a dis-*
obedient and contrary people.'

11 I ask, then, has God rejected his people? By no means! I myself am an Israelite, a descendant of Abraham, a member of the tribe of Benjamin. ²God has not rejected his people whom he foreknew. Do you not know what the scripture says of Eli'jah, how he pleads with God against Israel? ³ 'Lord, they have killed thy prophets, they have demolished thy altars, and I alone am left, and they seek my life.' ⁴But what is God's reply to him? 'I have kept for myself seven thousand men who have not bowed the knee to Ba'al.' ⁵So too at the present time there is a remnant, chosen by grace. ⁶But if it is by grace, it is no longer on the basis of works; otherwise grace would no longer be grace.

⁷What then? Israel failed to obtain what it sought. The elect obtained it, but the rest were hardened, ⁸as it is written,

'God gave them a spirit of stupor,
eyes that should not see and ears that should not hear,
down to this very day.'

⁹And David says,

'Let their feast become a snare and a trap,
a pitfall and a retribution for them;
¹⁰let their eyes be darkened so that they cannot see,
and bend their backs for ever.'

¹¹So I ask, have they stumbled so as to fall? By no means! But through their trespass salvation has come to the Gentiles, so as to make Israel jealous. ¹²Now if their trespass means riches for the world, and if their failure means riches for the Gentiles, how much more will their full inclusion mean!

¹³Now I am speaking to you Gentiles. Inasmuch then as I am an apostle to the Gentiles, I magnify my ministry ¹⁴in order to make my fellow Jews jealous, and thus save some of them. ¹⁵For if their rejection means the reconciliation of the world, what will their acceptance mean but life from the dead? ¹⁶If the dough offered as first fruits is holy, so is the whole lump; and if the root is holy, so are the branches.

¹⁷But if some of the branches were broken off, and you, a wild olive shoot, were grafted in their place to share the richness° of the olive tree, ¹⁸do not boast over the branches. If you do boast, remember it is not you that supports the root, but the root that supports you. ¹⁹You will say, 'Branches were broken off so that I might be grafted in.' ²⁰That is true. They were broken off because of their unbelief, but you stand fast only through faith. So do not

become proud, but stand in awe. ²¹For if God did not spare the natural branches, neither will he spare you. ²²Note then the kindness and the severity of God: severity toward those who have fallen, but God's kindness to you, provided you continue in his kindness; otherwise you too will be cut off. ²³And even the others, if they do not persist in their unbelief, will be grafted in, for God has the power to graft them in again. ²⁴For if you have been cut from what is by nature a wild olive tree, and grafted, contrary to nature, into a cultivated olive tree, how much more will these natural branches be grafted back into their own olive tree.

²⁵Lest you be wise in your own conceits, I want you to understand this mystery, brethren: a hardening has come upon part of Israel, until the full number of the Gentiles come in, ²⁶and so all Israel will be saved; as it is written,

'The Deliverer will come from Zion,
    he will banish ungodliness from Jacob';
²⁷'and this will be my covenant with them
    when I take away their sins.'

²⁸As regards the gospel they are enemies of God, for your sake; but as regards election they are beloved for the sake of their forefathers. ²⁹For the gifts and the call of God are irrevocable. ³⁰Just as you were once disobedient to God but now have received mercy because of their disobedience, ³¹so they have now been disobedient in order that by the mercy shown to you they also may^p receive mercy. ³²For God has consigned all men to disobedience, that he may have mercy upon all.

³³O the depth of the riches and wisdom and knowledge of God! How unsearchable are his judgments and how inscrutable his ways!
³⁴'For who has known the mind of the Lord,
    or who has been his counsellor?'
³⁵'Or who has given a gift to him
    that he might be repaid?'
³⁶For from him and through him and to him are all things. To him be glory for ever. Amen.

> ^{o} Other ancient authorities read *rich root*.
> ^{p} Other ancient authorities add *now*.

Romans 9.1–10.15, as we now have it, made up of Paul's original letter plus a number of theological comments, poses a problem for the Church. Anyone who read this part of *Romans* would have to try to reconcile a number of propositions. He would gather that Israel remained God's chosen people, even though a large part of Israel had not accepted the gospel; he would gather that God controlled men's response to his call, just as a potter controls the nature of the pots he makes; but he would also gather that God commissioned men to preach the gospel in the hope that Jews as well as Gentiles would respond. Righteousness, he would gather, was God's gift, given to those who accepted the belief that Jesus was Lord and God had raised him from the dead.

I have argued that these various propositions grew up gradually as Christian theologians tried to understand and expound Paul, and that in the attempt these theologians imported different ideas, sometimes misunderstanding his message and sometimes simply embarking on themes which he did not conceive of handling. For example, I think the predestinarian commentator in Chapter 9 misunderstood Paul, whereas the commentator who saw a christological creed in Deut. 30, which Paul had cited, was adding a reflection which did not suit Paul's present argument.

An editor who was trying to put *Romans* into order would not be in a position to sort out the layers in the way we have done; he could only try to explain how the various themes might be reconciled. His main problem was to show how God who controlled men's response to himself and who yet used words as the means of moving men's hearts could be justified in producing such striking obduracy among his own people, the Jews, and such striking faith among the Gentiles. God's ways are, of course, inscrutable, but a theologian given the clues to be found in 9.1–10.15 could at least sketch in an answer to the enigma of the uneven response among men to the gospel.

The section before us, 10.16–11.32, is, I believe, the sustained attempt by a theologian of the second century to suggest a pattern and a plan behind the history of Israel and the Church. His starting point is the glorification of the work of missionaries with which the previous section has closed. If, as I have argued, 10.6b–15 is already the work of a commentator on Paul, our present section is even more the work of a commentator. This last commentator addresses himself to the problems raised by the whole argument from the beginning of Chapter 9. His style is distinctive and his case complete.

What is he saying?

The problem is, Why have not all men who have heard the gospel obeyed? (10.16). It cannot be because God has not addressed all men, because even in nature God sees to it that men are spoken to about himself (10.18). Israel believed in one God, but Gentiles, too, had been able to deduce from the silent witness of nature that one God was responsible for creation. Our theologian's problem is that the first and best believers in God rejected his full revelation of himself in Christ. His answer is that, although Israel might have been expected to respond favourably first, in fact Israel has always been divided in its response: there were many examples of the bulk of the nation's not seeing, leaving only a remnant of faithful people. Furthermore, this obduracy, which might seem to be a defeat for God, is really part of God's plan.

The remnant in Israel included Paul (11.1–4). The fact of a remnant in Israel is meant to underline the truth that God saves men not for their works but only because of his own grace (11.5–10). But even God's rejection of the mass of Israel has its purpose, and in any case is not permanent. The Gentile mission only came about because of this rejection by Jews of the gospel (11.11, a theme to be found also in *Acts*).

Not only did Israel's transgression produce good results by providing an opportunity for Gentiles to come in, but the success of the Gentile Church will itself work to turn the Jews back to God. The Jews will become jealous, as Moses said they would (Deut. 32.21, cited in 10.19 and referred to in 11.11, 13 f.). Paul deliberately magnifies his ministry to the Gentiles in order to stir unbelieving Jews to greater fury (11.13–15).

Our theologian always has at the back of his mind a great challenge to his whole system of belief. This challenge interpreted the success of the Gentile mission not as a continuous part of the history of God's dealings with men which began with his choice of Israel, but as evidence that a higher and better God than the lower God of Israel had taken control, and that the Church should break free from its childish dependence on the Old Testament and from its traditional anxiety about the fate of the Jews. This challenge was mounted by Marcion above all, and the theologian who wrote Romans 10.16–

11.32 was trying to show that Paul's epistle should not be interpreted in a Marcionite sense.

Admittedly, there were ideas in Romans 1.1–10.16 which lent themselves to Marcion's view, ideas such as that Christ was the end of the Law (10.4) or that Christians were discharged from the Law, dead to the Law, and free from the Law (7.2, 4, 6). This sort of remark might lead people to think that Christianity preached a new and higher religion than the religion of the Old Testament, with a new and higher God than the God of the Old Testament.

Our commentator is undoubtedly right that Paul did not mean to teach this sort of doctrine. The way Paul constantly appeals to the Old Testament is proof enough of that. But he nevertheless has a powerful challenge to meet, and the way he meets it is to tell an allegorical story (11.16–24). In the story, a farmer takes the extraordinary step of grafting wild olive shoots into a cultivated olive stock, the exact opposite of what a normal farmer would do. The cultivated olive stock represents the Old Testament, which should have nourished and supported the Jews. However, the farmer, for reasons best known to himself, decides to cut off the good branches, the bulk of the Jews, and to graft in wild branches, representing Gentiles. The moral is that no Gentile branch should ever imagine that it could do without the root, the Old Testament. If he does so, he will very easily be cut out again. And any Jew who returns to faith will simply be grafted back into his natural position.

Finally, our theologian imparts his vision of the end to which God's double action of rejecting and accepting men will lead. The rejection of part of Israel now is for the sake of the Gentiles, and the response of the Gentiles will in turn lead to the salvation of Israel. God leaves no one outside his love and care and eventually all – or all who believe in one God – will be saved (11.25–32). God governs every event of history, and is able to use men's rebellion as well as their obedience to serve his mysterious purposes.

This is a theology of modified predestination. God controls the broad sweep of history so that blindness and vision are his work, although within the great plan individuals are free to join one side rather than the other. Although men may choose disobedience for a time, they cannot in the end be lost, for God wishes to save all, and his purpose cannot be finally thwarted.

Such a theology stands between a strict predestinarian view, according to which some are elect and some damned, and the general Biblical view, according to which men are free to choose salvation or damnation for themselves. The view in 10.16–11.32 was taken up by Irenaeus, and finds a powerful defender today in the writings of John Hick, whose book *Evil and the God of Love* is a notable exposition of universalism.

Paul himself seems to have held the normal Biblical view of human freedom, but his writings early fell into the hands of gnostic determinists who interpreted him as a strict predestinarian. We cannot but be grateful to the theologian who added the long reflective comment that we are considering here. He was not able to distinguish between Paul's words and the words of commentary, but he was able to offer a powerful and persuasive statement of another theodicy which, despite its weaknesses, makes it clear that God is a God of love.

The long section we are considering concludes with a doxology, 11.33–6, which is similar in tone to the floating doxology to be found at 16.25–7 (see note below). This doxology, too, was originally composed for use by Hellenistic Jews, and it had already found a place in *Romans* before our anti-Marcionite commentator inserted his long theological reflection, 10.16–11.32, since Marcion, who does not have our 10.5–11.32 in his Apostolicon, cites a shorter version of 11.33 f. We may even surmise that the doxology in praise of God's inscrutable ways prompted the theologian to try to make the divine purpose a little clearer and more understandable.

Notes

10.16

But they have not all heeded the gospel: literally, 'But not all have obeyed the good news'. Our theologian begins with his distinctive 'but', a word he uses as the first word of a sentence also in 10.18, 19; 11.4, 11. By *gospel* or 'good news' he means not the Christian gospel, nor even God's direct word through the prophets, but God's universal address to all men, for all men have heard of God in some way or other; man's distinctive quality is to have been addressed by God (10.18). The problem, then, is why men have not 'obeyed' God. God's purpose for men cannot be thwarted, and a theologian must try to understand why some men, who know God, are hostile to God.

for Isaiah says, 'Lord, who has believed what he has heard from us?': the citation of Is. 53.1 is from the LXX version, which contains the word *Lord* not found in the Hebrew. The theologian wishes to point out that his theological problem is not new; Isaiah asked the same question, and was puzzled by the fact that the most direct and obvious proclamation of God's might and power met with only partial response. The words *what he has heard from us* in the RSV represent three Greek words, literally 'our hearing'. According to context, this means either what we hear, or what others hear from us.

10.17

So faith comes from what is heard, and what is heard comes by the preaching of Christ: this sentence is extraordinarily hard to unravel. *What is heard* represents the same word as that discussed at the end of the previous note. In the previous verse 'hearing' most naturally means primarily the prophet's report, but in this verse 'hearing' most naturally means primarily the listeners' ability to hear. I suspect, however, that our theologian is deliberately exploiting the wide range of meaning contained in the Greek word 'hearing' in order to make a fundamental point about human capacity in relation to God. He wishes to say that faith depends on men's ability to hear, and the ability to hear depends on the fact that God has spoken. The word is what distinguishes men from all the rest of creation; all men can speak and hear and have faith and obey because of the existence of words, and words exist because of God. (A modern version of this view is to be found in the writings of Ernst Fuchs and Gerhard Ebeling.) Verse 17 may be paraphrased: consequently faith depends on men's ability to hear and speak or speak and hear, and this ability exists because of the medium of the word.

The text translated in the RSV is literally 'through the word of Christ', which the RSV takes to mean *by the preaching of Christ. Of Christ* is read by P⁴⁶, ℵ*, B, D* and the Latin tradition, but ℵᶜ, A, Dᶜ, K, Ψ, 33, 1984, sy, Clement of Alexandia read 'of God', and G, Hilary, Pelagius have neither, reading simply 'through the word'. 'Of God' is a correct interpretation, but the original was pretty clearly the shorter reading 'through the word'. 'Of Christ' was suggested by a scribe who thought that *the gospel* in v. 16 necessarily implied that the word was the word about Christ.

10.18

But I ask, have they not heard? Indeed they have: most commentators think that this question must be a question about Israel because Isaiah's question in v. 16 was about Israel, and that is the general theme of this section of the epistle. Formally, the subject must be the *all* of v. 16, so that the question is, Who are they? The quotation that now follows is from Psalm 19.4 (in the LXX version), a Psalm that opens with the assertion that *The heavens are telling the glory of God,* meaning that all men everywhere have heard witness to God's power. It is highly unlikely that Paul or anyone else would use these words to prove that all Jews had heard God's human messengers, and we must conclude with Calvin, that the Psalm is quoted in its original sense. It follows that the question at the beginning of v. 18 concerns all men, and that our theologian was establishing his fundamental point that God has seen to it that the sound of words (even if, in this case, a voiceless sound) has gone out to all men, and that all men have heard of God's glory. If all men have heard of his glory, the problem why all have not obeyed is excruciatingly acute. This statement of the problem leads the commentator on to his first main theme, the hostility of that part of mankind which might have been expected to recognize God first, and the receptivity of that part of mankind which might have been expected to be the last to find him.

10.19

Again I ask, did Israel not understand? First Moses says: the word *first* could just as easily be taken with the question as with the statement, and this alternative position seems to make much better sense (Zahn, following Bentley and Wettstein). Translate: 'But I ask, Israel knew first, didn't they?' The answer to that question is, Yes, but their knowledge only served to make them jealous of those not a nation and angry at a foolish nation. Israel's knowledge only made them more painfully aware of the privilege received by those who did come to obey God. God speaks in many ways, and his speaking can even be designed to move men to anger and jealousy instead of love. Those he has made his own nation and given his wisdom may have to be made furious and jealous by men who are *not a nation, a foolish nation.* The opposite of what we should expect to be God's intention for his people may turn out to be his deep intention.

10.20,21

The double quotation from the LXX version of Is. 65.1, 2 (with two transpositions of no importance) clinches the case. The elect are chosen for no seeking of their own, and Israel remains obdurate although God stretches out his hands to them. The logic of the last quotation at first sight does not seem to fit in with a scheme in which God is in control of the situation, but it really does. Our theologian does not deny that Israel had first knowledge of God, but he holds that, in God's purpose, only some heard. Similarly, the Gentiles had only the knowledge of God that could be derived from nature and yet, in God's purpose, some still heard. The opposite of what God might be thought to intend is what he actually intended.

11.1

I ask, then, has God rejected his people? By no means!: I ask, then is a favourite way for our theologian to begin a sentence, part of his rhetorical method (10.18, 19; 11.1, 11, 13, all different in small ways from 3.5; 4.9; 6.19; 9.1; 12.3; 15.8). The problem he is tackling is to understand why God, who is in control of history, seems to have failed in his original intention to make Israel a people for himself. It looks as though he has repudiated his people, but that cannot be the case, because God cannot make promises and then go back on his word. The theologian's question is phrased in terms drawn from Psalm 94.14 (cf. 1 Sam. 12.22; Jer. 31.37), where it is stated categorically that

> The Lord will not forsake his people
> And his inheritance he will not abandon
> Until righteousness again returns to the act of judgement
> And all the upright in heart possess it.
>
> (LXX Psalm 93.14 f.)

I myself am an Israelite, a descendant of Abraham, a member of the tribe of Benjamin: the first step in our theologian's argument is that God never leaves himself without a remnant of faithful Israelites. Speaking in Paul's name, he recalls Paul's own impeccable credentials (2 Cor. 11.22; Phil. 3.5). He thus prepares the ground for his argument that Paul, as a member of the faithful remnant, will not only be the instrument for turning Gentiles to God, but will also indirectly begin the process of rousing Israel to fury and jealousy so that they too will eventually be saved.

2

God has not rejected his people whom he foreknew: the patristic commentators all take *whom he foreknew* in a restrictive sense, to mean not the whole of Israel but the remnant within Israel. This is the natural way to take the words, but this idea contradicts the tenor of the chapter: 'The reference in this chapter is throughout to the election of the nation as a whole' (Sanday and Headlam). Sanday and Headlam, Lietzmann and others consequently wish to interpret the phrase adjectivally, of the nation as a whole, but the Greek will scarcely bear this meaning, and it is more likely that these words are the work of a glossator who assumed that *his people* was the spiritual Israel, the Church (cf. Gifford). The same phrase, *whom he foreknew*, appears as a gloss on v. 1 in P⁴⁶, A, D*, Chrysostom, Ambrosiaster, Augustine, and should be rejected as such in both places. The gloss is predestinarian either in a weak sense: whom God foreknew would be faithful (early Augustine, and the Greek commentators); or in a strong sense: whom God fore-ordained (later Augustine). Both senses undermine human freedom, for either men's actions are fixed by their natures so that God knows in advance what they will do, or men's actions are directly determined by God. Men could, of course, *feel* themselves free under either scheme, but that feeling would be an illusion.

2b–4

Do you not know what the scripture says of Elijah, how he pleads with God against Israel? The theologian draws a parallel between Paul and Elijah. Elijah was tempted to think that he might be the last faithful Israelite, and that he himself was in danger of being killed, but God tells him that he has other plans; he will preserve for himself seven thousand men who would not bow the knee to Baal. The theologian cites 1 Kings 19.10, 14, 18 in a translation not from the LXX but known to us also in the writings of Justin Martyr, where the passage is used to make a similar point (*Dialogue with Trypho the Jew* 39). Our theologian could well have written about the same time as Justin, towards the middle of the second century. *But what is God's reply to him?* (v. 4) is literally, 'But what does the divine answer say to him?' and the noun 'the divine answer' is an unusual term for God's speaking, found nowhere else in the New Testament, but used by the LXX, Philo, Josephus, and 1 Clement (Clement of Rome).

5, 6

These verses state our theologian's theory of election. The remnant exists only because of God's choice and grace. The theologian opposes grace and works, so that they are mutually exclusive: *if it is by grace, it is no longer on the basis of works; otherwise grace would no longer be grace* (v. 6). Paul, as we have seen in discussing 10.5, 6a, holds another view. For him, God's grace comes to the aid of men who stop trying to fulfil every one of the works of the Law and live instead by faith. Grace is still grace in being bestowed on those who live by faith, and men's choices and actions are taken into account by God in bestowing grace, without his goodness losing its gracious quality. Our theologian works rather with a sort of view of God which holds that unless God does everything he does nothing. On this view, God could not be just if he finally rejected any man, because such rejection would be due not to anything the man had done but to God's withholding his grace. Our theologian avoids this conclusion by affirming that God will eventually have mercy on all men, or at least on all men who believe in one God (11.32).

At the end of v. 6 B adds: 'But if it is on the basis of works it is no longer grace; otherwise the work would no longer be grace.' Almost all the other manuscripts that support B have changed the last word 'grace' to 'work' in order to make this sentence exactly parallel to the previous one, thus making nonsense of it. What B's version means is that the work *of God* would no longer be grace if it were on the basis of works. Because the change made nonsense, many old manuscripts omitted the sentence entirely (P⁴⁶, ℵ*, A, D, G, 1739, etc.), and this is the reading followed in the RSV. The reading in B is probably correct.

7–10

Our theologian turns to consider those in Israel whom God did not for the time being choose. He argues that they were *hardened* in accordance with Old Testament prophecies: Deut. 29.4 (enriched with a phrase from Is. 29.10) (v. 8), and Psalm 69.22 f. (vv. 9 f.). Neither passage, in context, supports a predestinarian theory: the first is a vivid way of admonishing the Israelites for their failure to see the obvious, and the second is a curse rather than a prophecy that is to be mechanically fulfilled. The second was probably used by the theologian to refer to the fall of Jerusalem, and this reference has led Lipsius to reject vv. 9 and 10 as a gloss.

The words *and bend their backs for ever* in v. 10 are a false translation by the LXX of the Hebrew *and make their loins tremble continually*. Our theologian can scarcely have wanted to accept the idea that the Jews' backs were to be bent *for ever*, since he goes on, in the very next verse, to deny that they have *stumbled so as to fall*. He probably took the phrase to mean, not *for ever*, but 'altogether, thoroughly', that is, completely. Their hardening was quite complete until the time came for them to be received again. B. Weiss translates the phrase in a temporal sense, continually, but takes it to mean continually during the fixed time of their hardening, which will eventually come to an end (cf. Althaus).

11, 12

Our theologian at last explicitly sets out his theory of why God has hardened the hearts of the majority of his people. Their stumbling and transgressing has led to the Gentiles' receiving salvation, to the fury of the Jews. But if their *transgression* and *failure* (or 'defeat') led to so much enrichment for the rest of the world, the final fulfilment of God's promises to them, when they all come back, cannot but produce unimaginable riches.

13, 14

The theologian, speaking on behalf of Paul, foreshadows his allegory of the olive tree by telling the Gentile Christians that he deliberately emphasizes his ministry to the Gentiles in order to move his own people to jealousy, in accordance with the divine plan laid down in Deut. 32.21 and already referred to in 10.19 and 11.11. *Now I am speaking to you Gentiles* implies that he is addressing a mixed audience made up of Jewish and Gentile Christians. Quite probably there were Gentiles in Paul's Rome who attended the Jewish Christian synagogues to which he directed his original epistle, but the tone of this argument would hardly fit them. The Gentiles here addressed sound much more like a large and dominant part of the Catholic Church who are in danger of thinking that the Church should wash its hands of the Jews. This is an attitude to the Jews of which we have strong evidence not only in the writings of Marcion, but also in other second-century writings like *The Epistle of Barnabas* and *The Epistle to Diognetus*. In the latter book, Chapters 3 and 4, Jews are equated with Gentile idolators (3.5). Our theologian stands in another tradition, the tradition of the writer of *Luke–Acts* and Justin Martyr, which is more sensitive to the difference between Jews and pagan worshippers, and which still longs for the conversion of Jews to their own Messiah.

The words *and thus save some of them* at the end of v. 14 do not contradict our theologian's belief that God would eventually have mercy on all Israel (11.28–32). He means that Paul (and, by implication, all missionaries) could only hope for the conversion of a few Jews by their own efforts. The great ingathering must wait for God, in the time immediately before the general resurrection.

15

life from the dead: the general resurrection, with which the messianic Kingdom of God on earth will begin (Lipsius). The usual spiritualizing interpretations are unlikely. This is the common Jewish view that when the bulk of Israel repents the Kingdom will come (cf. Acts 3.17–21).

16

if the root is holy, so are the branches: these words state the principle upon which the allegory that follows is based. The principle probably comes from the legend of the founding of Athens by Pallas Athene. She presented a holy olive tree to the city, and thereafter the olive branches were sacred.

The preceding principle, *if the dough offered as first fruits is holy, so is the whole lump,* probably refers to the practice of offering the first part of the dough made from the new season's corn (Numbers 15.18–21). The Old Testament, however, never says that the offering of part makes the rest holy, and it seems that this is our theologian's attempt to find some Old Testament analogy for the principle upon which the allegory hangs.

17–24

The story is completely improbable as a story – what farmer would be foolish enough to reverse his usual practice and graft wild shoots on to a good stock? – but that is just what the author requires. He wishes to emphasize the strangeness of the farmer's procedure in order to emphasize the unmerited favour of God. For this is an allegory, in which every element stands for something else. The farmer is God, the root is the Old Testament, the natural branches are the Jews, and the wild branches are Gentiles. If the Gentiles forget that they depend on the Old Testament for their life in God's Church, they too will be cut off again. The Jews lost their original place only because they did not give heed to the proper meaning of the Old Testament and rejected the Messiah there foretold.

The general grounds for denying Pauline authorship are given in the essay: Paul was not writing in this epistle to Gentile Christians, nor did he live at a time when a predominantly Gentile Church had to be warned against despising the Old Testament. Paul could assume that the Old Testament was scripture – partly because there was no other, the New Testament canon having not yet been enough formed so as to begin to be a possible rival to the Old Testament. The situation presupposed in the allegory is the second-century situation of a predominantly Gentile Christian Church challenged by Marcion, or the forerunners of Marcion, to cut itself free from the Old Testament.

Our general conclusion is supported by stylistic arguments. The allegory is addressed to an individual Gentile and is in diatribe form.

The Gentile is invited to draw conclusions from the details of the allegory, and is warned not to draw false conclusions. This is worked by numerous 'if' clauses (vv. 16, 17, 18, 21, 23, 24) and by putting into the Gentile's mind a conclusion, true in itself, but open to a false extension, which is stated in order to be refuted (v. 19 f.). Paul's style is much terser and less rhetorical than this; he rarely allows himself so much space to develop an argument, and does not elsewhere use allegory.

(I argue that similar passages in the Pauline corpus, passages like Romans 2 and Galatians 4.24 ff., are not by Paul either.)

25–27

The allegorist concludes his argument with a solemn warning to the Gentiles that they must not be *wise in* their *own conceits*; each stage in history is but part of God's mysterious purposes, and the temporary hardening of Israel for the Gentiles' sake will come to its determined end so that eventually *all Israel will be saved*. The *hardening* referred to in v. 25 is, of course, partial (*upon part of Israel* is the RSV translation), in that some Jews, like Paul, have not been hardened, but the Greek phrase possibly should here be given another meaning, 'temporarily': a hardening has temporarily come upon Israel until the fulness of the Gentiles come in (cf. Rom. 15.24: *for a little*, a translation of the same phrase). The Old Testament citation is a combination of Is. 59.20 f. and 27.9 in the LXX translation with small differences, and the author takes this to be a prophecy of the return of Christ.

28–32

The allegorist is not a strict predestinarian. Rather he sees history in a broad sweep as the history of peoples, all of whom live under the over-arching purpose of God that cannot be frustrated. He wants to emphasize that the enmity now existing between Christianity and Judaism is only temporary, just as the former pagan life of the Gentiles was only temporary. God himself ordains periods of disobedience for nations in order that he may have mercy on all nations and bring them back to himself. The disobedience of the Jews has led to God's having mercy on the Gentiles; God's having mercy on the Gentiles will, in its turn, lead to his having mercy on the Jews.

The argument is presented in the form of antitheses. Verse 28 states the basic antithesis between the Church and Judaism in the sharpest form: *as regards the gospel* (that is, from the point of view of the process of history by which God's news of his existence and power is spread to all men; cf. 10.16 and the note) they were made God's *enemies* so that

Gentiles would have their chance; *as regards election* (that is, from the point of view of the beginning of the process when God chose Israel) they remain God's loved ones because they are descendants of the patriarchs. Verse 29 reaffirms that God cannot go back on his promises. Verses 30 and 31 resolve the apparent contradiction between saying that the same people are both enemies of God and his loved ones by showing that God has hardened them and made them fight against him only for a time in order to give himself the opportunity to have mercy on other peoples, the Gentiles, who also have had their time of disobedience. When the time of the Gentiles is complete, then the Jews will again know his mercy (cf. Luke 21.24 for a similar view). God first called the Jews and then hardened them (most of them); the remnant of Jews like Paul were forced to turn to a Gentile mission, a mission which was highly successful in turning Gentiles from *disobedience*; but finally the Gentile obedience will lead to Israel's again receiving God's mercy. (The RSV text omits the word *now* at the end of v. 31 with P⁴⁶, A, G, and the Latin tradition against ℵ, B, D*, probably rightly. An early scribe may well have wanted to make the second half of the verse more nearly parallel the first half than the original author intended. The original author probably had no more hope for conversion of Jews in his own day than he ascribed to Paul, the hope that *some of them* would be saved by the exertion of missionaries (11.14). His ultimate hope would depend on God's good time, when the general hardening of Israel would be reversed.)

Verse 32, *For God has consigned all men to disobedience, that he may have mercy upon all,* cannot be read according to the strict predestinarian pattern that God will have mercy on all who are elect, because then it would have to mean, God has consigned all men to disobedience in order that he may have mercy on some (which is Calvin's interpretation). The whole point of the argument is that *all* who have been consigned to disobedience will *all* receive mercy; Gentiles who were once disobedient have received their mercy now, and Jews whose fathers were obedient, having been made disobedient in the meantime, will receive their mercy in the future. Yet it remains difficult to imagine that our theologian believed that all men without exception would be gathered into the Kingdom. However successful his Church was in converting Gentiles, he must have doubted whether all the Gentiles would receive mercy. The Gentiles he is addressing had once been disobedient but now have received mercy, and he seems to equate receiving mercy with being part of the visible Catholic Church, which certainly did not include all Gentiles. But he seems to make no distinction between Jews who will receive mercy and Jews who will remain outside: *the gifts and the call of God are irrevocable* (v. 29) and all Jews *are beloved for the sake of their forefathers* (v. 28).

The solution perhaps lies in 10.18. Our theologian is talking not about all men, but about all men who have heard God's witnesses to his glory, that is, all men who believe in one God, the Creator. These are the men who come within the scope of God's hardening and having mercy; God has shut all these men up unto disobedience in order to have mercy on all, to demonstrate that salvation depends on grace rather than on works (11.5 f.). Men are able to recognize God because of the witness his creation bears to him, but their final lesson, to be learnt only by passing through the period of disobedience and enmity, is that all depends on grace alone. Our commentator probably believed, then, that God's mercy would extend to all the Gentile members of the Church and all Jews.

33–36

The doxology contained in 11.33–36 was taken over from Hellenistic Judaism. There are no specifically Christian references, although the Church would completely accept all its sentiments. The doxology was already part of *Romans* before the theologian whose work we have been considering added 10.16–11.32. Marcion's *Romans* contained a shorter version of 11.33 f. immediately after 10.4. Marcion could, of course, have had 10.5–11.32 in his copy of *Romans* and removed them as not by Paul, but, whatever we think of 10.6b–15, 10.16–11.32 looks very much like a reply to Marcion. The argument in 10.16–11.32, furthermore, is not quite in harmony with the 11.33–36, in that our theologian tries to lift a corner of the veil of mystery covering God's inscrutable ways. He accepts the thesis of 11.33–36, that nobody can earn God's favour or tell God what he should do (Is. 40.13 and perhaps Job 41.11, cited in 11.34 f.), but he is seeking to show that God, by choosing Israel and then choosing the Gentile members of the Church has given a clear indication of how he works on the men he has chosen, and what his final merciful purpose will be. His *judgments* and *ways* are not entirely *unsearchable* and *inscrutable*.

The doxology originally belonged in Hellenistic Judaism. There is a good parallel in II Baruch 14.8, 9, the *Syriac Apocalypse of Baruch*, which was a translation from Greek.

But who, O Lord, my Lord, will comprehend Thy judgment,
Or who will search out the profoundness of Thy way?
Or who will think out the weight of Thy path?

Or who will be able to think out Thy incomprehensible counsel?
Or who of those that are born has ever found
The beginning or end of Thy wisdom?

(Trans. R. H. Charles)

The Judaism represented in our doxology, however, is also deeply influenced by Greek philosophy, as can be seen by putting alongside it this passage from the Meditations of the Roman Emperor Marcus Aurelius (emperor from A.D. 161 to 180), who had been trained in Stoic philsophy.

Everything is fitting for me, my Universe, which fits thy purpose. Nothing in thy good time is too early or too late for me; everything is fruit for me which thy seasons, Nature, bear; from thee, in thee, to thee are all things.

(*Meditations*, iv. 23, trans. A. S. L. Farquharson)

Note, however, that whereas Marcus Aurelius writes, all things are 'from thee, *in* thee, to thee', our passage says all things are *from him*, THROUGH *him*, *to him*. Judaism and Christianity never finally succumbed to the idea that all things occurred *in* God. God is not the atmosphere, as it were, within which events occur, but the Creator who wills that his creation be free although he govern the eventual outcome. The predestinarian commentators of *Romans* sailed uncomfortably close to Stoic determinism, but even they did not lose sight of the distinction between God and the universe. Our doxology ends by ascribing glory to God, and such worship of God who is Creator and redeemer is safeguard against determinism and pantheism.

Paul's thought as we have been able to disentangle it and let it stand in its own light is dominated by the search for a righteousness pleasing to God. This righteousness, he holds, has been revealed in the gospel, so that now all men may live as God requires them to live. If men will believe God's promises, recognize his Son, trust Jesus' death as sacrifice for their sins, and live day by day in this faith, they will become righteous. What God requires is not perfection but faith.

There is no division in Paul's mind between dogmatic theology and ethics, between belief and action.

It is rather surprising, therefore, that St Paul turns to a long section of moral exhortations without once referring to the doctrinal side of ethics. The word 'faith' disappears in its previous sense, and we hear no more argument or discussion about the old problem. Instead, we find nothing but excellent advice, sound moral precepts, improving thoughts.

All commentators admit the change of subject-matter, and account for the change by some such general reflection as that the Apostle now passes to the practical application of his previous theoretic discussion. A few commentators are more perceptive, and notice that the change in subject-matter is also matched by a change in form. Lietzmann, for example, remarks that there seems to be no order in the thoughts that follow, and Sanday and Headlam say about Chapter 12, 'the Apostle does not appear to follow any definite logical order, but touches on each subject as it suggests itself or is suggested by the previous ideas' (p. 351).

Here, I believe, lies the clue to the whole of the section that begins at 12.1 and reaches to 15.13. On close examination this section consists not of a connected argument, but of a series of aphorisms. The aphorisms are loosely related to one another in theme, but often the only connection between one saying and the next is a catchword or combination of catchwords, such as that between 15.4 and 5, where the mention of the *steadfastness and encouragement* to be gained from the Scriptures leads on to a distinct saying about *the God of steadfastness and encouragement.*

The aphoristic nature of the section is partly obscured for us by two passages where, to be sure, the method is still the collection of aphorisms, but the connection is much tighter and better organized. These two passages are 13.1–7 and Chapter 14, the first concerned with relations to the State, and the second with the problem of a community divided between enlightened members who see through all tabus about food and drink and lucky days, and weaker brothers who still think these things are important. Here we come closer to connected argument, although in Chapter 14 the very force exerted to make every verse serve the dominant theme betrays, by the violence and wrenching many of the sayings have undergone, that self-contained sayings expressing diverse sentiments have been turned to a new purpose. The original sayings in both these cases come much more directly out of Stoic philosophy than the sayings in the surrounding passages, and I have argued in the notes that both 13.1–7 and 14.1–23 were inserted later into the much looser framework of 12.1–21; 13.8–14; 15.1–13. This looser framework is mostly derived from the store of wisdom in Hellenistic Judaism. Hellenistic Judaism was also influenced by Stoicism and much else, but the piety of the Old Testament was never completely submerged under Greek influence, and we find here neither the unyielding submission to the 'powers that be' of 13.1–7 nor the elitism of 14.1–23. The theme in 12.1–21; 13.8–14; 15.1–13 is God's mercy to sinners, the naturalness of worshipping him, the call to forgive others, the injunction to love enemies as well as friends, the need to live as children of light, the search for peace, joy, and hope, the privilege of serving others and of worshipping God with single-minded devotion.

I have printed each aphorism from the original collection separately, giving first the RSV text and then, usually, my own translation. This is necessary in order to show the structure of each aphorism, for the difference in structure between one verse and the next is often the clearest sign that two originally distinct sayings have been put down side by side, and that there is really no tight connection between them, despite the general similarity of thought.

In the two sections 13.1–7 and 14.1–23 I have adopted a slightly different arrangement in order to show the peculiarities of these insertions. I have printed the RSV text of the whole passage at the beginning, then given a general essay on the passage as a whole, and then treated each of the constituent aphorisms separately, offering my own translation for each one. In this way I have tried to indicate that the individual aphorisms were much more firmly organized and subordinated to a single theme than was the case in the surrounding parts.

It is hardly necessary to say that St Paul was neither the author nor the collector of 12.1–21; 13.8–14; 15.1–13, much less of 13.1–7 and 14.1–23. There is nothing here that bears the stamp of his mind: no argument, no logical chain of connections, no personal address, no appeal, no sorrow or anger, no fears, no hopes; instead, the reflections of generations, wisdom distilled into aphorisms, thought worn smooth by exchange from hand to hand and generation to generation, sometimes profound, often trivial, usually sensible practical bits of advice that once made Greek-speaking Jews of the Dispersion the envy of their pagan neighbours for the moral excellence and wholesomeness of their lives, and were now to guide the lives of Gentile converts to Christianity and turn ordinary men and women into loving peaceful saints devoted to serving their fellow men and praising God. St Paul was not the author, but we can only be grateful to the commentator who inserted this moral and religious handbook a page or two before the end of the original letter to the Romans.

12.1–21

12.1

12 *I appeal to you therefore, brethren, by the mercies of God, to present your bodies as a living sacrifice, holy and acceptable to God, which is your spiritual worship.*

> Thus I exhort you, brothers,
> By the mercies of God:
> Offer your bodies

A living, holy, acceptable sacrifice:
Your rational rite.

This is a religious aphorism concerning the moral disposition men should adopt. They should not so much sacrifice animals as sacrifice themselves; this is the cult God really requires. Man as a rational creature fulfils his own nature only when he turns his whole being to the source of reason, God himself. God requires as sacrifice the offering of themselves by men who make themselves holy and virtuous.

The aphorism was probably coined in Greek-speaking Judaism. This is shown by one of the terms used: *mercies* in the plural is a literal translation of a Hebrew word that is usually plural. The general idea was widespread among Jews like Philo of Alexandria, who made the outward rites of the Law more acceptable to themselves (and their non-Jewish neighbours whom they wanted to convert) by spiritualizing the details without necessarily abandoning the outward observance. So, for example, Philo explains that God is not pleased by lavish sacrifices but rather delights in minds which love him, a fact symbolized by the two altars in the Temple, one made of stones near the steps for blood sacrifices, and the other made of gold hidden behind the first veil, seen only by priests who keep themselves pure. The divine command that the priest has to offer incense on the inner altar at dawn before he can offer a burnt offering outside 'is a symbol of nothing else than that, with God, it is not the number of things offered that is valued, but the purity of the rational spirit of the sacrificer' (*Special Laws*, i.271–279; the quotation is at the beginning of 277).

The whole idea, and even some of the terminology, particularly the word that I have translated 'rational' (RSV: *spiritual*), is drawn from current Greek philosophy which taught that man shared the divine nature because of his rationality, and must, therefore, devote himself to the divine if he would be true to himself. 'If I were a nightingale, I would be doing the things appropriate to a nightingale; if a swan, those appropriate to a swan. But since I am (a man and therefore) rational, it is necessary for me to sing hymns to God' (Epictetus, *Discourses* i.16.20).

This theme pervaded Hellenistic religious writings. Here are two examples of prayers from an Egyptian collection of tracts associated with the god Hermes Trismegistus.

Accept rational, holy sacrifices from a soul and heart stretched out towards you, you who are ineffable, not to be spoken of, named only in silence. (i.31)

I give you thanks, Father, energy of my powers; I give you thanks, God, power of my energies. Your Word hymns you through me; through me receive the All as a rational sacrifice by the Word. (xiii.18)

The form of the aphorism, Romans 12.1, shows that it is completely independent and not to be related to its context. The word *therefore* at the beginning, which I have translated 'thus' and made to refer forwards, is certainly not an indication that the saying follows on logically from the previous chapter in *Romans*.

The words *to God* in the phrase *acceptable to God* sometimes appear before the adjective and sometimes after, and I think should be omitted as a gloss – a correct gloss, but unnecessary.

The aphorism, then, consists of five nearly-equal lines; the first two give the source of the appeal, the next two the substance of the appeal, and the last the basis on which the appeal rests. Man as man must engage himself in the rite appropriate to his rational nature.

12.2

²*Do not be conformed to this world*[a] *but be transformed by the renewal of your mind, that you may prove what is the will of God, what is good and acceptable and perfect.*[r]

[a] Greek *age.*
[r] Or *what is the good and acceptable and perfect will of God.*

> Do not be conformed to this world
> But be transformed by the mind's renewal
> So that you may discover what is God's will,
> What is good and acceptable and perfect.

This aphorism urges the reader to stand against the subtle and insidious pressures of society and to allow himself to be inwardly and completely transformed. Only by such transformation will he discover God's will, that is, the good, acceptable, and perfect life a man should live.

The aphorism is connected with v. 1 by neither thought nor form and style.

The thought could not possibly be connected, because v. 1 uses the image of the sacrifice of men's bodies to convey a very similar idea to the idea contained in the phrase 'the transformation of the mind' in v. 2; no one author is likely to have employed body and mind in the same paragraph to express identical rather than contrasting entities.

The first aphorism consists of five short lines. The second consists of four longer lines of remarkably even length and stress; indeed, if we can omit the first word 'and' with 1739, the syllables of each line are 13, 16, 16, 13.

The phrase 'this world' or 'this age' is a Jewish expression (IV Ezra 7.12 f.), but the general tone shows that the author had lived in a Hellenistic environment in which men were looking for total transformation rather than partial correction; conversion not simply improvement. (See A. D. Nock, *Conversion: The Old and the New in Religion from Alexander the Great to Augustine of Hippo*, Oxford, 1933, reprinted.) I should guess that this too, like v. 1, was a Jewish saying before it was taken over into the present collection, but I must be cautious, because one word, *renewal*, is not found outside Christian writings (its earliest appearance, after Rom. 12.2 and Tit. 3.5, is in the *Vision of the Shepherd of Hermas* 3.8.9). Nevertheless, the word without its prefix is in Josephus *Antiquities* 18.230, and I see no real reason, apart from this word, for concluding that the saying is specifically Christian.

12.3

³*For by the grace given to me I bid every one among you not to think of himself more highly than he ought to think, but to think with sober judgment, each according to the measure of faith which God has assigned him.*

> For by the authority given me I say to every man who is among you, Do not think proudly, above what it is fitting to think, but think so as to think soberly; to each I say, let him think just so highly of himself as God has portioned out warrant.

This aphorism is a solemn admonition from a wise teacher who has been entrusted by God with the task of helping men to form a just estimation of their own capacities and so to live in the light of this self-knowledge. Each man is given a certain ability by God, and each man has the duty of discovering the extent of this ability and thinking of himself just so highly as the facts warrant.

The aphorism is written in prose, but a rhetorical and formal prose; note particularly the grand emphasis of 'I say . . . to every man who is among you . . . to each (I say) . . .', and the play on words ('think proudly . . . think . . . think . . . think soberly'; 'as God has portioned the portion').

Paul could scarcely have written this saying. The word *faith* is used not to describe man's trust in God, nor God's saving faithfulness to men, but rather to describe a virtue in man, the level of ability God has pledged and granted to each individual; 'faith' means trustworthiness rather than trust. After making such a feature of faith in a quite different sense, Paul could scarcely have resorted to this new sense in such a casual manner.

The emphasis on conforming to the necessity of things, of thinking as it is fitting or necessary to think, is a favourite theme in popular Greek philosophy and religion. This saying is another form of the common warning against Hubris, overweening and unwarranted self-confidence.

12.4, 5

4*For as in one body we have many members, and all the members do not have the same function,* 5*so we, though many, are one body in Christ, and individually members one of another.*

> For as in one body we have many members
> And all members have not the same function,
> So we many are one body through Christ,
> And each members to one another.

The analogy between the human body made up of different members – each with its own function, and each necessary to the harmonious existence of the whole – and the 'body politic' is a commonplace in writings of this period. The most famous example is the fable of Menenius Agrippa (Consul at Rome in 503 B.C.) who is said to have persuaded the plebeians who had seceded from Rome to return by telling this story (here given in the version found in *Aesop's Fables*, translated by V. S. Vernon Jones).

The Members of the Body once rebelled against the Belly. 'You', they said to the Belly, 'live in luxury and sloth, and never do a stroke of work; while we not only have to do all the hard work there is to be done, but are actually your slaves and have to minister to all your wants. Now, we will do so no longer, and you can shift for yourself for the future.' They were as good as their word, and left the Belly to starve. The result was just what might have been expected: the whole Body soon began to fail, and the Members and all shared in the general collapse. And then they saw too late how foolish they had been. (Cf. Josephus, *Jewish War*, 5.27,279; *Antiquities* 7.66; Dionysius of Halicarnassus, *Roman Antiquities* 3.11.5; 6.54.2 etc.) This theme is applied in *Romans* to the men and women who have been brought together in one community by Christ. (The phrase is literally *in Christ*, but there is no need to import into this saying any idea of Christ as a body with Christians as members; the point of the saying is not the special nature of the Christian union, but the ordinary consequences that follow from *any* union of people into one communion. The preposition *in* is frequently used to form instrumental phrases.)

The aphorism consists of four even lines, and the structure perfectly suits the thought: as in *a b* follows; so in *a' b'* must follow. Bultmann in his first book (*Der Stil der paulinischen Predigt und die kynisch-stoische Diatribe*, Göttingen, 1910, pp. 75 f.) noticed the poetic structure of the saying, but wrongly linked it with vv. 6–14, which are quite different from this, and themselves contain more than one different form.

12.6–8   TWO APHORISMS

[6]*Having gifts that differ according to the grace given to us, let us use them: if prophecy, in proportion to our faith;* [7]*if service, in our serving; he who teaches, in his teaching;* [8]*he who exhorts, in his exhortation; he who contributes, in liberality; he who gives aid, with zeal; he who does acts of mercy, with cheerfulness.*

6–8a Since we have gifts that depend on the grace given to us,
    Excellent according to the proportion of faith,
      If one of us serves, let him devote himself to service,
      If one of us teaches, let him devote himself to teaching,
      If one of us consoles, let him devote himself to consolation.

8bc Let him who gives give liberally;
    Let him who cares care zealously;
    Let him who helps help cheerfully.

Two lists of gifts seem to have been combined into one. The triad in
v. 8bc, however, separates itself fairly obviously from the preceding
saying. First, each injunction specifies the manner of exercising the
named function ('liberally', 'zealously', 'cheerfully') and not the
warning to use fully what is given, as in vv. 7, 8a (literally, 'in service',
'in teaching' 'in consolation'). Second, the triad in v. 8bc is perfectly
regular in a way the earlier list is not. This evident regularity may
even extend to the number of Greek syllables, ten in each line, if we
accept the spelling of the verb in the second line given in א.

The triad is concerned with the way in which charity should be
exercised. The second line could be translated to refer to the exercise
of a particular office in the Church, and this ambiguity has made it
easier to run together our two sayings, but the immediate context, in
between alms-giving and works of mercy, makes it almost certain
that general care of the weak is meant, not Church administration.

The first saying, in vv. 6–8a, raises more difficulties.

Verse 6, as it stands, is puzzling. The two words translated by the
RSV as *gifts that differ* are a noun and an adjective, but they are separated by the phrase *according to the grace given to us*. Further, the phrase
in proportion to our faith is formally parallel to *according to the grace given
to us*, but in thought quite cut off by the first gift in the list, the gift of
prophecy. Finally, it is hard to see why service, teaching, and exhortation should be exercised in serving, teaching, and exhortation, while
prophecy alone has to be exercised *in proportion to our faith*.

My guess is that the words *if prophecy* were originally a marginal
note by a commentator who thought one of the necessary offices in
the Church had been omitted. He may have read the verb *Having* at
the beginning of the verse as related to the verb *are* in the previous

verse, and this would make it easier to suggest that prophecy could be inserted here.

When the words *if prophecy* are omitted, we recover a lucid introduction to the three functions listed in vv. 7, 8a. The adjective 'different' can also mean 'excellent', and should be taken this way; it now goes with the phrase *in proportion to our faith*, and this phrase applies to the three following gifts, not just to the one gift of prophecy: 'Since the gifts are given to us, and become excellent in proportion to the faith with which we use them, let us serve, teach, and comfort as hard as we can.'

Perhaps the three lines referring to gifts were originally a little more regular than they are in our present text. There is a case for accepting the reading of ℵ, 1, 69 in the first line, so that all three would begin with participles, 'If anyone is serving, teaching, consoling'.

12.9

⁹*Let love be genuine; hate what is evil, hold fast to what is good;*

> Let love be unfeigned:
> Abhor evil
> And cling to good.

Love, *agape* in Greek, is a rather rare Greek word, which Greek-speaking Jews adopted to express moral love between people, and between God and man. This saying particularly emphasizes the moral character of true love. The same sort of theme is expressed in the *Testament of Benjamin,* one of the *Testaments of the XII Patriarchs,* a late Jewish tract: 'You, my brothers, flee evil, envy, and hatred of your brothers, and cling to goodness and love' (8.1).

The three lines are of very even length. If we accept the reading of 999 in line 3, each line consists of nine syllables.

12.10

¹⁰*love one another with brotherly affection; outdo one another in showing honour.*

> As loving one another dearly with brotherly love
> Lead the way in showing honour to one another.

The verb in the second line is much disputed. Its normal meaning is 'to lead the way', and I have tried to keep to that meaning in my translation. Unfortunately, the words dependent on the verb seem to be in the wrong cases for this meaning to hold, and various other possibilities are put forward: the RSV suggests *outdo one another in showing zeal*, although again *one another* seems to be in the wrong case; and Sanday and Headlam, Lietzmann, Zahn, Langrange, Barrett prefer 'esteem one another most highly in honour' referring to Phil. 2.3, *count others better than yourselves*. Whatever the correct meaning of the verb, the drift of the aphorism seems to be that brotherly love should not mean the doing away with order and courtesy; those who love one another sincerely should also pay respect and honour to each other.

Both lines in this aphorism begin with a noun in the dative case, and that has led the collector to add three more aphorisms which also begin each line (with one exception) in the dative. Despite this one formal similarity, they are really very different from one another in overall form, and in thought.

12.11

¹¹*Never flag in zeal, be aglow with the Spirit, serve the Lord.*

> Never flag in zeal,
> Burn in spirit
> Serve at every opportunity.

In line 3 of this aphorism the RSV has followed the majority text, *serve the Lord*, but the word *Lord* has almost certainly been substituted for the harder original reading, 'serve the time', found in D*, G and some Latin Mss. 'Serve the time' could too easily be taken in a bad sense, and scribes changed the word to the very similar-looking word *Lord*; it is hard to imagine a scribe's making the other change, from *Lord* to 'time' (Zahn).

When the original sense of line 3 is restored, it is clear that 'spirit' in line 2 refers to the human spirit and not to the Holy Spirit. The saying recommends the glowing devotion that never misses an opportunity to serve.

The three lines each contain seven Greek syllables.

12.12

¹²*Rejoice in your hope, be patient in tribulation, be constant in prayer.*

> Rejoice over the hope you have,
> Stand firm in tribulation,
> Persevere in prayer.

The three lines of v. 12 are concerned with how to resist the pressures to abandon God in trouble, and the advice is: remember what you hope for and be glad, be firm in the face of trouble, and don't stop praying.

The three lines contain 7, 8, and 9 syllables respectively, and perhaps this ascension was intentional.

12.13

¹³*Contribute to the needs of the saints, practise hospitality.*

> Share in meeting the needs of the saints;
> Devote yourselves to hospitality.

The beginning of the first line of this saying is still in the dative, like the beginnings of every line in vv. 10–12, but in the dative plural, not the dative singular like the rest. The second line breaks the pattern, by beginning with an accusative.

The aphorism recommends generous giving to meet the needs of poorer members of the community, and the exercise of hospitality. *Saints* is a Jewish term for those who remain faithful to God, and does imply moral purity on their part (e.g. Is. 4.3 f.).

12.14

¹⁴*Bless those who persecute you; bless and do not curse them.*

> Bless persecutors,
> Bless and don't curse.

Here is clear proof that a collector of aphorisms is at work, not an author writing a continuous moral discourse. The verb 'to persecute' also means 'to pursue, devote oneself to', and has been used in that second sense at the end of v. 13. The compiler has mechanically put together a saying that ends by recommending devotion with another saying that begins by recommending persecutors to be blessed!

This aphorism could have gone back to Jesus himself (cf. Matt. 5.44; Luke 6.27 f.), although it is not completely without analogy in the Old Testament (Ex. 23.4 f.; Prov. 25.21 f.; see Rom. 12.20). The more likely solution is that this is a Jewish saying from before the time of Jesus that has gladly been accepted into Christian teaching.

12.15

> ¹⁵*Rejoice with those who rejoice, weep with those who weep.*

> Rejoice with rejoicers,
> Weep with weepers.

Show sympathy with men in both joy and grief. Each line contains seven syllables, and the imperative is, for the first time, expressed by the Greek infinitive.

12.16ab

> ¹⁶*Live in harmony with one another; do not be haughty, but associate with the lowly;*^a

> ^a Or *give yourselves to humble tasks.*

> Regard everyone equally;
> Don't be proud
> But get along well with the humblest.

Line 1 means literally 'think the same to one another', and the commentators take this to be a reference to harmony in the community (cf. 2 Cor. 13.11, where the same phrase is used). Some commentators refer this line back to the previous verse, and put a full stop at its end, but this is unlikely, since the verb is a participle, not an infinitive as in v. 15. I myself would relate line 1 much more firmly to lines 2 and 3 by suggesting the translation 'think equally of one another' rather than *live in harmony with one another*. Then it becomes even more likely that the RSV text *associate with the lowly* is preferable to the rendering in the note, *give yourselves to humble tasks*.

12.16c

never be conceited.

> Do not become wise in your own estimation.

The compiler quotes Prov. 3.7a (in the plural, to fit this context, rather than in the original singular) to supplement the previous saying. No attempt has been made, beyond the change to the plural, to graft this proverb into the other.

12.17a

¹⁷*Repay no one evil for evil.*

Proverbs 17.13 said,
> If a man returns evil for good
> evil will not depart from his house.

To this Rabbi Simeon bar Abba (about A.D. 280) said, Not only whoever returns evil for good, but also whoever returns good for evil, from his house evil will not depart (Genesis Rabba 38.3). Jesus' advice was just the opposite (Matt 5.38 ff.; Luke 6.29 f.). The saying in front of us can scarcely be said to stem from the teaching of Jesus, since it lacks the positive note that requires a disciple to return good for evil. I think, then, that the proverb in *Romans* is a pre-Christian Jewish proverb, which arose in Greek-speaking Judaism, and was gladly accepted into the corpus of Christian wisdom because of its obvious affinities with the rulings of Jesus.

12.17b

but take thought for what is noble in the sight of all.

> Plan deeds noble in all men's sight.

The LXX of Prov. 3.4 has taken this verse in a quite different sense from the sense the original Hebrew probably warranted, and it is the LXX that is followed here. The point is that Christians (or Jews, the original audience) should not be indifferent to what men outside regard as good and noble, but should consider this when planning their actions.

12.18

¹⁸*If possible, so far as it depends upon you, live peaceably with all.*

This is a very sensible proverb. Live at peace with all men, it says, so long as that is at all possible, and if the peace has to be broken, make sure that you are not the one responsible for the breach.

Although the theme of the aphorism is in general akin to the theme of the preceding and following sayings, being concerned with relations to outsiders or enemies, there is no actual connection between being the last to break the peace and either planning to impress outsiders by the nobility of one's actions or never taking revenge. In the second case, v. 18 envisages the possibility of a reply to an enemy that v. 19 would seem to rule out entirely. I do not mean the sayings are contradictory; simply that they do not come from the pen of one man pursuing a connected theme.

12.19

¹⁹*Beloved, never avenge yourselves, but leave it*ᵗ *to the wrath of God; for it is written, 'Vengeance is mine, I will repay, says the Lord.'*

ᵗ Greek *give place.*

The RSV correctly takes the phrase 'give place to anger' in the sense *leave it to the wrath of God*, as the citation of Deut. 32.35 shows. The citation is a better rendering of the original Hebrew than the LXX manages, and it is interesting to note that Deut. 32.35 is given in exactly the same Greek rendering in another New Testament context, Hebrews 10.30.

12.20

²⁰*No, 'if your enemy is hungry, feed him; if he is thirsty, give him drink; for by so doing you will heap burning coals upon his head.'*

Another hand has added from the LXX a quotation from Prov. 25.21 f.

The *burning coals* should probably be interpreted, following the Targum, as *coals* of burning shame leading to repentance and reconciliation.

12.21

²¹*Do not be overcome by evil, but overcome evil with good.*

> Do not be conquered by evil
> But conquer evil with good.

This saying also probably stemmed from Greek-speaking Judaism. There is a close parallel in the *Testament of Benjamin* 4.3 (one of the *Testaments of the XII Patriarchs*): the good man 'by doing good conquers evil'.

13.1–7

13 *Let every person be subject to the governing authorities. For there is no authority except from God, and those that exist have been instituted by God. ²Therefore he who resists the authorities resists what God has appointed, and those who resist will incur judgment. ³For rulers are not a terror to good conduct, but to bad. Would you have no fear of him who is in authority? Then do what is good, and you will receive his approval, ⁴for he is God's servant for your good. But if you do wrong, be afraid, for he does not bear the sword in vain; he is the servant of God to execute his wrath on the wrongdoer. ⁵Therefore one must be subject, not only to avoid God's wrath but also for the sake of conscience. ⁶For the same reason you also pay taxes, for the authorities are ministers of God, attending to this very thing. ⁷Pay all of them their dues, taxes to whom taxes are due, revenue to whom revenue is due, respect to whom respect is due, honour to whom honour is due.*

This section is self-contained, and was incorporated into the larger ethical section, 12.1–15.13, at a pretty late stage, perhaps even after that section was itself incorporated into *Romans*. Ernst Barnikol ('Römer 13: Der nichtpaulinische Ursprung der absoluten Obrigkeitsbejahung von Römer 13.1–7' in *Studien zum Neuen Testament:*

Erich Klostermann zum 90. Geburtstag dargebracht, Texte und Unter-suchungen, Vol. 77 (Berlin, 1961), pp. 65–133) argues that no Christian writer refers to Rom. 13.1–7 before A.D. 150, or even before A.D. 180. James Kallas argues a similar thesis ('Romans XIII 1–7: An Inter-polation', *New Testament Studies* 11 (1965), pp. 365–74).

Romans 13.1–7 is neither Christian nor Jewish in origin. Both Christian and Jewish tradition commanded respect for earthly rulers, but never the absolute obedience laid down in this section. Indeed, Jewish and Christian teaching is remarkably unanimous on this point. Rulers are given authority by God (Wisdom of Solomon 6.3; Josephus, *War*, ii. 140 (8.7)) and must therefore be obeyed (Mark 12.17), but their authority is naturally subordinate to God's authority (Psalm 82; Wisdom of Solomon 6.1–11) and no one should ever disobey God, even if the ruler command it (Mark 12.17; Acts 5.29): 'Render to Caesar what is Caesar's, and to God what is God's'; 'It is necessary to obey God rather than men'.

The passage here is made up of eight injunctions, collected together by a Stoic teacher and given Stoic philosophical grounding in the first saying (v. 1). Stoicism held that everything that existed was derivative from God and, in a derivative sense, *was* God. Everything that happened was determined, and the wise man was the man who knew that, and adjusted his life to this grim knowledge. Rulers owed their power to God absolutely, and they had to be submitted to of necessity: when the Stoic philosopher and courtier Seneca (c. 4 B.C.–A.D. 65) was ordered by Nero to take his own life, he did so with absolute calmness despite the unjustness of the charge against him. The freedom he had was the freedom to submit.

The collection only gained a foothold in the Christian setting because of two circumstances, one material and the other almost accidental. The material circumstance is the agreement of the teaching in the insertion with one strand of the Jewish-Christian tradition, the strand which acknowledges the divine source of earthly rulers' power, their authority to collect taxation, and their right to expect obedience and respect and prayers for their well-being. The almost accidental circumstance is the purely verbal agreement between Romans 13.8 and the last sentence of the Stoic collection, Romans 13.7: v. 8 says 'Owe nothing to anyone' and v. 7 'Give everyone what they are owed'. The verbal similarity, with the complete difference in concepts, is just what would appeal to a compiler of aphorisms or a glossator of aphorisms, for whom word-play is everything.

The ultimate reason for the incorporation of this section is that the later Church would feel the need for some guidance in relations with the State in an apostolic letter to the Romans; surely, they would feel, the apostle had something to say about the power of Rome when writing to the Romans. This little collection about the theme was probably ancient at the time of its incorporation; and we can only hope that the time of its incorporation was a time of peace and prosperity, when the Roman empire was being just and fair, when the authorities were *ministers of God, attending to this very thing* (v. 6).

These seven verses have caused more unhappiness and misery in the Christian East and West than any other seven verses in the New Testament by the licence they have given to tyrants, and the support for tyrants the Church has felt called on to offer as a result of the presence of Romans 13 in the canon.

13.1

> Be subject to all the governing powers:
> For there is no power except from God,
> And the powers that be have been ordained by God.

The teaching of this ethical maxim is that human life is ruled by a series of 'powers', both heavenly powers, who govern men's fate and determine everything that happens to them, and earthly powers, rulers and potentates who are the agents of the heavenly powers. Wisdom consists in complete submission to what the powers ordain, for it is futile to go against authority, which ultimately derives from God. No distinction between powers is possible; all are ordained by God, however malignant they appear, and all must be submitted to.

The text I have translated at the head of this note differs from the text translated in the RSV. They have followed the majority of manuscripts in reading *Let every person be subject,* but the true reading seems to be that of P⁴⁶, G, 'Be subject to all . . .' This text was changed to soften the absoluteness of the saying, and to bring it into line with v. 2 by making it also a direct address to each subject of the Empire rather than a statement of the claims of every one of the powers that be.

Verse 1 is quite distinct from v. 2. The form is different, because v. 1 consists of three lines, each containing fourteen Greek syllables, whereas v. 2 originally, before it was incorporated into this collection, consisted of a sentence that split evenly into two parts, each of twelve syllables. More important, the subject-matter is distinct. Verse 1 is the philosophical grounding for a position of absolute submission to the State, but a philosophical grounding which depends on the metaphysical connection between earthly powers and their heavenly controllers. Verse 2, on the other hand, is simply an assertion that to rebel against earthly rule is to rebel against authority God has ordained.

Some commentators, notably Oscar Cullmann in his book *The State in the New Testament* (London, 1957), have argued that Paul wrote this injunction against the larger background in his own thought of the theory that Christ had dethroned and forced the heavenly powers to submit. Unfortunately, there is no support in this verse or in the passage as a whole for this theory, and it must be counted a vain attempt to incorporate what is really a foreign body into the tissue of Paul's theology.

13.2a

Consequently:

> He who withstands authority
> withstands the ordinance of God.

The author of this aphorism was counselling absolute obedience to ruling authority in the State. He was well aware that rulers could be unjust and tyrannical, but nevertheless counselled submission. What he was not aware of was the possibility that rulers could actually successfully defy God's ordinance – successfully, that is, in the short run. The author was probably a determinist who held that rulers, like everyone else, were under divine necessity.

Jewish and Christian theology, however greatly it emphasized the divine right of rulers to rule, always knew that there could come a time when one had to obey God rather than man. The disobedience to man that was required might be passive disobedience, but it had to be disobedience nevertheless, because, in such a conflict of loyalties, loyalty to God remained paramount.

The teaching given here in v. 2 could only find its way into a Christian collection because loyalty to rulers was regarded as important, and the duty of disobeying them when conflict with loyalty to God arose was assumed.

The regularity of the sentence (two parts of twelve syllables each) leads me to suppose that the introductory 'consequently' was added by the compiler who put v. 1 at the head of the collection. Verse 1 is wider in scope and more philosophical in intent than the rather blunt command in v. 2.

The word 'consequently' is not quoted by Ambrose and Augustine, and perhaps should be omitted.

13.2b, 3a

Rebels will receive judgement on themselves, for rulers are not a terror to the good deed, but to the bad.

This is a general warning against rebellion, based on the simple observable fact that rulers armed with absolute power are difficult to oppose, and on the assumption that such power is basically benign.

The saying hangs together in form and content, and it is inadvisable to join v. 2b, the first part of the sentence, with the previous saying, as the RSV has done. The previous saying is addressed to the individual who is tempted to rebel, whereas the saying in vv. 2b and 3a is a general statement about rebels and rulers.

13.3b, 4a

> You wish not to fear authority:
> Do good and you will have praise from authority,
> For authority is God's servant to you for good.

The first sentence, either a statement or a question, is the typical introduction to a Stoic diatribe (Bultmann, *Der Stil der paulinischen Predigt und die kynisch-stoische Diatribe*, Göttingen, 1910, pp. 15 ff.). The problem raised in the opening sentence is resolved in two further sentences, the first giving the right course of action and the second the metaphysical grounding for the action. Again, the author of the saying is prohibited by his view of the universe from envisaging successful disobedience to God on the part of a ruler. However bad the ruler appears, he must be God's servant to thee for good.

4b

> If you do evil, tremble with fear,
> For he does not bear the sword in vain,
> The avenger on him who does evil.

I suspect that this saying was originally made up of three lines only, and that the statement *he is the servant of God* was introduced from the previous saying in order to give some theological justification for what is otherwise rather a bare affirmation of the unvarying justice of rulers.

There is no textual evidence for that conjecture, but there is good evidence for the omission of 'unto wrath' in the last line, the words being omitted by G. 'Unto wrath' was added to bring this saying into line with what the glossator thought was the message in v. 5, namely, that rulers' punishment was the legitimate expression of divine wrath against unrighteousness.

When the two Greek words are removed, we are left with three lines of ten syllables each.

The saying expresses the irresistible power of the ruler, which cannot possibly be avoided, against everyone who does evil.

13.5

> This is why subjection is necessary:
> Not only because of fear of punishment,
> But also because of conscience.

The word *wrath* means not God's wrath but simply fear of the punishment able to be meted out by the ruler. God is not mentioned explicitly in the Greek, and it is much easier to suppose that the writer is making a contrast between submission to a ruler out of fear and submission for conscience's sake, that is, for God's sake ultimately, than to suppose a contrast between submission to God's wrath and submission for conscience's sake which is also therefore submission to

God. The contrast is between outward and inward submission, not between submission to two aspects of God's demand.

The form of the aphorism is very regular; lines 1 and 3 consist of ten syllables, and line 2 of eight.

Bultmann (1947 in *Exegetica*, Tübingen, 1967, pp. 281 f.) argued that v. 5 was a gloss that broke the connection between vv. 4 and 6. Verse 5 is certainly a self-contained unit, but so are vv. 4b and 6, and they are but three examples of the eight aphorisms that go to make up 13.1–7.

13.6

> This is the reason you pay taxes:
> They are God's ministers,
> Devoting themselves to this very service.

The advice contained in this aphorism is severely practical, quite different from the advice in v. 5, although the form is very similar, and there are also ten, eight, and ten syllables respectively in each line.

The word *ministers* has sacred overtones, although here it applies strictly to the ruling authorities of the State. Taxation is their right because running the State is a divinely given office.

Jews and Christians were very willing to pay taxes, and even to overlook the divine titles the rulers sometimes took to themselves, provided they did not have to commit idolatry, but it is doubtful whether a Jewish or Christian writer would have ever chosen to use the word *ministers* in this context, although the word could be used in an ordinary unreligious sense (Phil. 2.25).

13.7

> Give to all what is owed:
> To him due tax, tax;
> To him due excise, excise;
> To him due fear, fear;
> To him due honour, honour.

This is another injunction urging absolute loyalty to civil authority. It consists of an opening general statement followed by four lines of equal length, the first pair dealing with taxation (direct and indirect) and the second pair with respect (negative and positive).

The saying nicely rounds off the collection by being general and comprehensive. The only element it lacks is reference to the divine sanction behind the necessary obedience, but that, of course, is assumed.

13.8–10

13.8a

⁸Owe no one anything, except to love one another ...

> Owe nothing to anybody
> Except to love each other.

All other obligations to each other can be, and ought to be, punctiliously discharged; the only obligation that never comes to an end and is never fully discharged is the obligation to love one another.

This is a perfect couplet consisting of two lines with nine syllables in each line. The assonance in the Greek is rather striking:

> mēdeni mēden opheilete,
> ei mē to allēlous agapan.

The saying probably originally came from Greek-speaking Judaism. The Testaments of the Twelve Patriarchs are full of injunctions to love one another (Testament of Reuben 6.9; Testament of Simeon 4.7; Testament of Issachar 5.2; Testament of Zebulun 8.5; Testament of Dan 5.3; Testament of Gad. 4.2; 7.7; Testament of Joseph 17.2; Testament of Benjamin 3.3–5; 8.1). The Qumran writings also enjoin love for the brotherhood (e.g. 1QS X. 26), even if it be combined with hatred for God's enemies. Compare 1 John 3.11, 23; 4.7, 12.

13.8b

for he who loves his neighbour has fulfilled the law.

> The man who loves his neighbour
> fulfils the Law.

I think this was originally an isolated saying. It is a sentence falling into two parts, not a saying in lines like the one preceding and the one following.

The idea belongs in the teaching of Jesus (Mark 12.28–31; cf. Matt. 22.40), but it was probably found in Judaism before his day (Rabbi Hillel, b. Sabbath 31a; Philo, *Special Laws* ii.63). The other New Testament references to love of neighbour as fulfilling the Law, and the one reference in the Apostolic Fathers, all appear to me to have been derived directly from Hellenistic Judaism (Gal. 5.14; James 2.8; Didache 1.2). Jesus reaffirmed this summary of the Law, and the Church gratefully quoted from earlier Jewish sources to show that Jesus did indeed fulfil the highest vision of his people and the best understanding of the Old Testament.

13.9

⁹*The commandments, 'You shall not commit adultery, You shall not kill, You shall not steal, You shall not covet,' and any other commandment, are summed up in this sentence, 'You shall love your neighbour as yourself.'*

> The commandments You shall not commit adultery, You
>   shall not kill,
> You shall not steal, You shall not covet
> And whatever other commandment you name
> Are summed up in this word,
> 'You shall love your neighbour as yourself'.

This saying consists of five lines. If we omit the link-word 'for' at the beginning, and the superfluous words before the citation of Lev. 19.18 at the end (following B, G, and the Latin tradition) we are left with nine syllables in lines 1–3 and thirteen syllables in lines 4, 5. The selection of commandments was made for poetic purposes rather than for any other special reason.

Like the preceding saying, this also probably originated in Greek-speaking Judaism.

13.10

¹⁰*Love does no wrong to a neighbour; therefore love is the fulfilling of the law.*

The RSV translation, with its use of the semicolon, nicely brings out the structure of this little saying.

The argument is that, since the Law is designed to protect every one from harm, love fulfils the Law by never inflicting evil on anyone. Paul's argument that no one actually does completely keep the Law is quite outside the range of the Hellenistic Jewish writer who first wrote this aphorism. Paul would have agreed with the aphorism (cf. Gal. 5.6), but his problem was the case where love failed. He could hardly have written this aphorism himself, however, without touching on the weightier argument in Romans 7 and 8.

13.11–14   FIVE APHORISMS

11Besides this you know what hour it is, how it is full time now for you to wake from sleep. For salvation is nearer to us now than when we first believed; 12the night is far gone, the day is at hand. Let us then cast off the works of darkness and put on the armour of light; 13let us conduct ourselves becomingly as in the day, not in revelling and drunkenness, not in debauchery and licentiousness, not in quarrelling and jealousy. 14But put on the Lord Jesus Christ, and make no provision for the flesh, to gratify its desires.

13.11a

> And this I say: Know the time,
> That the hour is already here
> For you to awake from sleep.

The whole theme of spiritual renewal as waking from sleep is a commonplace in the mystery religions of the day, and was taken over into Greek-speaking Judaism. Awaking from sleep was naturally linked with break of day (cf. Eph. 5.14), so that this saying provided a good opening to the little collection of five sayings which form the unit we are considering.

13.11b

For now is our salvation nearer than when we first believed.

The compiler of the collection wishes to anchor (in space and time) the moral admonitions he has collected; aphorisms that originally referred to the timeless spiritual state of every man are here made more pressing and urgent by a theologian who believes that the return of the Lord and the day of judgement cannot be long delayed. This belief, that the end of all things was nearer than when the group to which the theologian belonged had been converted to Christianity, cannot be used to date the collection, since such beliefs have always sprung up from time to time in the Church's history. All that we can conclude is that the community in which the collection was made was young in the faith.

13.12a

> Night is fading, day is near.

This was originally a separate aphorism, akin to the opening saying, v. 12a. It is a call to awake from spiritual sleep. The collector, whose own words we have just noticed (v. 12b), has interpreted the image as a reference to the approaching day of the Lord.

13.12b

> Put off the works of darkness;
> Put on the weapons of light.

This is a perfect couplet, each line consisting of twelve syllables. The word *then* ('therefore') is either not original (cf. the Syriac), or has no strict logical force linking the couplet to what goes before, because this saying does not depend on the objective passing away of darkness as day breaks, but rather applies whatever the time. Under all circumstances one must renounce the deeds of darkness and put on the weapons necessary to fight on the side of light.

13.13

> Let us walk nobly as in the day:
> Not in revelling and drunkenness,
> Not in sexual excesses and debauchery,
> Not in bitter strife and rivalry.

This saying lists the enemies of the good life: sensual excess of table and bed, and dissension. These are things condemned by all moral codes worthy of the name.

The verse is not related either to what follows or to what precedes: its task is simply to list the dangers and to condemn them as ignoble. The imagery is about 'walking', and the saying came into the collection because of the reference to 'day'.

13.14

> Now put on the Lord;
> Do not lavish great attention on the flesh.

There is textual evidence that this saying originally had the short form I have translated above. The majority of manuscripts read, *put on the Lord Jesus Christ*, but B has 'put on the Messiah (Christ) Jesus' and P⁴⁶ 'put on Jesus Christ our Lord', and this is evidence that 'Jesus Christ' was originally a marginal note which was either substituted for *Lord* or inserted in one or other of the possible positions.

The word *and* that links the two clauses is omitted by D* and G, and this short hard reading seems preferable. Finally, the awkward words at the end, *to gratify its desires*, are omitted by one Latin manuscript (M), and seem to be an explanation of how devoting attention to the flesh is bad: in pandering to the flesh's desires.

The shorter text consists of two equal and parallel lines, each of ten syllables. There is no direct connection between this saying and the preceding one, since the word *but* at the beginning is a common device to strengthen a command.

The first line is a very bold image, which would not be quite at home in Judaism. The nearest parallel in Jewish writings is in the Odes of Solomon 33.12, where Wisdom personified as a Virgin says, 'I am your judge; and they who have put me on shall not be injured . . .' Greek religious writings, however, were more accustomed to speaking of men as 'god-bearing', and the saying was probably informed by this sort of imagery. Paul has already adopted it for baptism in Gal. 3.27, but here it is more directly a moral clothing oneself with the Lord that is in question.

The saying was probably originally Jewish. When it was incorporated into a Christian context, everyone would assume that the Lord was the Lord Jesus Christ, but the textual tradition suggests that this was only made explicit by a marginal gloss rather late in the history of transmission.

The contrast is between clothing oneself with the Lord, living entirely with mind fixed on him, and living for the flesh, the outward senses. The whole of mysticism depends on this contrast.

14.1–23

14 *As for the man who is weak in faith, welcome him, but not for disputes over opinions.* [2] *One believes he may eat anything, while the weak man eats only vegetables.* [3] *Let not him who eats despise him who abstains, and let not him who abstains pass judgment on him who eats; for God has welcomed him.* [4] *Who are you to pass judgment on the servant of another? It is before his own master that he stands or falls. And he will be upheld, for the Master is able to make him stand.*

[5] *One man esteems one day as better than another, while another man esteems all days alike. Let every one be fully convinced in his own mind.* [6] *He who observes the day, observes it in honour of the Lord. He also who eats, eats in honour of the Lord, since he gives thanks to God; while he who abstains, abstains in honour of the Lord and gives thanks to God.* [7] *None of us lives to himself, and none of us dies to himself.* [8] *If we live, we live to the Lord, and if we die, we die to the Lord; so then, whether we live or whether we die, we are the Lord's.* [9] *For to this end Christ died and lived again, that he might be Lord both of the dead and of the living.*

[10] *Why do you pass judgment on your brother? Or you, why do you despise your brother? For we shall all stand before the judgment seat of God;* [11] *for it is written,*

'As I live, says the Lord, every knee shall bow to me,
and every tongue shall give praise" to God.'
[12] *So each of us shall give account of himself to God.*

[13] *Then let us no more pass judgment on one another, but rather decide never to put a stumbling block or hindrance in the way of a brother.* [14] *I know and am persuaded in the Lord Jesus that nothing is unclean in itself; but it is unclean for any one who thinks it unclean.* [15] *If your brother is being injured by what you eat, you are no longer walking in love. Do not let what you eat cause the ruin of one for whom Christ died.* [16] *So do not let what is good to you be spoken of as evil.* [17] *For the kingdom of God does not mean food and drink but righteousness and peace and joy in the Holy Spirit;* [18] *he who thus*

*serves Christ is acceptable to God and approved by men. ¹⁹Let us then pursue
what makes for peace and for mutual upbuilding. ²⁰Do not, for the sake of
food, destroy the work of God. Everything is indeed clean, but it is wrong for
any one to make others fall by what he eats; ²¹it is right not to eat meat or
drink wine or do anything that makes your brother stumble.^v ²²The faith
that you have, keep between yourself and God; happy is he who has no
reason to judge himself for what he approves. ²³But he who has doubts is
condemned, if he eats, because he does not act from faith; for whatever does
not proceed from faith is sin.^w*

^u Or *confess.*
^v Other ancient authorities add *or be upset or be weakened.*
^w Other authorities, some ancient, insert here Ch. 16.25–27.

A Christian teacher has collected together a great number of wise
sayings about how stronger members of the community should deal
with those other members who were weighed down with scruples.
The scruples are mainly about food and drink, although scruples
about special days are also mentioned (vv. 5, 6a), and some of the
sayings are quite general in application.

The situation in which the collection was made is hard to describe,
because the sayings themselves were probably almost all traditional
pieces of wisdom by the time they were collected: the content of the
individual sayings is quite general and timeless, even though the
occasion of the collection may have been particular.

Negatively, however, we can be pretty sure that the collection of
sayings was not made by Paul and does not apply to his day. It is unlikely that Paul should have discussed the observance of food tabus or
tabus about certain days without explicitly mentioning the crucial
difficulties that Jewish Christians had to face so long as they counted
themselves, and were counted by their fellow Jews, as members of
Israel.

Paul's own position would have been that the Jewish Christian
congregations should continue to observe the Law, and that the
Gentile Christian congregations were not bound to observe the Law
in these respects. Paul reproached Cephas (Peter) in Antioch (Gal.
2.11–21) not because he was continuing to live like a Jew but because
he had, by changing his perfectly permissible custom of eating with

Gentiles, suggested that Gentile Christians were bound to assume the yoke of Jewish food laws. In Paul's eyes, Cephas was perfectly free to go on as a Jew, so long as he never suggested that Gentile Christians had to follow him.

Romans 14, on the other hand, assumes a unified Church made up of people with scruples about food, drink, and days, and people who were free of such scruples. The sayings are addressed to the strong, those without scruples, to urge them to respect the difficulties of the weak. The strong are even to adopt the scruples of the weak, if that will help the weak to remain within the fellowship and prevent them from being scandalized. In other words, the initiative now lies with the strong; and the weak – who may even be Gentiles, although more probably Jews – are to be dealt with in a kind and charitable way in case they be lost.

The situation is different from Paul's, and the remedy is consequently also different. The source of the remedy is not so much the Old Testament or the wisdom of Israel but the practical wisdom of the Graeco-Roman world which had been hammered out in efforts to help diverse factions in city-state and empire to live together in harmony and peace for the common good.

The collection has an immediate purpose of helping a community divided by sharply different customs to live in harmony and peace, but time and time again we find that the sayings now turned to this purpose originally had a wider aim. They are mostly drawn from Stoic ethics, the main theme of which is to enable wise men to live self-contained lives, unshaken in their inner moral purposes, and determined to be unmoved by outward fortune or misfortune. The collector of the sayings obviously sympathized with this ideal, but his purpose was to make the rather lonely and isolated Stoic into a useful member of the community, not despising men less enlightened than himself, but doing everything possible to make the community harmonious and peaceful.

Chapter 14 seems once to have been a self-contained unit. It is devoted to one theme, and the twenty-two aphorisms that make up the chapter, whatever their original scope and purpose, are now pressed into service and marshalled into line for that one specific duty, the promotion of toleration and peace within a divided community.

Certainly Chapter 15 starts with sayings designed to serve the same purpose, but they are much less tidy, and soon the chapter moves on to other themes in the manner with which we are familiar from Chapter 12 and Chapter 13.8–14. I conclude, therefore, that Chapter 14 was once an independent collection, added to *Romans*, like 13.1–7, when 12, 13.8–14, and 15.1–13 were already firmly part of the epistle.

The chapter ends, according to many manuscripts, with the doxology usually printed as Romans 16.25–27 (L, Ψ, 614, 1984, etc.). This is further evidence that Chapter 14 was added to *Romans* as an insertion rather late in the history of the development of the book, after the section 12, 13.8–14, and 15.1–13. The addition of Chapter 14 before the similar part of the earlier collection, 15.1–13, possibly left a space at the end of a codex sheet when the floating doxology could be conveniently copied, since 15.13 and 15.33 already were doxologies, and would not so easily accommodate such an addition. That, at least, is a possible theory to explain the evidence. (See 16.25–27 for a fuller discussion.)

Chapter 14 is, then, a collection of aphorisms, many of Stoic origin, which has been carefully designed to serve the one purpose of uniting a Church divided between those who abstained from various food or drink, or regarded certain days as propitious, and those who regarded all such practices as mere superstition.

14.1

> Assist the man who is weak in faith,
> Doing nothing to arouse hesitations over doubtful matters.

The usual translations of this verse make it appear that the man weak in faith is a newcomer or stranger who must be taken in and welcomed, but not in order to get him involved in disputes about his erroneous opinions. Nowhere else in the passage, however, is it suggested that the weak are newcomers; if anything, they are long-standing members of the Church who are in danger of being driven out. Furthermore, the great danger to be guarded against, according to all the other sayings in the collection, is not so much disputation over opinions as the sort of shock and horror in the offended weaker brothers that would lead them to walk out of the community altogether.

It seems better, therefore, to adopt a translation more like the one given at the head of this note. The verb 'welcome' also has the perfectly ordinary sense of 'assist', and the *disputes over opinions* can just as well be 'waverings over doubts' (cf. 4.20 for the cognate verb in the sense of 'to waver') (Lipsius).

The saying is aphoristic in form, and does not lead on in thought to the next verse.

Faith here is religious faith in general, the virtue of those who are so strong and self-confident in their faith that they are not troubled by scruples and tabus.

The saying was possibly current in Hellenistic philosophical circles; it can be paralleled by other similar sayings that advise philosophers, who can see through the cruder materialistic superstitions of ordinary pious folk, not to upset their beliefs, but rather to help them to hold on to the religious values enshrined in the outward customs.

14.2, 3

> One man confidently eats everything,
> Another man eats only vegetables:
> Let not him who eats despise him who does not eat,
> Nor let him who does not eat condemn him who eats;
> For God accepts him.

The last line probably does not refer just to the man who eats anything, but to both sorts of men; God accepts each. The saying as a whole is designed to promote tolerance in the community, by cutting at the root of divisiveness: contempt for the vegetarian by the man without fear, and condemnation of the man who eats anything by the one who denies himself.

We have no way of identifying the vegetarians. The Orphics, devotees of the cult of Dionysus, Pythagoreans and Neo-Pythagoreans, and many others who followed Hellenistic mystery religions were vegetarians, and in Judaism the Therapeutae described by Philo (*Contemplative Life* 37), James the Just, the brother of the Lord (Hegesippus in Eusebius, *Ecclesiastical History* ii.23.5) and possibly whole groups of others were also vegetarians.

This isolated saying gives us no positive clue to its specific application. It owes its place in the collection to its general theme, and to the fact that it employs the same verb 'to accept' as v. 1, although with a quite different reference.

14.4

> Who are you to condemn someone else's servant? Whether he stands or falls depends on his own master alone. He will stand, for his master is able to make him stand.

This saying was originally coined in a situation where many gods were worshipped and many cults were possible within the one set of myths. The devotee of one god should not condemn the devotee of another for his strange practices. Each god had power to protect his own follower, and someone outside that cult should leave the members of the cult to the protection of their own god.

In a Jewish and Christian setting the saying has to be interpreted rather differently. There is only one Lord, and each believer stands in a unique relationship to the Lord and must not be condemned by another believer for the form which his devotion takes.

14.5

> One man thinks one day is different from another;
> One man regards all days alike:
> Let each be absolutely convinced he is right in his own mind.

This saying could scarcely have come originally from a Jewish or Christian setting. It did not refer to the Sabbath or the Christian Sunday or to festival days; it referred rather to astrological superstitions about lucky and unlucky days. The extraordinary thing is that these superstitions are not condemned; rather, those who hold the superstition and those who do not are both told to act with full unwavering conviction. Plainly the author of the saying is a philosopher who stands above the conflict, and values simplicity and sincerity of purpose above argument about the content of religion.

The saying gains its position because of the verb 'to judge', but there is no real connection between the judging in v. 3 or v. 4 and the judging in v. 5.

14.6b

> He who eats, eats thinking of the Lord
> Because he gives God thanks,
> And he who does not eat certain foods also eats thinking of
>   the Lord
> Because he too gives God thanks.

The first part of v. 6, 'He who observes a day, observes it for the Lord', was probably an early gloss designed to link v. 5 with the self-contained saying translated at the head of this note.

The saying without the gloss is perfectly regular and balanced. It is a Jewish version of the principle contained in the previous non-Jewish sayings. Jews (and Christians) say grace at all meals, giving thanks to God the Creator and Sustainer of the world, from whose goodness they receive life and enjoy food. Whatever food regulations they observe, they are united in giving thanks to the Creator, and therefore are united in the all-important respect.

14.7, 8

> Indeed none of us lives for himself,
>   And none dies for himself.
> If we live
>   we live for the Lord;
> If we die
>   we die for the Lord.
> Whether we live
>   or whether we die
>   We are the Lord's.

This is a beautiful poem of resignation to God. Whatever happens, life or death, we belong to him. The spirit is rather more Stoic than Jewish or Christian, although one should not be too dogmatic about the distinction between the two attitudes to death. Paul in Romans 8 regards death rather differently, as the enemy whose ravages are to be reversed by the glorious resurrection of the body. Philippians 1 comes closer in tone to this saying (e.g. v. 21, *For me to live is Christ, and to die is gain*), but perhaps Philippians is not directly from Paul.

Parallels are hard to find in Jewish and Christian writings, but they are common in Greek philosophical and religious works, beginning from Plato's account of Socrates' address to the judges who condemned him: 'no evil can come to a good man in life or death . . . he is not forgotten by God'; 'now the time is come to go away, you to live and I to die, but which to the better destiny is known only to God' (*Apology* 41D, 42).

14.9

> This is why Christ died and lived:
> To be Lord of both the dead and the living.

It is hard to tell whether this saying is as profound as it looks or not. In general it states that Christ's death and resurrection make him rule over both those who are dead and those who are alive. But when we come to any particular relation between Christ's death and his resurrection and the lot of the dead and the living, the saying offers no specific direction to our thoughts.

The verb that refers to Christ's resurrection is the ordinary verb 'to live', which is most unusual. It was probably adopted in order to provide an exact parallel for the participle 'the living' in line 2, but its strangeness has led to a number of textual variants, all of which arise because of the marginal addition of the usual word for 'he rose'.

14.10

> You here: why do you condemn your brother?
> Or you there: why do you despise your brother?
> We shall all stand before the judgement seat of God.

The form of this saying is the familiar form of diatribe, question and answer adopted in order to involve the reader in a living consideration of the problem. Dissension in any brotherhood arises either from disparagement of one another or from condemnation of one another (cf. v. 3 above). But all such imperfect judgements are beside the point, since final judgement lies with God. A man should fix his attention there, and stop weighing and judging his brother's behaviour.

The saying probably arose in Hellenistic Judaism. The idea that only God is competent in the end to weigh men's deeds is common in both Greek philosophy and religion and in Judaism, but it is Judaism's particular contribution that there will come a day when all men have to stand before the seat of judgement to give account of their lives.

The theme is, of course, prominent in the teaching of Jesus, but there is no trace of evidence that this verse is directly derived from that source. The present form was probably originally older than the time of Jesus.

14.11, 12

> Now it is written:
> As I live, says the Lord, every knee shall bow to me
> And every tongue confess to God.
> So each of us must give account of himself.

The scriptural quotation is from Is. 45.23 with an introduction, 'As I live, says the Lord' from Is. 49.18 etc. The verb I have translated 'confess' in its original context probably means either sware allegiance or sing praise, but the author of this saying, whose comment appears in v. 12, takes it in a more usual Greek sense to mean to confess fully what one has done. The saying, therefore, arose in Greek-speaking Judaism.

14.13

> So let us no longer judge one another,
> But rather adjudge this to be the proper course of action:
> Not to put any obstacle in a brother's path, or stumbling-block.

This aphorism makes play with the verb 'to judge'. In Greek this verb can mean either to judge and condemn or to judge something to be right. The advice in line 3 comes back to the general theme of the whole collection: care for the brother's spiritual progress is far more important than carping criticism and condemnation of his foibles or superstitions.

14.14

> I know and am persuaded by the Lord
> That nothing is intrinsically common.

Except:
> To him who counts anything common
> To such a man it *is* common.

The word 'common' in Jewish circles meant ceremonially unclean, not to be touched or eaten by a man who would keep himself pure in the Lord's eyes. 'Common' was also used in ordinary Greek to mean despicable, although this usage was pretty rare. It seems best to take this saying, then, as referring to food declared unclean in the Old Testament.

The phrase translated literally by the RSV as *in the Lord Jesus* is a quite usual way to express agent and has no special sense of the incorporation of the one who believes and is persuaded into the Lord Jesus: 'I am persuaded by the Lord Jesus'. The reference is to the saying of Jesus, Mark 7.14–23; Matt. 15.10–20 (Jülicher, Zahn, Lagrange). The word 'Jesus' should perhaps be omitted, with the Ambrosiaster, but the omission makes no difference to the sense.

I have set the second part of the verse rather differently from the first, because it seems to be making a rather different point, and to be written in a rather different style. The point is not about intrinsic or inherent uncleanness but about how the subjective attitude of a man makes things clean or unclean. If someone can't bear to touch something for fear of defilement it is for him unclean. The teaching of Jesus, on the other hand, seeks to convince people that however unclean they may fear some food to be it is not really unclean at all. Jesus's teaching is designed to free men from fear; the second half of the verse is designed to make men who have no fear of uncleanness respect the scruples of those who have such fear. I suspect that two sayings, once distinct, have been put together.

14.15, 16

> Now if your brother is distressed through food
> You are no longer walking lovingly;
> Do not by your food destroy him
> For whom Christ died.

The teaching here is found at greater length in 1 Cor. 8.7–13. The issue there is not one of clean and unclean food but of food which has been used for pagan sacrifice. A Jew or Christian, who believed the pagan deities did not exist and knew that nothing happened to food and drink employed in pagan ritual, might well decide to ask no questions about the food he bought in the market or the food he was offered by an unbelieving friend. But another Jew or Christian might well believe that the pagan deities existed, existed as malevolent demons which had the power to contaminate the food offered to them and so to attack the pure. These Jews or Christians might be deeply upset to see fellow-believers rashly eating and drinking what could well hurt them and the whole community.

The advice both here and in 1 Cor. 8 is that, although the man who eats food offered in pagan ceremonies will take no harm, he should abstain if his action should so distress the scrupulous fellow-believer that he destroys his mental balance and peace.

The word 'destroy' can also mean 'kill', although it is used here metaphorically. However, the image suggested to the author, or to a later glossator, that the attitude of the heartless believer who went on eating food that caused such distress to his brother was in stark contrast to the attitude of Jesus, who died for his brothers and did not stand on his own rights.

14.16

Never let your good be ill spoken of.

This is a general proverb added to the collection at this point as a summary of the specific advice just given.

The aphorism originally belonged to the common stock of sayings on one side of the debate about whether the wise man should take any notice of what the world thought of his actions.

Plato's Socrates advised Crito to take no notice of what *hoi polloi* said of his actions, but only of the verdict of the rare man who could distinguish right and wrong, and the verdict of Truth herself (48A). This was the tradition followed by the Stoics, represented notably, at the time of the collection we are considering, by the philosopher-emperor Marcus Aurelius (iii.4 etc.).

Against such disdain for the opinion of others may be set the criticism of Cicero (*on Duty* i.99) and of Tacitus: 'By contempt of fame, virtue is treated with contempt' (*Annals* iv.38).

The aphorism in *Romans* neatly makes the same point, and it is futile to speculate about what specific good is being referred to. The saying is clearly distinct from v. 15 because the second person pronoun is plural, not singular.

14.17

> Now the Kingdom of God is not eating and drinking
> But righteousness and peace and joy in spirit.

The point of this aphorism is that disputes about eating and drinking, whether some food or drink is forbidden or not, miss the central fact about membership of the Kingdom of God. Those who are members of the Kingdom are members because they share the spiritual blessings of the Kingdom and live righteously, peaceably, and joyfully, and not because they have made a fuss, one way or the other, about food and drink.

I suspect that originally the word *Holy* was not in the text; its addition would be natural enough, but actually it partially obscures the point, that the Kingdom is spiritual and not material in nature.

14.18

> He who is pleasing to God
> Is also respected by men.

I have tentatively reconstructed here what I think was the original form of this saying. The message would have been much the same as the message in v. 16.

The original saying was subsequently glossed, either before or after it had been incorporated into our collection, to make it more specifically Christian: the man who follows all the precepts laid down and so serves Christ will please both God and men.

14.19

> Let us then pursue what makes for peace
> And for the strengthening of our common life.

The aphorism is a perfect couplet which recommends peace and a

strong common life as the highest goal. The image for the common
life together is the building; hence our word 'edification', the giving
of one another the sort of help and advice that builds us up as a good
community (a word that has become a little debased in ordinary use).

14.20a

> Do not destroy God's work because of food.

The aphorism reflects the situation already described in the comment
on vv. 15 and 17. 'God's work' here is probably the community.

14.20b

> All things are clean, but it is wrong for a man to eat if in
> eating he offends others.

This saying repeats the point already made in vv. 13, 14a, 15, 17 and
19 that no one has a right to disregard the scruples of fellow-members
of the community, even although those scruples and fears are ground-
less.

14.21

> It is not good to eat flesh or drink wine or do anything to
> which your brother takes offence.

This is the extreme statement of the principle that, for the sake of the
community, the enlightened member must observe all the tabus of
less-enlightened members.

We cannot deduce from the saying that there existed a group within the community who abstained from both meat and wine, for the
wording is meant to be all-embracing rather than specific; whatever
the tabu, the enlightened must respect it.

This aphorism, taken literally, represents a sort of philosophical
temper that is far from the vigour and openness of the Jewish and
Christian ideal. Jewish and Christian communities were not afraid of
argument about tabus, and could find room for great variety of
practice. As long ago as the prophet Jeremiah the Rechabites were
tolerated and admired for their rejection of wine and houses and the
luxuries of city life without other Jews feeling obliged to follow their
example in daily life (see Jeremiah 35).

14.22a

> The faith that you have
> Keep to yourself.

This saying does not, of course, refer to Christian faith, but to faith in the sense of the key characteristic of a man who has turned away from external things to cultivate and perfect his own moral purpose (Epictetus, *Discourses* i.4.18). A faithful man no longer cares what other people say about him (for the opposite idea, cf. v. 16 above), but devotes himself to developing the most perfect part of himself 'in which faith, self-respect, truth, law, a good divinity come into being' (Marcus Aurelius, *Meditations* x.13). The rule such a man must observe is, 'Guard your own good in everything' (Epictetus, *Discourses* iv.3.11), and this is the rule recommended in Romans 14.22, 'The faith that you have, Keep to yourself'.

An early scribe or commentator thought that the reference of such faith to God, whose faithfulness man should imitate, was called for (Epictetus *Discourses* ii.14.11–13) and added the gloss 'before God'. The words do not appear in ℵ*, 1927, Chrysostom, and should be omitted.

The saying represents a central idea in Stoic ethics. The reason it was incorporated into this Christian collection, however, was not because of its wider meaning, but because it could apply to the narrower issue of the behaviour of free and independent men towards other members of the community who were bound by tabus and superstitions. The wise man should keep his faith to himself, meaning that he should condescend to observe other men's tabus for the sake of peace and harmony in the community, hiding his own strength and freedom.

14.22b

> Happy is he who does not feel anxious about what he has come to the conclusion is right.

Epictetus, *Discourses* ii.13, has a long chapter on anxiety, urging the wise man not to be anxious or diffident about his own words and actions. 'When I see a man in anxiety, I say to myself, What can it be that this fellow wants? For if he did not want something that was outside of his control, how could he still remain in anxiety?' (translated by W. A. Oldfather, Loeb Classical Library).

The saying in *Romans* was originally meant to carry exactly the same message. What is under a man's own control, the rightness and wrongness of his own actions, should be decided on and acted on without self-doubt or hesitation.

In the context of the Christian collection, the saying was probably meant to warn the self-confident free man not to do anything which could merit censure because of its bad effects on community life; he himself might be quite certain he is right to act in a certain way, but he must also remember the wider consequences of his action. 'Happy is the man who will not have reason to condemn himself for doing what he himself approves.'

14.23

> The man who eats, doubting whether to eat, is condemned,
> for he acts not with conviction, for:
>> Everything that does not spring from faith
>> Misses the mark.

This, the concluding saying in the collection, is the only one directed to the man with scruples. He is counselled not to try to act against his instinctive convictions, because the most important thing about behaviour is its inner certainty and direction.

Again a precept of Stoic ethics is cited (the couplet at the end of the verse) to support a narrower application, although originally it had a wider and rather different purpose. Originally the aphorism was a call to the wise man to be true to himself and otherwise indifferent; he settled the principles of his actions within himself, resolving not to seek or avoid anything external which lay outside his own control, and then, in everything he did, he acted as a faithful, self-respecting man: got up, washed, ate, and lived (Epictetus, *Discourses* i.4.18–21).

In the present setting the principle of inner direction is applied not to the strong, independent man, but to the weak and wavering man. He should not try to live beyond his scruples. The assumption behind this advice is that the community will be strong and harmonious if the independent spirits hide their independence and observe the customs of the less free and enlightened, and if the less free and enlightened don't struggle to act beyond their psychic strength. Stoic ethics are made communal and the divisive elite is tamed and made to contribute to the harmonious corporate life of the community.

15.1–13

15.1

15 *We who are strong ought to bear with the failings of the weak, and not to please ourselves;*

> We who are able should bear the weaknesses of the unable
> and not please ourselves.

This saying gave occasion for the insertion of Chapter 14, which has a clear and definite notion of who are strong and who are weak, but there is no such clear picture present here: those who are able are simply those who have strength at any particular time to carry the burdens of others. Those who are able to help one day may themselves be in need of help the next. Cf. Gal. 6.2: *Bear one another's burdens.*

15.2

²*let each of us please his neighbour for his good, to edify him.*

> Let each of us
> Please his neighbour:
> For good,
> To build him up.

The last two lines are meant to qualify strictly the force of 'please' in line 2. The duty of pleasing a neighbour is not the duty of gratifying his every whim, but rather the duty of waking and satisfying his desire for true good and for growth in the moral life.

The saying is self-contained, and not part of a connected argument running from v. 1 to v. 3.

15.3

³*For Christ did not please himself; but, as it is written, 'The reproaches of those who reproached thee fell on me.'*

> Now Christ did not please himself,
> But, as it is written,
> The reproaches of those who reproach you
> Have fallen on me.

If this saying is related strictly to the context provided by v. 2, we should probably have to conclude that the 'you' in the citation from Psalm 69.9 has been taken to refer to the neighbour, not to God, as in the original setting (Lietzmann). But this is such an unlikely twisting of the Psalm that I prefer to say that v. 3 is an independent aphorism which was put in this context simply because of the verb 'to please', the word that has already brought together vv. 1 and 2.

The saying was originally a theological statement about the nature and dignity of the Messiah, showing the necessity of his suffering by reference to Old Testament scripture. Like a similar credal statement in Phil. 2.5–11, this has been cited in order to make a moral admonition for believers; just as Christ did not please himself, neither should we. But originally the saying was designed to point out that Christ had to suffer in order to fulfil the Old Testament prophecy that the Messiah must take on himself the reproaches men heap on God.

The statement was originally made by a Greek-speaking Christian. Not only is the citation taken from the LXX, but the arrangement of the words is quite regular, the lines as printed above containing 12, 7, 12, 7 syllables respectively in the Greek.

15.4

⁴*For whatever was written in former days was written for our instruction, that by steadfastness and by the encouragement of the scriptures we might have hope.*

> Now whatever was written beforehand
>   was written for our instruction
> In order that by patience and by the comfort of the scriptures
>   we might have hope.

The citation in v. 3 no doubt suggested to the compiler of the collection that here would be a good place to insert an old saying about the use of scripture, which also fitted in to the general theme of the collection.

Scripture is understood to refer not simply to the time when it was written but to future times. Jewish exegetes would expect to find everywhere in scripture, not just in the obvious places, directions about how to live, as well as prophecies about the coming of the Messiah.

The emphasis in this saying is on the moral teaching scripture provides, to enable the present generation to persevere in the good life in face of adversity. Notice that *all* that was written beforehand is said to be 'written for our instruction'. This conviction led sometimes to what we should regard as fantastic exegesis, which relied either on allegory or on far-fetched analogy for its point. But the results are sometimes moving and apposite, working by a poetic insight into the meaning of the old writings; v. 3 above is not at all a bad example of the method in action. Compare Rom. 4.23 f.; 1 Cor. 9.10; 10.11; 2 Tim. 3.16, for similar statements about the use of scripture.

15.5, 6

⁵*May the God of steadfastness and encouragement grant you to live in such harmony with one another, in accord with Christ Jesus, *⁶*that together you may with one voice glorify the God and Father of our Lord Jesus Christ.*

> May the God of patience and comfort give you grace to agree among yourselves according to the will of Christ Jesus; in order that united with one voice you may glorify God, Father of our Lord Jesus Christ.

This blessing came into the collection because of its description of God as 'the God of patience and comfort', which made it a natural sequel to the saying about scripture's working 'by patience and comfort' (v. 4). But there is no inner connection of thought, apart from the word-play, although the general theme of the collection, the need for unity and brotherly-love, makes the collection naturally hospitable to such a blessing.

The expression *God of steadfastness and encouragement* means God who is the source of patience and comfort. This way of speaking first rose in Hellenistic Judaism as a translation of a semitic idiom ('Blessed be the God of truth', 1 Esdras 4.40; 'God of the fathers and Lord of mercy', Wisdom of Solomon 9.1), and is found in the New Testament in 2 Cor. 1.3; Eph. 1.17 (cf. Acts 4.36).

The words *glorify the God and Father of our Lord Jesus Christ* can also be translated 'glorify God, Father of our Lord Jesus Christ' (Gifford). The same formula, drawn no doubt from the Church's liturgy, is also to be found in 2 Cor. 1.3; 11.31; Eph. 1.3; and 1 Peter 1.3 (cf. Col. 1.3). The RSV translation is possible (cf. Eph. 1.17: '*the God of our Lord Jesus Christ, the Father of glory*'), but in the present context God is assumed to be already clearly known, and the blessing asks that the congregation may now unite with one voice to praise him as 'Father of our Lord Jesus Christ'.

Father and Son are terms taken over from court usage, meaning the King and the Prince whom he enthrones at his right hand; they are used in the Old Testament and later Judaism for God and the Messiah (2 Sam. 7.14; 1 Chron. 17.13; Psalm 2.7; (Psalm 110.1 ff.); Qumran Manual of Discipline, Annexe (1QSa II. 11 f.); Qumran Florilegium (4QFlor)), and already Judaism had reckoned with the mystery of the unity of God and his Son (Philo, *On the Tilling of the Earth* (*De Agricultura*) 51: God, shepherd and king, rules (all parts of nature) according to order and law, appointing over them his right reason (*Logos*) and first-born Son, who is to receive charge of this sacred company as lieutenant of the great King).

15.7

7 *Welcome one another, therefore, as Christ has welcomed you, for the glory of God.*

> So receive one another
> As Christ himself received us
> For the glory of God.

Again there is no movement of thought from v. 6 to v. 7, or from v. 7 to v. 8, and yet all share the same theme of Christ's humble ministry and its beneficent effects.

This saying argues that an overriding concern for God's praise led Christ to welcome sinners into his company and should lead us also to be welcoming to each other and not critical of faults and failings.

Note the assumption behind the pronoun 'us' (the reading of B, D*, P, 1984, which I prefer, as harder, to the *you* found in ℵ, A, C, Ψ, 33, 1739). There is no elite among Christians; all need to be accepted by Christ despite their weaknesses, and all need both to accept one another and to be accepted by one another. This aphorism does not make the distinction between strong and weak Christians that dominates Chapter 14.

15.8

[8]*For I tell you that Christ became a servant to the circumcised to show God's truthfulness, in order to confirm the promises given to the patriarchs.*

> I tell you that Christ became a servant of circumcision
> To serve God's truth
> In order to confirm the promises made to the fathers.

A predominantly Gentile Church soon began to ask why the saviour had to be a Jew. The answer given in this aphorism is simply that God was the God of the Jews, and that his promises to the patriarchs had to be fulfilled. Provided the Church kept to the Old Testament, she was committed to God as spoken of in those pages, and he was a God who made promises for the future, which he would surely not break.

The saying arose at the time when gnostics in general and perhaps even the theologian Marcion in particular were questioning the place of the Old Testament in the Church, and were reluctant to allow Jewish Christians to go on observing their Jewish customs.

The grammatical form of this verse and the next is not such as to allow v. 9 to be read as a continuation of v. 8. They are separate sayings, put together because one talks about the Jews ('the circumcision') and the other about Gentiles. A further link is provided by the references to the glory of God (vv. 7 and 9) and the truth of God (v. 8).

Friedrich Spitta (*Zur Geschichte und Litteratur des Urchristentums. Dritter Band, erste Hälfte: Untersuchungen über den Brief des Paulus an die*

Römer, Göttingen, 1901) argued from the connection between the theme of 15.8 ff. and the end of Chapter 11 that the original *Romans* consisted of 1.1–11.36; 15.8–33; 16.21–27, and that this original *Romans* was enlarged by a second shorter letter, consisting of 12.1–15.7; 16.1–20. I agree that there is a surprising change of subject in Chapter 12, and that 15.8 ff. returns to the earlier theme of the Church and the Jews, but I see no tight connection in thought between 11.36 and 15.8. A better theory would seem to be the theory that a collection of aphorisms (12; 13.8–14; 15.1–13) was inserted into *Romans* after Chapters 1–11 partly because this collection, too, ended with a treatment of the place of Gentiles in a Church whose roots were in Judaism and the Old Testament.

15.9–12

⁹*and in order that the Gentiles might glorify God for his mercy. As it is written,*
  '*Therefore I will praise thee among the Gentiles,*
   and sing to thy name';
¹⁰*and again it is said,*
  '*Rejoice, O Gentiles, with his people*';
¹¹*and again,*
  '*Praise the Lord, all Gentiles,*
   and let all the peoples praise him';
¹²*and further Isaiah says,*
  '*The root of Jesse shall come,*
   he who rises to rule the Gentiles;
   in him shall the Gentiles hope.'

    Let the Gentiles glorify God for his mercy;
    As it is written:
        For this I shall praise you among the Gentiles,
        And I shall sing to your name;
    And again it says:
        Rejoice, Gentiles, with his people;
    And again:
        Praise the Lord, all Gentiles,
        And let all peoples lift praises to him;

And again Isaiah says:
> There will be a root of Jesse,
> And he will arise to rule the Gentiles;
> On him the Gentiles will set their hope.

This is a collection of proof-texts from the Old Testament to support the call to the Gentiles to glorify God which stands at the head of the catena. The verb in this opening call is an infinitive, but used to represent the imperative; it is necessary for the Gentiles to glorify God. The infinitive cannot be parallel to the infinitive in the clause *in order to confirm the promises*, v. 8, as the RSV takes it.

The first two proof texts (Psalm 18.49; Deut. 32.43) are cited in order to show that Jews will stand together with Gentiles in praising God; the third (Psalm 117.1) is a direct call to the Gentiles to praise the Lord; and the fourth (Is. 11.10) is a reminder that the Gentiles set their hope on the King who is Son of David. All the citations are taken from the LXX, with occasional slight variations, and the second and fourth differ markedly from the Hebrew.

If the strict meaning of the citations can be pressed, the man who chose them would seem to be a Jew who wishes to show that Jews and Gentiles are to unite in praising God: 'I shall praise you among the Gentiles', 'Rejoice, Gentiles, with his people'. If Jews are to be mingled with Gentiles in praising God, the Gentiles in turn are to recognize that the one who has arisen to rule them is 'the root of Jesse', the Davidic Messiah.

Paul himself can hardly have been responsible for this passage. He worked from the Hebrew text of the Old Testament, making his own Greek translation, and he wanted not so much the mingling of Jews and Gentiles in one Church as the recognition by the Jewish Christian synagogues of the Gentile congregations he was founding.

15.13

¹³*May the God of hope fill you with all joy and peace in believing, so that by the power of the Holy Spirit you may abound in hope.*

> May the God of hope fill you
> With all joy and peace in believing
> That you may abound in hope
> [Through the power of the Holy Spirit].

God is the source of hope, who is ready to give men the conditions for living hopefully. When he fills them with trust in his promises, which they accept with joy and serene confidence, then they will never despair in any difficulties or trials.

There is no manuscript evidence for omitting the last line, which I have bracketed off, but it does not seem to fit the tightly packed order of the first three lines, each of which contains 13 syllables. I suspect a commentator wished to explain that God helped men abound in hope by the power of the Holy Spirit: true, but not necessary to be said. Without the last line, the thought is beautifully arranged and complete. The third line balances the first, and the second line shows how the completion of which the first and third lines speak is accomplished.

This blessing was put here partly because of the key-word 'hope', which linked on to the end of the catena of quotations in vv. 9–12, and partly because it provided a fitting conclusion to the whole collection, which began with pleas for a similar transformation of life, 12.1 f.

15.14–33

[14]*I myself am satisfied about you, my brethren, that you yourselves are full of goodness, filled with all knowledge, and able to instruct one another.* [15]*But on some points I have written to you very boldly by way of reminder, because of the grace given me by God* [16]*to be a minister of Christ Jesus to the Gentiles in the priestly service of the gospel of God, so that the offering of the Gentiles may be acceptable, sanctified by the Holy Spirit.* [17]*In Christ Jesus, then, I have reason to be proud of my work for God.* [18]*For I will not venture to speak of anything except what Christ has wrought through me to win obedience from the Gentiles, by word and deed,* [19]*by the power of signs and wonders, by the power of the Holy Spirit, so that from Jerusalem and as far round as Illyr'icum I have fully preached the gospel of Christ,* [20]*thus making it my ambition to preach the gospel, not where Christ has already been named, lest I build on another man's foundation,* [21]*but as it is written,*

'They shall see who have never been told of him,
and they shall understand who have never heard of him.'

[22]*This is the reason why I have so often been hindered from coming to you.* [23]*But now, since I no longer have any room for work in these regions, and since I have longed for many years to come to you,* [24]*I hope to see you in passing as I go to Spain, and to be sped on my journey there by you, once I have enjoyed your company for a little.* [25]*At present, however, I am going to Jerusalem with aid for the saints.* [26]*For Macedon'ia and Acha'ia have been pleased to make some contribution for the poor among the saints at Jerusalem;* [27]*they were pleased to do it, and indeed they are in debt to them, for if the Gentiles have come to share in their spiritual blessings, they ought also to be of service to them in material blessings.* [28]*When therefore I have completed this, and have delivered to them what has been raised,ˣ I shall go on by way of you to Spain;* [29]*and I know that when I come to you I shall come in the fulness of the blessingʸ of Christ.*

[30]*I appeal to you, brethren, by our Lord Jesus Christ and by the love of the Spirit, to strive together with me in your prayers to God on my behalf,* [31]*that I may be delivered from the unbelievers in Judea, and that my service for*

Jerusalem may be acceptable to the saints, ³²so that by God's will I may come to you with joy and be refreshed in your company. ³³The God of peace be with you all. Amen.

ˣ Greek *sealed to them this fruit.*
ʸ Other ancient authorities insert *of the gospel.*

Paul's aim in writing to the Roman Christians has been not to instruct them, not to preach to them, but to remind them of his own special function of preaching to the Gentiles, and to win their prayers for his work.

His reason for not coming to them sooner, although he had long intended to make the journey, was that he had to complete the work of preaching assigned to him in the eastern Mediterranean. Now that his task there was completed, he was about to set out on a journey to Spain, calling at Rome on the way. First, however, he had to take to Jerusalem the money contributed by the Gentile Christians in Macedonia and Achaea for the relief of the poor Christians in Jerusalem.

He asks for the Romans' prayers that the gift would be acceptable and that he might not be hurt by those in Judaea, of which he had once been a supporter, who were hostile to Christianity in general and his work in particular. We know that this last prayer was not answered, although his prayer to come to Rome with joy by God's will was answered in an unexpected way. Paul was brought to Rome as a prisoner, there to die a martyr's death.

Paul's view of his work is that of a priest before God. The Gentiles who turn to God and believe the good news about the righteousness God requires are an offering to God which Paul presents. As priest, he is responsible for the purity of the offering, and if his boast is in the importance of his office, his care is only to act in response to the commission and continuing support of Christ himself. He is, then, both insisting on his right to go out to establish purely Gentile congregations, and assuring the Jewish Christian congregations in Rome that the Gentile congregations are the result of Christ's working, and are pure and acceptable to the Father.

I have put all the emphasis on the image of Paul as priest, responsible for the purity of the Gentile offering to God, and have made almost nothing of another feature of the passage which has aroused a great deal of discussion. Paul seems to be saying that his preaching in the eastern Mediterranean, *from Jerusalem and as far round as Illyricum* (v. 19), is complete: *I no longer have any room for work in these regions.* This assertion has been both dismissed as absurd and taken as the key to the understanding of Paul's missionary strategy. It is dismissed as absurd by Lipsius, who has followed the unusual course, for him, of deleting part of v. 19 (from *so that from Jerusalem* to the end), part of v. 20 and the first word of v. 21 (the words, *not where Christ has already been named, lest I build on another man's foundation, but*), and all of vv. 22–24, and of supposing that v. 28 ended *I shall go on* to you, instead of *I shall go on by way of you to Spain*. On the other hand, Johannes Munck sees in the geographical references the vital clue to Paul's work. Paul's view, according to Munck, was one of 'representative universalism', whereby the response of Gentiles in the chief towns represented the response of the Gentiles as a whole. Paul had set himself the task, or rather, God has set it for him, of gaining the necessary response from the Gentiles in preparation for the Second Coming of Christ. Paul believed that the Jews would not respond themselves until the Gentiles had believed; then the Jews, moved to jealousy, would also come in. The only disagreement he had with the Jerusalem leaders was over priorities, and at his memorable visit to Jerusalem recorded in Gal. 2 he had gained their support for his attempt, although they themselves preferred to persevere with their own direct efforts to convert the Jews.

So when Paul says in Romans 15.17–24 that his work is finished 'his meaning must be this: it was never his intention that every individual was to hear the Gospel and make a decision with regard to it; but all Gentile nations were to do so, and by deciding on their attitude to the Gospel in, say, Corinth, Ephesus, or Philippi, the people in question would decide to be for or against Christ' ('Israel and the Gentiles in the New Testament', *Journal of Theological Studies*, new series ii (1951), pp. 3–16 at p. 8; see also *Paul and the Salvation of Mankind*, London, 1959. The same point was made in 1904 by William Wrede in his little book, *Paulus*, Tübingen, pp. 31 f.

Munck seems to me to be right to point out that Paul had a distinct and separate strategy from that of the Jerusalem leaders. His strategy

was to go to the Gentiles and to establish purely Gentile congregations alongside synagogues that believed in Jesus Christ, whereas
theirs was to keep working at persuading synagogues that Jesus was
Messiah, with no particular concern for Gentiles except in so far as
they joined the synagogue.

But Munck's idea of 'representative universalism' seems to be
going beyond the evidence. Paul certainly moved on quickly once he
had established a new congregation, and he does seem to have en-
visaged the bold move westward of going to Spain to continue his
mission, but I do not think he was as clear about what completion
meant as Munck supposes.

As I argue in the notes, there is no need to press the translation of
v. 19, *I have fully preached the gospel of Christ*, to mean 'I have done all
the preaching that anyone needs to do', nor to press v. 23, which is
literally 'now I no longer having place in these regions', to mean
since I no longer have any room for work in these regions.

Paul is arguing for his divine commission to go straight to the
Gentiles, and is insisting that his results are good and pure, that the
Gentiles who believe really do attain the righteousness of God and are
an acceptable offering to him. I do not think Paul was concerned
about times and seasons, about when exactly Christ would return, the
dead be raised, and judgement completed. Nor was he working to
achieve certain conditions for that desired consummation. His only
call was to be obedient to his special mission, to do nothing *except
what Christ* had *wrought through* him (v. 18).

Although I do not wish to follow Munck completely, I think he
has pointed in the right direction. On the other hand, Lipsius's
attempt to eliminate all the geographical references seems to me quite
wrong. The very difficulties to which he draws attention – the idea of
Paul's starting from Jerusalem, the lack of evidence about a mission in
Illyricum, the complete absence of reliable evidence about Spain,
either in intention or in accomplishment – all seem to me to be indications of authenticity. No glossator would have fabricated such unknown movements and intentions.

Paul is writing to Jewish Christians in Rome to win their prayers
and their support for his particular mission to the Gentiles. This
passage, then, does provide an important key to the interpretation of

the Epistle to the Romans. Paul did have one urgent and specific purpose in writing to Rome and here it is, stated more clearly and explicitly than anywhere else. Because he had one such urgent purpose, that called out all his powers of theological exposition and argument, he wrote a letter which provided a secure foundation for the addition of a great deal of more general theological reflection by later theologians and editors, but when we know his purpose and hold it firmly in our mind we have a touchstone for distinguishing his work from the work of his successors. Not the only touchstone, for there are numerous other tests, tests of inconsistency, of difference in vocabulary and style, as well as other external indications provided by textual criticism, but this touchstone is the one test that applies in every case, and is relatively simple to use.

Paul is justifying himself to his own people for his work among the Gentiles. He argues, he pleads, he wrestles with objections, but he never apologizes, for he is proud of his office and sure of his faithful priestly service of the gospel.

Notes

14

With a *captatio benevolentiae*, Paul prepares the Jewish Christians in Rome for a succinct statement of the argument he does wish to press on them, the case he does want to win. Although it is a *captatio benevolentiae* it is not for that reason insincere. Paul does admire and praise their goodness, their grasp of the truth, and their ability to teach one another (or even 'others', if Origen's reading be right). He has written so strongly and persuasively in favour of his particular position partly because the Roman Churches are strong, powerful, and influential.

The fact that this concluding section of the epistle began with a glowing praise of the Romans' goodness provided just the opportunity for an editor to insert before the peroration his ethical collection, 12.1–15.13. Strictly speaking, if the Romans were so ethically skilled they would not need instruction, but the editor would draw just the opposite conclusion from this praise: he would conclude that other readers, when they read of the Romans' goodness and knowledge, had a right to know in detail the maxims of their moral existence.

15 f.

As the sentence stands, Paul's boldness in writing is meant to cover a multitude of subjects, with no one particular subject being mentioned, and the bulk of the sentence is given up to a statement of Paul's warrant for writing: *because of the grace given me by God to be a minister of Christ Jesus to the Gentiles* . . . This is a most unlikely line of argument. The praise of v. 14 is almost all taken back by the implication that they do need bold instruction, and the basis for this instruction is a long statement of Paul's special mission which, if the audience is indeed mostly Jewish, is beside the point. What we expect, and do not really get, is a second object for the verb 'to remind'; we need to be told of what he has written to remind them. Some commentators (e.g. Lipsius) make the clause *to be a minister of Christ Jesus* into an object and translate, 'I have written boldly . . . as reminding you . . . that I am a minister of Christ Jesus to the Gentiles', but I do not think the Greek will support this rendering, attractive as it is from the point of view of sense. The true solution seems to be that a scribe has destroyed the original meaning by inserting a familiar *because of* before the words *the grace given me by God* (v. 15). In fact the *because of* would normally take the genitive case, were this the original (cf. 12.3), but here it has to take the accusative case, which is grammatically possible but odd, simply because the original was a second accusative after the verb 'to remind'. The original sentence would have read, 'But I am writing to you so very boldly in part that I may remind you of the grace given me by God to be a priest of Christ Jesus, performing priestly service in preaching the gospel of God, so that the Gentiles' offering might be acceptable, sanctified by the Holy Spirit'.

There is no direct textual evidence for this conjecture, but the indirect evidence is quite strong. One early and important manuscript, P[46], repeats the preposition *because of* as the first word of v. 16, and this I take to be evidence that the preposition once stood as a marginal note, which one scribe, at least, took to be a substitute for the next similar preposition rather than as an addition higher up in his manuscript.

16

to the Gentiles: omitted by B, and probably rightly. The word *minister* can imply service to fellow men as well as the more strictly priestly service to God, but the emphasis at this stage of the sentence is on service to God. Because he is God's servant or priest, he has to exercise his *priestly service of the gospel of God* – his priestly work of preaching – in order to ensure that the Gentiles he presents to God as an offering are truly pure and holy.

17

In Christ Jesus, then, I have reason to be proud of my work for God: the phrase *in Christ Jesus* has a causal meaning: 'Because of Christ Jesus I can boast about my service to God' (Büchsel, *Zeitschrift für die neutestamentliche Wissenschaft*, 42 (1949), pp. 142 ff.; cf. 1 Cor. 15.31; Phil. 1.26).

18

For I will not venture to speak of anything: I suspect that the reference to boasting in v. 17 has led a scribe to insert an unnecessary infinitive, *to speak*, after the verb *I venture*. The infinitive itself is variously read, different in different manuscripts, and its position is unsure. If we omit it, we get a reference to what Paul has done, which is real ground for boasting, rather than a confused reference to what he will say. If we accept this conjecture and read the verb in the present tense, with B and other manuscripts, we get much better sense. 'For I do not dare anything except what Christ has wrought through me to win the Gentiles' obedience, by word and deed, by power of signs and miracles, by power of the Spirit . . .'

19

so that from Jerusalem and as far round as Illyricum I have fully preached the gospel of Christ: v. 23, which the RSV translates *since I no longer have any room for work in these regions*, points in the direction of taking the verb 'to fulfil' in v. 19 in a spatial sense, and vv. 20 and 21 seem to clinch the matter; Paul seems to be saying that the work he has done in the eastern Mediterranean has actually completed all the preaching that needed doing there. But this is absurd. If he really meant this, he could hardly have written to the Corinthians or the Galatians or the Thessalonians in expectation that more and more Gentiles would hear the gospel, respond to it, and join the Christian company. What he could well have meant was that his special function was complete in the area from Jerusalem round to Illyricum (roughly, present-day Yugoslavia, without the province of Macedonia), and this seems to be the simple and obvious force of v. 23. Verse 19, then, can hardly mean that the gospel of Christ has been fully preached in this area. The meaning must be that wherever Paul has preached, from Jerusalem round to Illyricum, he has properly fulfilled his duty as a preacher of Christ: the message he has delivered has been backed by Christ's authority, has been purely delivered, and has produced real purity in the Gentiles who have obeyed.

20 f.

Paul explains both why he has ranged so far as to go right to Illyricum and why he is about to set out on an even more ambitious journey to Spain. His aim always is to go where Christ has not *already been named*, that is, has not already been preached. It does seem, from the accounts we have in *Acts*, that Paul rarely, if ever, preached where Christ had already been named – Ephesus is the possible exception (Acts 19.1) – but the ambition to preach *not where Christ has already been named* would not rule out his preaching also where Christ had been named. He did hope to preach in Rome (1.15). But his great aim was to go where no other missionaries had been before, and to use one successful congregation as the springboard for mission into the regions beyond (cf. 2 Cor. 10.13–16). There is no need to press the meaning of the words in v. 19, *I have fully preached the gospel of Christ*, to mean that Paul thought there was no more preaching that needed to be done in the circuit from Jerusalem to Illyricum or to mean that *all* the towns where Christ was not named had been visited. Verse 23, as translated by the RSV, seems to suggest that Paul thought that he had visited every place where Christ had not been named, but the words *since I no longer have any room for work in these regions* mean rather 'since now I no longer have opportunity in these regions' and need imply nothing more than that he had done all that seemed possible at the time and that there was no urgent reason why he should make any more sorties into those parts. There is no suggestion that he feels impelled to complete a programme for visiting representative towns in every part of the known world. His aim is to go where no other missionaries had been before him, not to complete single-handed a grand plan upon which God's purposes for drawing history to a close would depend. Johannes Munck's theory depended very much on reading these verses in the light of the overall view of history presented in Chapter 11 but, as we have argued above, there are good reasons for ascribing Chapter 11 to a theologian writing long after Paul. Paul himself acted boldly to take the gospel to new areas where Christ had not been heard of before, but he left the out-. come of these efforts in the hands of God. His warrant was Is. 52.15 (according to the LXX, but the textual evidence suggests that possibly Paul's original was different from the LXX, and later scribes have changed the wording to conform to the familiar version). This is a clear case of Paul's taking an Old Testament passage about the Suffering Servant as a reference to Christ, and he may well have had the context of Isaiah 52 and 53 in mind (cf. Romans 4.24f.).

23 f.

. . . since . . . and since . . . I hope to see you in passing as I go to Spain:

the RSV has accepted an inferior text, that given in G (omitting the conjunction 'for' with *I hope*), in order to rescue the grammar of the sentence. I think that the rescue operation is unnecessary, and that there is no real difficulty in putting a full stop after Spain, and beginning a new sentence with the words 'For I hope, in passing through, to see you . . .' The previous sentence lacks a main verb (in the best manuscripts), but the main verb is perfectly obvious and it is grammatically correct to leave a verb unexpressed. A fairly literal translation, in which I add in brackets the words understood, would be: 'But now no longer having opportunity in these regions, and having the desire to come to you for many years, (I shall come at last) when I am going on my way to Spain'.

25–28

The collection for poor Christians in Jerusalem was always an important part of Paul's work. He had gladly accepted the obligation when in Jerusalem getting the approval of the 'pillar' authorities for his Gentile congregations (Gal. 2.10), and the collection is often mentioned in later epistles (1 Cor. 16.1–4; 2 Cor. 8; 9 etc.). Apart from sheer charity, this help to the poor saints in Jerusalem was a sign that Old Testament prophecy was being fulfilled, when the wealth of nations would be brought to Jerusalem in homage to Israel's God (Is. 60.5 etc.).

27

I find this explanation a little tame and pedestrian, and suspect a gloss, but can produce no final objection against the verse.

30–32

Paul asks for strenuous intercessory prayer. He has three requests he wants the Romans to join him in making to God: for safety from enemies in Judaea, for willing acceptance of the Gentiles' offerings by the Jerusalem believers, and for a happy outcome of his desire to visit Rome. According to *Acts*, and there is no reason to doubt the substantial accuracy of that account, the second prayer was granted, but the partial failure of the first led to the partial granting of the third; the success of Paul's enemies in Judaea led to his coming to Rome all right, but as a prisoner.

The last two words in v. 32, translated *and be refreshed in your company*, literally 'lie down and sleep with you', are omitted by P[46] and B, and are a gloss by a scribe who would refer to Paul's martyrdom in Rome. Sleep is a metaphor for death.

33

The simple blessing, *The God of peace be with you all*, has been supplemented in P⁴⁶ by the addition of 16.25–27.

Romans 16

16 I commend to you our sister Phoebe, a deaconess of the church at Cen'chre-ae, ²that you may receive her in the Lord as befits the saints, and help her in whatever she may require from you, for she has been a helper of many and of myself as well.

³Greet Prisca and Aquila, my fellow workers in Christ Jesus, ⁴who risked their necks for my life, to whom not only I but also all the churches of the Gentiles give thanks; ⁵greet also the church in their house. Greet my beloved Epae'netus, who was the first convert in Asia for Christ. ⁶Greet Mary, who has worked hard among you. ⁷Greet Androni'cus and Ju'nias, my kinsmen and my fellow prisoners; they are men of note among the apostles, and they were in Christ before me. ⁸Greet Amplia'tus, my beloved in the Lord. ⁹Greet Urba'nus, our fellow worker in Christ, and my beloved Stachys. ¹⁰Greet Apel'les, who is approved in Christ. Greet those who belong to the family of Aristobu'lus. ¹¹Greet my kinsman Hero'dion. Greet those in the Lord who belong to the family of Narcis'sus. ¹²Greet those workers in the Lord, Tryphae'na and Trypho'sa. Greet the beloved Persis, who has worked hard in the Lord. ¹³Greet Rufus, eminent in the Lord, also his mother and mine. ¹⁴Greet Asyn'critus, Phlegon, Hermes, Pat'robas, Hermas, and the brethren who are with them. ¹⁵Greet Philol'ogus, Julia, Nereus and his sister, and Olym'pas, and all the saints who are with them. ¹⁶Greet one another with a holy kiss. All the churches of Christ greet you.

¹⁷I appeal to you, brethren, to take note of those who create dissensions and difficulties, in opposition to the doctrine which you have been taught; avoid them. ¹⁸For such persons do not serve our Lord Christ, but their own appetites,* and by fair and flattering words they deceive the hearts of the simpleminded. ¹⁹For while your obedience is known to all, so that I rejoice over you, I would have you wise as to what is good and guileless as to what is evil; ²⁰then the God of peace will soon crush Satan under your feet. The grace of our Lord Jesus Christ be with you.ᵃ

²¹Timothy, my fellow worker, greets you; so do Lucius and Jason and Sosip'ater, my kinsmen.

²²*I Tertius, the writer of this letter, greet you in the Lord.*
²³*Ga'ius, who is host to me and to the whole church, greets you. Eras'tus, the city treasurer, and our brother Quartus, greet you.*^b

²⁵*Now to him who is able to strengthen you according to my gospel and the preaching of Jesus Christ, according to the revelation of the mystery which was kept secret for long ages* ²⁶*but is now disclosed and through the prophetic writings is made known to all nations, according to the command of the eternal God, to bring about the obedience of faith –* ²⁷*to the only wise God be glory for evermore through Jesus Christ! Amen.*

^z Greek *their own belly* (Phil. 3.19).
^a Other ancient authorities omit this sentence.
^b Other ancient authorities insert verse 24, *The grace of our Lord Jesus Christ be with you all. Amen.*

Paul ends with a recommendation of Phoebe on her visit to Rome (vv. 1 f.); a series of greetings to those at Rome he knows, beginning with Prisca and Aquila (vv. 3–16a); and a list of people who wish their greetings to be united with Paul's (vv. 21–23).

In addition to this material, there are two pieces that sit awkwardly in the text, and are probably later additions.

The first is vv. 16b–20, from *All the churches of Christ greet you* to *The grace of our Lord Jesus Christ be with you.* This is a warning against heresy. The heresy is hard to define exactly, but its general features are a challenge to accepted orthodox teaching, an emphasis on the importance of food tabus (which seems to be the meaning of the charge that they do not serve our Lord Christ but rather their own belly, v. 18), a smooth line of talk, and an indifference to morality. The language and tone of the passage do not seem at all like the language and tone of Paul, and we especially miss any theological argument. Those commentators who insist that Paul wrote these verses have to suppose a sudden and violent change of mood in Paul, which is immediately succeeded by the old tone in vv. 21 ff. It is easier to suppose that an editor has inserted an old letter, which begins *All the churches of Christ greet you,* just before the final list of greetings in the original *Romans* beginning, *Timothy, my fellow worker, greets you . . .*

The second foreign body is vv. 25–27, the doxology. This is entirely omitted from *Romans* by Marcion and some manuscripts; it appears at the end of Chapter 14 in others; both at the end of Chapter 14 and at the end of Chapter 16 in yet others; at the end of Chapter 15 alone in P⁴⁶; and at the end of Chapter 16 alone in the best manuscripts (for details, see the Notes). Very many commentators now agree that Paul was not the author, and the discussion centres on what its position tells us about the original contents of *Romans*. Did *Romans* once end at Chapter 14, or at Chapter 15? Is Chapter 16 a part of *Romans*, or was it originally addressed by Paul to Ephesus?

The theory that Chapter 16 was first written to Ephesus and then, by mistake, added to *Romans* was first put forward in 1829 by David Schulz (1779–1854), and was later advocated by Lipsius (for vv. 1–20), Jülicher, and Feine. One of their arguments was the sharp tone of vv. 17–20, scarcely to be expected from Paul in a letter to an unknown congregation. The other arguments were the general unlikelihood of Paul's knowing so many people in a congregation he had never visited, and, more specifically, the unlikelihood that Prisca and Aquila, who had been expelled from Rome under an edict of the Emperor Claudius, who had settled in Corinth and moved to Ephesus, should again be settled in Rome with their house again open to a house-church (Acts 18; 1 Cor. 16.19; 2 Tim. 4.19).

The first argument, about the sharp tone of vv. 17–20, disappears if this section be an interpolation. The second and third arguments are more weighty, but not insuperable. Lietzmann lightens the second by pointing out that Paul did not have to know all these people intimately in order to send greetings; indeed, the plethora of greetings, not found in the other epistles, may indicate precisely that he did not know the Church well, and wished to make the most of every possible contact (Zahn).

Finally, Lietzmann seems to me to dispose of the third argument by pointing out that a rich Jewish merchant could possibly have retained his business in Rome under a slave as agent, and returned there on Claudius's death in A.D. 54, when the edict against him would lapse.

A self-contained letter of greeting, even with the argument of vv.

17–20 included, is hard to imagine as written to Ephesus or anywhere else. The simplest solution is to accept vv. 1–16a and 21–23 as the original ending to *Romans*.

The doxology does not so much indicate that *Romans* once ended elsewhere than at 16.23 as that editors were eager to use a splendid liturgical doxology somewhere at the close of *Romans*. They either put it last, or inserted it where there was a space (the end of Chapter 14), or where a blessing seemed to offer scope for a doxology as well (the end of Chapter 15).

The original Chapter 16, as Paul wrote it, is a reminder of the great movement of people from all parts of the Empire into Rome, of the diversity of races and background of the Christians who came there, and of the potential importance of Rome, even in those early days, for the life of the Church.

Notes

1

our sister Phoebe, a deaconess of the church at Cenchreae: sister means fellow-Christian. The term 'Christian' had probably not yet been invented, and 'Church' was still a word confined to a local congregation (as here) and could not be used to describe Christians in general in the way we say 'member of the Church'. The fundamental fact about being a Christian or being a member of the Church was that one spoke to God as Father and so belonged to the brother– and sisterhood that was devoted to the Lord Jesus.

Deaconess is probably the right translation here, although the word could simply mean 'servant', 'helper'. Just as *sister* refers to a life-long status, so does *deaconess*. The specific function that went with the status is referred to in v. 2: *she has been a helper of many and of myself as well*, possibly by welcoming visitors and the destitute into her own home.

2

in the Lord: the phrases *in Christ, in Christ Jesus,* and *in the Lord* occur eleven times in this chapter (in vv. 2, 3, 7, 8, 9, 10, 11, 12 (twice), 13, and 22). G. Adolf Deissmann has argued, in an immensely influential book (*Die neutestamentliche Formel 'in Christo Jesu'*, Marburg, 1892), that the preposition 'in' with a name or personal pronoun in the singular must indicate a place in standard Greek, and yet standard Greek could not possibly understand what was meant by saying that some men were 'in' another man. Since Paul wrote standard Greek, he must have known what he was doing; he must, therefore, have been coining a technical term to convey the new and startling idea that Christians live 'in' the exalted Christ, as in an element, in the way an animal lives 'in' the air, a fish 'in' water, or the roots of a plant 'in' the soil (pp. 84 f.). Deissmann's theory has been challenged, notably by Johannes Weiss and Friedrich Büchsel (*Zeitschrift für die neutestamentliche Wissenschaft* 42 (1949), pp. 141–58), yet its influence strangely persists. The Achilles' heel of the argument is that Paul wrote standard Greek, and once that theory is disproved all the rest falls to the ground. Phrases made up of 'in' with a name or personal pronoun in the singular are not technical terms, but are ordinary phrases open to a host of different interpretations according to the many possibilities to be found in ordinary Greek and in Greek influenced by semitic idioms.

The repetition of the phrases *in the Lord, in Christ, in Christ Jesus* in this chapter does suggest that we require a fairly uniform meaning for each occurrence, but Deissmann's suggestion of 'in the spiritual atmosphere which is the Lord' does not seem very likely. It seems artificial to ask that Phoebe be received in the spiritual atmosphere which is the Lord (v. 2), to say that Apelles was tried or approved in that sphere rather than in the world of trial and temptation (v. 10), or to say that one was taking a letter at dictation in that atmosphere (v. 22). A much more natural meaning would be 'for the Lord', 'on account of the Lord' (cf. Gal. 1.24, they glorified God 'in me', i.e. for me). This fits almost every case quite easily. Paul is asking the Romans to greet friends who are beloved for Christ's sake, who live for the Lord, and who work for the Lord. In v. 2 he asks them to receive Phoebe for the Lord's sake, in a manner worthy of saints. Christ is the living Lord for whose sake Christians receive strangers, love one another, resist temptation, and work. The one difficult case is v. 13, Rufus 'chosen in the Lord', but possibly here we should adopt the common instrumental meaning, 'chosen by the Lord' (Büchsel). Whatever translation we plump for here, 'chosen in the spiritual atmosphere which is the Lord', Deissmann's meaning, is unlikely.

4

all the churches of the Gentiles: this casual phrase is precious evidence for Paul's distinctive apostolic work. Jewish synagogues that believed in Jesus Christ did indeed have room for Gentiles, like all the synagogues of the day, either as proselytes who became Jews or as less fully committed attenders. What was distinctive about Paul was his work in establishing purely Gentile congregations. Prisca and Aquila stand at the head of those in Rome Paul greets because they, being Jews like him, are witnesses to his work in establishing Gentile congregations, and a living testimony to the whole argument of his letter to the Romans.

5
greet also the church in their house: Jews at this time worshipped in synagogues, special buildings set aside for the purpose of worship and instruction, or at places of prayer in the open by a river (Acts 16.13, 16), or possibly in private houses, provided at least ten men were present. The house was always a place of prayer and instruction, however informal, and nothing was more natural than that the large houses of more prosperous Jews would become meeting-places for those who believed in Jesus Christ. Elsewhere in Paul there is reference to the congregation that met in Aquila and Prisca's house in Ephesus (1 Cor. 16.19), to the congregation in Nympha's house in Laodicea (Col. 4.15), and to the congregation in Philemon's house (Phlm. 2). Possibly the groups of Christians mentioned in Rom. 16.14 and 15 are separate congregations meeting in houses in Rome. Zahn holds that those mentioned in vv. 5–13 all belonged to the church in Prisca and Aquila's house, but I do not think that is so likely, since no specific indication of their unity is given.

Greet my beloved Epaenetus, who was the first convert in Asia for Christ: literally, 'the first-fruit of Asia to Christ'. Paul thinks of the Gentiles as a sacrifice presented to Christ (cf. 15.15 f.).

7
Andronicus and Junias . . . they are men of note among the apostles: Lipsius, followed by most commentators, takes this to mean that Andronicus and Junias were apostles, that is, belonged to the much wider circle than the Twelve of those who were missionaries of the gospel (cf. 1 Cor. 15.7; Acts 14.4, 14). But it is possible that Andronicus and Junias were not themselves apostles; rather, men held in high regard by the apostles. *Of note among the apostles* is ambiguous, and in favour of the second interpretation we may well ask why Paul did not write 'they are noted apostles' if that is what he meant (F. C. Baur, Zahn). Against the second interpretation is that Paul links these men with himself, and he certainly held that he was an apostle.

they were in Christ before me: see note on v. 2 above for the suggested translation, 'they were for Christ before me'.

11

Greet those in the Lord who belong to the family of Narcissus: see note on v. 2 above for the translation, 'Greet those of the house of Narcissus who are for the Lord'. The implication is that not all this household believed.

13

Greet Rufus, eminent in the Lord: see note on v. 2 above for the translation, 'chosen by the Lord'. 'Chosen for the Lord' is also possible, meaning chosen by him for some special destiny.

his mother and mine: Paul must have once received special care from Rufus's mother, but we know no details.

14, 15

See the note on house-churches, v. 5 above.

16

Greet one another with a holy kiss: the same request appears at the end of both letters to the Corinthians, 1 Thessalonians, and 1 Peter (1 Cor. 16.20; 2 Cor. 13.12; 1 Thess. 5.26; 1 Peter 5.14). It could simply be an expression of Paul's desire that all the Christians in the towns to which he is writing remain united in the bond of love, this being shown by their greeting one another, whenever they meet, with a holy kiss. However, the holy kiss was well established by the middle of the second century as part of worship. Immediately after the prayers and before the bread and wine were brought to the president to be blessed, the congregation saluted one another with a kiss (Justin Martyr, *Apology* 65). This custom has led to the suggestion, first put forward by Rheinhold Seeberg (1859-1935), that Paul meant his letters to be read during worship before the eucharist. Some support is given to this theory by the strict command which follows immediately on the injunction to greet all the brethren with a holy kiss in 1 Thessalonians, *I adjure you by the Lord that this letter be read to all the brethren* (1 Thess. 5.27). If the letter is to be read to all the brethren, then the best place to do so would be when they gathered for worship. Nevertheless, the context in *Romans* does not support the suggestion that here the letter was meant to be read at one assembly, after which the eucharist followed. Rather, Paul is addressing the established synagogues in Rome that believed in Jesus Christ, or simply their leaders, asking them to convey special greetings to three house assemblies and to scattered individuals. The injunction *Greet one another with a holy kiss* looks more like an expression of the expectation that when the Roman leaders convey these greetings they will do so with the usual holy kiss. The holy kiss here is the greeting of a messenger carrying good news from Paul to his friends and acquaintance rather than a liturgical direction. This does not exclude the possibility that *Romans* was meant to be read at public worship, but simply that this verse can be called in support of that hypothesis.

16b–20

As suggested in the essay above, these verses are not by Paul, and were interpolated into *Romans* at the point where Paul switches from greeting people in Rome to conveying greetings from outsiders (v. 21). The address, tone, style, and vocabulary of vv. 16b–20 all show that Paul was not the author. The address is from one who claims to represent *all the churches of Christ*, an assumption of authority Paul never made (see Hans Windisch, Kittel's *Theologisches Wörterbuch*, i.499). The tone is peremptory in the middle of a peaceful passage. The style is dogmatic and neither admits argument nor gives argument. The vocabulary is not Paul's, the following words and expressions not being found elsewhere in Paul's writings: *the churches of Christ* (16b), *difficulties* (in the plural, 17), *our Lord Christ* (18), *fair . . . words* (18), *the simpleminded* (18), *is known* (19), *soon* (20), *crush* (20). It is a self-contained letter beginning with an address (which D* and G omit and add to v. 21), and ending with a benediction (omitted by D and G, who put it at the end of Paul's letter, at v. 24). Probably the author was a bishop of Rome who was warning a particular Church to resist the seductive talk of gnostic heresies and to hold to orthodox teaching. The heretics were causing dissension, making scruples about food, and confusing the morality of the congregation, whose obedience to God had previously been so well spoken of. The Church is to resist heresy as a temptation of Satan, whom God was soon to crush beneath their feet as he brought in his kingdom of peace.

19
I would have you

> (be) *wise as to what is good*
> *and guileless as to what is evil.*

The writer quotes a well-known saying, which consists of two equally balanced lines. It is strange that Jesus' form of the idea is not quoted (Matt. 10.16b), but perhaps the standard proverb was more apt to a situation where moral temptation was the danger.

21
Timothy: son of a Jewish mother and Greek father, therefore by Jewish

Law a Jew; since he had not been circumcised, circumcised by Paul. Referred to in Acts 16.1; 17.14 f.; 18.5; 19.22; 20.4; 1 Cor. 4.17; 16.10; 2 Cor. 1.1, 19; Phil. 1.1; 2.19; Col. 1.1; 1 Thess. 1.1; 3.2, 6; 2 Thess. 1.1; 1 Tim. 1.2, 18; 6.20; 2 Tim. 1.2; Phlm. 1; Heb. 13.23.

Sosipator: possibly the Sopater of Beroea, son of Pyrrhus, who accompanied Paul from Greece at the beginning of his last journey from there to Syria and Jerusalem, Acts 20.4.

22

Tertius, the writer of this letter: Paul was accustomed to dictate his letters (as is implied by 1 Cor. 16.21; Gal. 6.11; Col. 4.18; 2 Thess. 3.17; Phlm. 19). Perhaps this was because of his poor eyesight, which made his own writing too large (Gal. 6.11).

23

Gaius, who is host to me and to the whole church: men of the name Gaius are mentioned five times in the New Testament; Gaius the Macedonian, one of Paul's companions seized by the crowd in Ephesus (Acts 19.29); Gaius of Derbe, who was with Sopater, Timothy and others for the first stage at least of Paul's last journey from Greece to Jerusalem (Acts 20.4); Gaius one of the only two whom Paul baptized in Corinth (1 Cor. 1.14); and Gaius to whom John the Presbyter wrote the third letter (3 John 1); and this Gaius. Perhaps this Gaius is the Corinthian one. He was not *host to the whole church* in the sense that the whole Church met in his house, or that all Christians were welcome to visit Paul there when he was staying with Gaius, but that he willingly gave hospitality on the congregation's behalf to all Christian travellers who were passing through (Lagrange).

Erastus, the city treasurer: presumably of the city from which Paul is writing, which, if Gaius is Gaius of Corinth, would be Corinth. This Erastus is therefore different from Paul's companion mentioned in association with Timothy in Acts 19.22 and 2 Tim. 4.20.

25–27

Compare the similar ascriptions of praise in Eph. 3.20 f.; 1 Tim. 1.17; Jude 24 f.; Martyrdom of Polycarp 20.2. Jude 24 f. gives the first clue to the origin of such doxologies, for some manuscripts (K, P, etc.) omit the only reference to Christ, *through Jesus Christ our Lord,* and this omission is likely to be the original text, for it is easier to imagine the words' having been added than omitted (although it is possible, but not likely, that a scribe's eye jumped from one *our* to the next). That suggests that doxologies have been taken over from Greek-speaking Judaism into Christianity. The doxology in *Romans* betrays signs of the same process. First, the words *through Jesus Christ* in v. 27 disturb the grammar of the doxology by suggesting that the doxology might be meant to be directed to him rather than to God the Father, as is clearly the case at the outset. Second, the reference to *Jesus Christ*, with the reference to *my gospel* in v. 25, looks very like an explanation of the clause *according to the revelation of the mystery which was kept secret for long ages.* Origen omits *and the preaching of Jesus Christ*, but the preceding words *according to my gospel* fall under equal suspicion.

Difficulty is also caused by two further parts of the doxology. The doxology is primarily concerned about a new revelation that was previously kept secret. If that is so, it is hard to see how the *prophetic writings* are the vehicle of this revelation, for they are presumably the Old Testament scriptures, which had long been known and preached from by the Jews of the Dispersion. These *prophetic writings* could be incorporated into a scheme which talked of a new revelation, but scarcely without more explanation than is offered here.

Secondly, the reference to what is *made known to all nations* (i.e. the Gentiles) is very much more awkward in the Greek than in the RSV. It follows directly on a phrase in the same grammatical form, the phrase translated by the RSV *to bring about the obedience of faith.* It seems likely that this latter phrase is the original, and the reference to the Gentiles a gloss to bring the doxology more into line with the theme of *Romans*.

I suggest that the original Jewish doxology consisted of the words printed below. I have put the Christian interpolations in brackets to the right of the lines to which they refer.

To him who is able to strengthen you
    [according to my gospel
    [and the preaching of Jesus Christ
According to the revelation of the mystery
Kept silent for long ages;
    [now manifest through the prophetic writings
According to the command of the eternal God
Made known to the obedience of faith;
    [to all Gentiles
To the only wise God
    [through Jesus Christ
To him be glory for ever.   Amen.

The original doxology began with a line directing the worshippers' minds to him who could strengthen them; then followed two couplets, each beginning with 'according to', which assured the believers that what was once silent may now be heard, provided it is received with faithful obedience; and finally the object of praise was named, 'the only wise God', and eternal glory offered to him.

Paul neither wrote this doxology nor took it over for his epistle, since it is missing in the Greek side of F, in G, 629, and Marcion. The Ms. D probably did not originally contain it, as it is written continuously and not in sense-lines like the rest of the epistle; the doxology was added to D some time after D had first been written out.

The thought of the original doxology was Jewish, but springing from Judaism of a particular kind. The theme of this Judaism was God's speaking out of silence.

For while quiet silence clothed all things
And night in its swiftness was at midpoint,
Your all-powerful Word down from heaven from the royal thrones
Leapt, a relentless warrior, into the middle of doomed earth,
Bearing a sharp sword, your sure decree;
And standing, he filled all things with death,
And he both touched heaven and stood on earth.

(Wisdom of Solomon 18.14–16)

The same theme is found in the theology of Ignatius of Antioch, who speaks of Jesus Christ, God's Son, 'who is his Word proceeding from silence' (To the Magnesians 8.2; cf. Ephesians 15.2; 19.1), and the idea is also to be found in Valentinian Gnosticism.

Notice how the process of incorporation into the Christian letter is a process which adds reference to the Old Testament and to the mission to the Gentiles. The Jews had not been left in silence, for they had the scriptures, and the coming of Jesus Christ led to the proclamation of the gospel to Gentiles, who were hitherto without revelation.

The position of 16.25–27 in various manuscripts, and the bearing of the evidence on the composition of Romans

The doxology occurs in different positions in different manuscripts.

(i) At 16.25–27 only	ℵ, B, 1739, the Latin tradition, Clement of Alexandria, Origen
(ii) At 16.25–27 and after 14.23	A, P, 33, 88, Armenian
(iii) After 14.23 only	L, Ψ, 1984, syʰ, Chrysostom
(iv) After 15.33 only	P46
(v) Omitted altogether	Fᵍʳ, G, (D), 629, Marcion

Many scholars have argued from these various positions that *Romans* originally existed in longer and shorter recensions; there were once a Romans 1–14, a Romans 1–15, and a Romans 1–16. But the various positions do not necessarily show that *Romans* ever ended at either of the earlier points.

Let us take the peculiar reading of P46 first (iv above). When P46 was discovered and published in the 1930s, scholars who on other grounds had entertained the hypothesis that Chapter 16 of *Romans* was once a separate letter now hailed the discovery as positive proof that there had once existed a *Romans* without Chapter 16. However, Lietzmann's arguments against this theory still seem to be compelling; above all else, it is very hard to see Chapter 16 as a self-contained letter. Nor is the hypothesis that *Romans* once ended at Chapter 15 the only hypothesis that will explain the presence of a doxology at that point. Doxologies occur earlier in *Romans*, at 1.25; 9.5; and 11.36 (cf. Gal. 1.5; Eph. 3.21; Phil. 4.20; 1 Tim. 1.17; 6.16; 2 Tim. 4.18; Heb. 13.21; 1 Peter 4.11; 5.11; Rev. 1.6; 7.12), and indeed it is rare to find a doxology at the very end of an epistle (the only New Testament cases being 2 Peter 3.18 and Jude 24 f.). If a doxology was to be added, a scribal editor might well look for an appropriate place near the end, but not at the end, on the analogy of Philippians, 1 and 2 Timothy, Hebrews, and 1 Peter. The evidence of P46, therefore, need not at all indicate that this scribe possessed a copy of *Romans* without Chapter 16.

The case for seeing the position of the doxology at the end of Chapter 14 as evidence that *Romans* once ended there is somewhat stronger (iii above, and cf. ii). Marcion's edition of *Romans* probably did not contain Chapters 15 and 16, nor do Irenaeus, Tertullian, or Cyprian ever cite these two chapters. Tertullian may even have implied, in *Adversus Marcionem* v.14.14, that *Romans* ended about Romans 14.10. Finally, some chapter-headings preserved in the Latin Codex *Amiatinus* make Chapter 50 our Romans 14.14–23 and Chapter 51 our Romans 16.25–27, with nothing more on *Romans*.

External evidence for *Romans* having ended here is far stronger than for its having ended with Chapter 15, but the internal evidence is immeasurably weaker. Chapters 15 and 16 belong stylistically with Chapters 1–13, whatever their relation to Chapter 14, and if we did not have this external evidence no one would have thought to draw a line under Chapter 14 and to ascribe the addition of Chapters 15 and 16 to a later editor.

I have tentatively suggested in the commentary on Chapter 14 another explanation for the external evidence. I have argued that

Chapter 14 was originally an independent unit which was inserted into the fabric of Chapters 12–15.13 at what seemed to be an appropriate place. It is possible that the inserted passage was written on leaves in such a way that there was space on the last page. This space provided room for the insertion of the doxology, and it also caused tired and careless scribes to think they had come to the end of *Romans*.

The hypothesis that there was once space at the end of Chapter 14 is not simply a guess. One manuscript that omits the doxology altogether, the Ms. G, has a space at the end of Chapter 14. Editors sometimes assume that this meant the scribe was doubtful whether or not to insert the doxology, but the more likely explanation is that he was faithfully producing a feature of the archetype of our *Romans*: the archetype itself had a space after Chapter 14 simply because that was the blank end of a sheet bearing an independent section which had to be inserted into the continuous flow of *Romans*.

The scribe who wrote G reproduced the space, but other scribes inserted the doxology. The insertion is quite appropriate, given that doxologies customarily occurred scattered throughout epistles. The theme of 14.23, *for whatever does not proceed from faith is sin*, could well lead on to an ascription of glory to him 'who is made known to the obedience of faith' (16.26).

The conclusions to be drawn from the various positions of the doxology seem to be, then, not that *Romans* once existed in two or three recensions, short, longer and longest, but that the doxology was added in three different places for a variety of reasons: at the end, because it provided a good ending; after Chapter 15, because doxologies often preceded the final greetings; and after Chapter 14, because there was room, and because a doxology could well occur at a place that would clinch a particularly important theme (cf. 1.25; 9.5; and 11.36).

The most important conclusion to be drawn from the various positions of the doxology in our manuscripts of *Romans* is that *Romans* was added to by later scribes, right up to the time when our text was becoming settled. The peculiar character of this addition, and its late coming into *Romans*, have left far more detailed evidence of the process than we otherwise have, but there is good reason to suspect that the process had been going on for some time, and that many other passages besides 16.25–27 were interpolated into the letter Paul once wrote to Rome.

A RECONSTRUCTION OF
PAUL'S ORIGINAL LETTER
TO THE ROMANS

1 Paul, servant of Christ Jesus, called to be an apostle *on his behalf to all the Gentiles; 7to all those at Rome who are called to be saints: Grace to you and peace, from God our Father, and the Lord Jesus Christ.

8First, I thank my God through Jesus Christ for you all, because your faith is world-renowned. 9For God is my witness, whom I freely serve in preaching the gospel of his Son, that I am constantly making mention of you, 10always in my prayers asking whether I shall finally succeed, by God's will, in coming to you. 11For I long to see you in order to impart to you some spiritual gift, so that new firmness may result, 12I mean, the mutual reception of comfort in your company, through the faith that is in each of us, your faith and mine.

13I want you to be in no doubt, brothers, that I have often intended to come to you (but have been prevented up till now) in order to gather some fruit in your city too, as I have done among Gentiles elsewhere. 14I have a duty to Greeks and to barbarians, to wise and to foolish – 15hence my desire to preach also to those in Rome. 16For I am not ashamed of the gospel, for it is the power of God, bringing salvation to everyone who believes, first to Jew, then to Greek. 17For the righteousness acceptable to God is revealed through the gospel to the man who goes forward with ever increasing faith; as it is written, 'The righteous man shall live by faith' (Hab. 2.4).

3 What then is the advantage of being a Jew, or what is the value of circumcision? 2Great in every way. For, above all, they are the ones who were entrusted with God's oracles. 3What follows? If some Jews were faithless, their untrustworthiness does not nullify God's faithfulness, does it? 4Impossible. It must be conceded that God is still faithful even if 'every man prove liar', as scripture says (Psalm 116.11). 5But if our unrighteousness finds a way to adopt a righteousness acceptable to God, what shall we say?

264

The God who brings his wrath to bear on men is not unjust, is he? ⁶That could not be. If the truth of God in the case of my lie has magnified his glory, what shall we say? I too am still to be judged as a sinner. And this is not – is it? – (as we are slanderously accused of implying, and as some assert we actually say), 'Let us do evil that good may result.' The condemnation of people who say that is completely right.

⁹What, then, do we put up as a defence? We have argued that Jews and Greeks are all subject to sin: ¹⁰as it is written, 'There is no righteous man, not one' (Psalm 14.3); ¹¹'The man who really understands does not exist; the man who is searching for God does not exist' (Psalm 14.2b). ¹⁹As we know, the Law says what it says in order that every mouth be stopped, and the whole world be answerable to God. ²⁰Consequently, for doing the works prescribed in the Law 'no mortal man who appears before him is acquitted' (Psalm 143.2), for through the Law comes knowledge of sin.

²¹But now the righteousness acceptable to God has been manifested separately from the Law, although witnessed to by the Law and the Prophets, ²²God's righteousness through faith, accessible to all, for all who believe. For there is no distinction, ²³for all have sinned and come short of reflecting God's glory, ²⁴but they will be freely vindicated by his grace in virtue of the redemption from death of Jesus Christ, whom God set before men in blood, as a means of expiation, to show the righteousness he requires ²⁶in this present age, namely that the righteous man is the man who lives by faith.

²⁷What place is there for boasting? It has been excluded. Through what? Through works? No, through faith. ²⁸For we hold that a man is vindicated by aith, apart from the duties the Law requires. ²⁹Or is God God only of the Jews and not also of the Gentiles? Yes, of the Gentiles too. ³⁰As, then, God is one, he will vindicate the Circumcision because of their faith, and the Uncircumcision because of their faith.

³¹Are we destroying the Law with faith? That is unthinkable. On the contrary, we are confirming the Law.

4 We shall speak, then, about Abraham, our forefather according to the flesh. ²For if Abraham was vindicated because of works, he, logically, has reason to boast. ⁵But for the man who does not perform what is required, but trusts the one who acquits the guilty, faith is counted as righteousness. ⁹For we say (with Gen. 15.6) that 'faith was reckoned to Abraham for righteousness.' ¹⁰Under what circumstances, then, was it reckoned? When he was

circumcised or when he was uncircumcised? Not when he was circumcised, but when he was uncircumcised. [11]*And he received the sign of circumcision as a seal of the righteousness he had while uncircumcised, which rested on faith, so that he is father of uncircumcision, in order that faith may be reckoned as righteousness to them too;* [12]*and father of circumcision, in order that faith may be reckoned as righteousness not to those who are merely circumcised, but to those who, in addition, also walk in the footsteps of the faith of our father Abraham.* [13]*For the promise to Abraham and his seed that he and his should be heir came not through the Law but through the righteousness of faith.* [16]*For this reason the inheritance is based on faith, so that it might be according to grace, so that the promise should be sure for all the seed, not the seed that keeps the Law only, but the seed that also lives by the faith of Abraham, who is father of us all,* [18]*who, against hope, believed with hope that he would become 'father' according to the promise that said, 'so will be your seed'* (Gen. 15.5); [19]*and, not weakening in faith, he did not pay attention to his own body – he was nearly a hundred years old – nor did he pay attention to the barrenness of Sarah his wife.* [20]*He did not let lack of faith make him doubt God's promise but, empowered by faith, he gave glory to God,* [21]*being fully convinced that God was able to do what he had promised.* [23]*'It was reckoned to him'* (Gen. 15.6) – *this was recorded not only for him,* [24]*but also for us, to whom it is going to be reckoned, who believe in him who raised Jesus our Lord from the dead, who was put to death for our transgressions* (Is. 53.5).

5 *Therefore, since we are found righteous because of faith, we have peace with God through our Lord Jesus Christ,* [2]*through whom we have access to this grace in which we stand, and we exult in the hope of sharing God's glory;* [3]*not only that: but we also exult in our sufferings,* [5]*because knowledge of God's love is poured out in our hearts through the Holy Spirit given to us.* [6]*If only Christ – we say sometimes when we are weak – had died for the guilty! For it is rare even to find someone who will die for a righteous man!* [8]*But God shows his own love for us in that, while we were still sinners, Christ died for us.* [9]*Since we are now found righteous in receiving his blood, we shall, all the more, be saved through him from the effects of God's wrath.* [10]*For if while we were enemies we were reconciled to God through the death of his Son, now having been reconciled, we shall, all the more, be saved in receiving his life.* [11]*Not only that: but we also exult in God*

through our Lord Jesus Christ, through whom we have now received this reconciliation.

6 *What, then, shall we say? Shall we continue in sin, so that there may be even more grace? ²Never! How shall we, who have died to sin, continue to live in it? ³Surely you know that all who were baptized for Christ were baptized for his death ⁴in order that, as Christ was raised from the dead, so we too should walk in newness of life. ⁸If we died with Christ, we believe that we shall also live with him, ⁹knowing that he who is raised from the dead dies no more: death no longer rules over him. ¹⁰For in that he died, he died to sin once for all; in that he lives, he lives to God. ¹¹ And so count yourselves dead to sin and alive to God through Christ Jesus.*

¹²Do not, then, let sin reign in your mortal body; do not obey sin. ¹³Do not present your members to sin as instruments of unrighteousness, but present yourselves to God as those who will be alive from the dead, and your members to God as instruments of righteousness. ¹⁴For sin shall not rule over you, for you are not under Law but under grace.

¹⁵What, then? Let us sin because we are not under Law but under grace? Never! ¹⁶Do you not know that, if you present yourselves as slaves in obedience to someone, you really have to become servants of him you obey: servants of sin or servants for righteousness. ¹⁷Thanks be to God, because you were once servants of sin. ²¹What fruit did you then have from the things of which you are now ashamed? For the end of them is death. ²²But now, freed from sin and having passed into God's service, you have your fruit in sanctification, and the end is eternal life. ²³For the wages paid by sin is death, but the gift of God is eternal life with Christ Jesus our Lord.

7 *⁴Consequently you, my brothers, have died to the Law through receiving the body of Christ (or through the body. ⁶We have now been released from the Law by dying to the way in which the Law used to keep us captive, so that we serve in the newness of the Spirit and not in the old way of the letter.*

⁷What, then, shall we conclude? That the Law is sin? Impossible! But I should not have known the full meaning of sin had it not been for the Law. For I should not have known the significance of covetousness had not the Law said, 'You shall not covet' (Ex. 20.17; Deut. 5.21). ¹²So the Law is holy and the commandment is holy, and righteous, and good. ¹³Then did the good come to be death for me? Inconceivable! But sin, so that it would appear as sin, brought about death in me through the good; sin became exceedingly sinful through the commandment.

8 So there will be no condemnation with Christ Jesus. ³As for that powerlessness of the Law, the respect in which it was weak, God sent his own Son in the likeness of sin and for sin, and in the flesh condemned sin, ⁴so that the just requirement of the Law might be fulfilled by us.

¹¹If the Spirit of him who raised Jesus from the dead dwells in you, he who raised from the dead will make your mortal bodies alive. ¹⁵For you have not received a Spirit of bondage to fear, but you have received a Spirit of adoption as sons. When we cry 'Abba! Father!' ¹⁶the Spirit itself bears witness with our spirit that we are God's children. ¹⁷If children, then heirs, heirs of God and heirs with Christ, provided we suffer with him in order also to be glorified with him. ¹⁸For I reckon that the sufferings of this present age are not worth comparing to the coming glory that is to be revealed to us. ¹⁹(²⁰)For the eager expectation of creation waits in hope for the revelation of the sons of God. ²¹Therefore creation itself will also be freed from its bondage to decay to enjoy the freedom of the glory of God's children. ²²For we know that the whole of creation groans and labours until now.

²³That is not all. Although we have the Spirit, we too groan to ourselves, waiting for adoption, the redemption of our body. ²⁴For by hope we have been saved. Hope seen is not hope, for why hope for what anyone sees? ²⁵When we hope for what we do not see, we wait in patience. ²⁶As we might expect, the Spirit also helps us in our weakness, for we do not know how to pray as we ought. ²⁸But we do know that, for those who love God, he works all things for good.

³¹What shall we say, then, in the light of these things?

If God is for us, who is against us? ³²He who did not spare his own Son, but gave him for us all, how shall he not, with him, generously give us all things? ³⁴Who is to condemn? It is Christ Jesus who died, rather, who is raised, who is at the right hand of God, who intercedes for us. ³⁵Who shall separate us from God's love? Tribulation or distress or persecution or famine or nakedness or peril or sword? ³⁷No, in all these things we are more than conquerors through him who loved us.

9 I am speaking the truth; I am not lying; my conscience bears me out: ²the sorrow I have is great and there is ceaseless pain in my heart, ³for I could even wish myself anathema to Christ for the sake of my brothers, my kinsmen in the flesh. 6It is not as if the word of God has failed, for not all from Israel are Israel, 7nor all the children Abraham's seed, 8but the children of the promise are reckoned as seed, 9for this word is a word of promise: 'at the appointed time I shall come' (Gen. 18.14, cf. 10). 10Not only that; but Rebecca conceived two quite different twins after intercourse with one man, Isaac our father. 25As God says to Hosea, 'I shall call Not-my-people My-people and Not-beloved Beloved' (Hos. 2.23); 26'and it shall come to pass in the place where it was said to them, "You are not my people", there they shall be called "sons of the living God"' (Hos. 1.10). 27Isaiah cries out for Israel's sake, 'Even if the number of the sons of Israel were as great as the sand of the sea, only a remnant will be saved' (Is. 10.22).

30What, then, shall we say? That Gentiles, who were not seeking righteousness, have attained righteousness, righteousness which is based on faith, 31but Israel, in seeking the Law, did not measure up to the Law. 32Why? Because they did not act in faith, but as though it could be achieved by works. They stumbled against 'the stone of stumbling' (Is. 8.14), 33as it is written, 'Behold, I am laying in Sion a stone of stumbling and a rock of offence, and he who trusts in that will not be put to shame' (Is. 28.16; 8.14).

10 Brothers, the desire of my heart and the prayer I make to God for them is for their salvation. 2I can testify of them that they have a zeal for God, but it is not well informed, 3for they do not know the righteousness God requires, and in seeking to set up their own they have not given allegiance to the righteousness of God. 4For the goal of the Law is righteousness for everyone who has faith. 5For Moses writes that he who practises the righteousness that is of faith shall live by that faith; 6he speaks in this fashion: 'Do not say in your heart "who shall go up to heaven?"' (Deut. 9.4; 30.12).

15 14I am myself completely satisfied about you, my brothers, that you are full of goodness, complete in knowledge, able also to instruct one another. 15I write to you so boldly and at length to remind you of the grace given me from God 16to be Christ Jesus' minister, performing priestly service in preaching the gospel of God, so that the Gentiles' sacrificial offering of themselves may be acceptable, being sanctified by the Holy Spirit. 17Because of Christ Jesus I have reason to boast of my service to God, 18for I dare nothing except what Christ, with the aim of winning the obedience of the

Gentiles, has prepared to be achieved through me, by word and deed, ¹⁹by power of signs and miracles, by power of the Spirit; so that I have properly carried out the task of preaching Christ, from Jerusalem round to Illyricum. ²⁰So I have preferred not to preach where Christ was already named, in order not to build on another's foundation, but, as it is written, ' Those shall see, to whom no proclamation about him has come, and those who have not heard shall understand' (Is. 52.15).

²²You can gather why I have been so often prevented from coming to you. ²³But now, since there are no more opportunities in these parts, I am looking forward to realizing the ambition I have had for many years of coming to you, ²⁴on my way to Spain. For I hope to see you as I pass through, and to be speeded on my way there by you after I have first enjoyed your company for a while. ²⁵At the moment I am on my way to Jerusalem to serve the saints, for Macedonia and Achaia have been pleased to make a certain collection for the poor among the saints in Jerusalem. ²⁷I say they have been pleased, but really it is their duty. For if the Gentiles share in the spiritual riches of the Jews, they ought to serve them in their material needs. ²⁸When I have done this and given the fruit of the collection to them under my seal, I shall set off for Spain, coming to you on the way. ²⁹I know that when I come to you I shall come with the full blessing of Christ. ³⁰I beg you, brothers, through our Lord Jesus Christ and through the love the Spirit engenders, to join me in concentrated prayers to God on my behalf. ³¹Ask that I may be rescued from those in Judea who are not persuaded about the gospel; ask that the act of service I have to carry out in Jerusalem may be acceptable to the saints; ³²ask that I may come to you in joy, if that is God's will.

³³May the God of peace be with you all.

16 I recommend to you Phoebe our sister who is a deaconess of the church at Cenchreae, ²and ask you to receive her for the Lord in a way worthy of saints, and to help her with whatever she needs of you, for she herself has been of great help to many people, including me.

³Greet Prisca and Aquila, my fellow-workers for Christ Jesus, who have risked their own heads to save my life. I am not the only one to give thanks for them; all the Gentile churches have equal reason to give thanks. ⁵And greet the church that meets in their house.

Greet my dear friend Epaenetus, who was the first-fruit of Asia to be offered to Christ. ⁶Greet Mary, who has worked immensely hard among you.

⁷*Greet Andronicus and Junias, my fellow-countrymen and my fellow-prisoners, men of special value to the apostles, who were for Christ before I was.*

⁸*Greet Ampliatus, loved by me for the Lord's sake.* ⁹*Greet Urbanus our fellow-worker for Christ, and my beloved Stachys.* ¹⁰*Greet Apelles, approved by Christ. Greet those from Aristobulus's house.* ¹¹*Greet my fellow-countryman Herodion. Greet those of Narcissus' house who are for the Lord.* ¹²*Greet those workers for the Lord, Tryphaena and Tryphosa. Greet dear Persis; she has worked hard for the Lord.* ¹³*Greet Rufus chosen by the Lord, and greet his mother and mine.* ¹⁴*Greet Asyncritus, Phlegon, Hermes, Patrobas, Hermas, and the brothers who are with them.* ¹⁵*Greet Philologus and Julia, Nereus and his sister (Olympas, is she?), and all the saints with them.*

¹⁶*Greet each other with a holy kiss.*

²¹*My fellow-worker Timothy greets you, and Lucius and Jason and Sosipater, my fellow-countrymen.* ²²*I, Tertius, who write this letter for the Lord's sake, greet you.* ²³*Gaius my host, and host to strangers on behalf of the whole church to which he belongs, greets you. Erastus, who is city treasurer here, greets you, and Quartus the brother.*

²⁴*The grace of our Lord be with you all.*

VERSES NOT ASCRIBED TO
PAUL AND VERSES DIFFERENTLY
READ FROM THE GREEK
TEXT USED IN THE RSV

Verses not by Paul
    either
      unmarked
      (in brackets that part of the verse which is not by Paul)
    or
      **emended from the Greek text used in the RSV
    or
      † interpolated into a non-Pauline context
Verses by Paul
    * emended from the Greek text used in the RSV.

1.1 (*the gospel of God*)	3.5*
2	3.6 (*For then how could God judge*
3	*the world?*)
4**	3.9*
5** (all except *among all the*	3.10–18 (all the citations from the
nations)	LXX)
6**	3.19*
11*	3.21*
15*	3.24*
1.18–2.29	3.25*
1.32**	3.26*
2.1**, 3**	3.27*
2.14†, 15†	4.1*, 2*
2.21**	4.3, 4
2.28**, 29**	4.6–8, 9 (first sentence)
3.4 (citation from Psalm 51)	4.11 f*, 4.13*

4.14, 15
4.17
4.18★
4.19★
4.22
4.25★
5.3, 4, 5 (and hope does not disappoint us)
5.6★, 7★
5.12–21
5.12★★
5.13★★, 14★★, 20★★
5.14★★, 15★★, 16★★
6.3★
6.4 (We were buried therefore with him by baptism into death) (by the glory of the Father)
6.5–7
6.9, 11★
6.12★
6.16★
6.17 (who ... have become obedient from the heart to the standard of teaching to which you were committed)
6.18–20
7.1
7.2
7.3
7.4 (so that you may belong to another, to him who was raised from the dead in order that we may bear fruit for God)
7.5
7.8–11
7.14–25
7.25★★

8.1★
8.2
8.3★
8.4 (who walk not according to the flesh but according to the Spirit)
8.5–10
8.11★
8.11 (through his Spirit which dwells in you)
8.12–14
8.15★
8.20 (bar the words in hope)
8.26 (but the Spirit himself intercedes for us with sighs too deep for words)
8.27
8.28 (who are called according to his purpose)
8.29, 30
8.33
8.35★
8.36
8.38, 39
9.1★
9.4, 5
9.5★★
9.7 (but 'Through Isaac shall your descendants be named')
9.8 (This means that it is not the children of the flesh who are the children of God)
9.9★
9.11–13
9.14–23
9.22★★, 23★★
9.24
9.28★★

9.29
9.31*
10.4*
10.5*
10.6*
10.6b (from (*that is, to bring Christ down*)) −15
10.16–11.32
10.17**
11.2**
11.6**
11.33–36
12.1–15.13
12.1**
12.7**
12.9**
12.11**
13.1–7†
13.1**
13.2a**
13.4b**
13.9**

13.14**
14.1–23†
14.6b**
14.14**
14.17**
14.18**
14.22**
End of 14: 16.25–27**
15.7**
15.13**
15.14*
15.15*
15.16*
15.18*
15.27?
15.32*
16.16b (*All the churches of Christ greet you*)
16.17–20
16.24*
16.25–27

MANUSCRIPTS CITED WITH NOTES

The Manuscripts of Romans

Paul dictated his original letter in Greek to his secretary, Tertius. The letter was to all the Christians in Rome, not just to their leaders, and would probably be read at their meetings for worship. Although it would have apostolic authority, it would not be regarded as 'scripture'.

We can only conjecture from scraps of evidence what would have happened to the letter then. Possibly the letter would be read again at intervals, particularly after Paul had been martyred at Rome, but there would have been no thought that it was part of the body of writings that every Christian should know about. Nevertheless, because *Romans* was so useful and good, copies would be made, and these copies would be carried by Christians travelling from Rome to other parts.

The high authority of the letter from an apostle and martyr would mean that teachers and preachers would use *Romans* in their work. It is generally admitted that the original text would attract marginal notes (glosses) as it was copied and as it was annotated. For example, in Romans 5.2 someone added the explanatory remark *by faith* to the words *Through him we have obtained access to this grace*, to produce *Through him we have obtained access by faith to this grace*.

In the commentary I have been arguing that additions of this sort were more numerous than modern scholars have generally thought. Not only that: I think it likely that teachers and preachers inserted quite long meditations on the original, in order to make Paul's letter the vehicle for a fuller and more systematic exposition of the Christian faith than Paul had intended. As time went on, additions of yet another kind would be made, consisting of other traditional material, particularly moral instruction, which had also been handed down from the past and which, by its antiquity, had a claim to be incorporated into the sacred document.

At some stage an effort would be made to collect and edit all of

Paul's epistles and to make them into a manual for the use of the Church everywhere. This would be done in regions where Paul was particularly honoured, and that was not everywhere. Only in the second half of the second century did the idea take hold that Paul's letters were part of the staple diet of all Christians, an idea that the heretic Marcion had done something to foster. His edition of Paul helped to prod the main Church to produce a fuller edition, and gradually this became standardized. By the end of the century, Paul's letters were being bound together with other apostolic letters and added to the Gospels to make up a New Testament which was used along with the Old Testament in public worship as sacred scripture.

All our copies of *Romans* go back to the text as standardized by the Church. We actually possess parts of a copy of *Romans* which was written about A.D. 200, the Chester Beatty Papyrus (P⁴⁶). We also possess later copies of the writings of teachers, men like Irenaeus and Tertullian, who lived in the second century and who quoted from the standard *Romans*.

Every copy of *Romans* was made by hand by a scribe, and therefore every copy contains mistakes, since no copy of any writing is perfect. That fact was recognized by Christian scholars at the time. For example, Origen in his commentary on Matthew 15.14 said, 'The differences among the manuscripts have become great, either through the negligence of some copyist or through the perverse audacity of others; they either neglect to check over what they have transcribed, or, in the process of checking, they make additions or deletions as they please' (cited by B. M. Metzger, 'Explicit References in the Works of Origen to Variant Readings in New Testament Manuscripts', *Historical and Literary Studies: Pagan, Jewish, and Christian*, Leiden, 1968, pp. 88–103, at p. 88). Consequently, Church leaders would begin to see the necessity of editing the scriptures to be used in their area, and would set scholars to work to establish as good a quality text as possible, and they would make this the standard text for their Churches.

Textual critics in the eighteenth and nineteenth centuries collected as many manuscripts as they could find and, by comparing them, began to group together manuscripts according to the great standard archetypal editions they probably represented. They discovered evidence for two great efforts of standardization and control, an early one, probably made in Alexandria, and a later one, probably made in Asia Minor. The names given to these groups differ, but the best terms are Beta for the earlier one and Alpha for the later one. These terms were suggested by Kenyon. (The Beta controlled text-type is called Neutral plus Alexandrian by Hort, Eta by von Soden, B by Lagrange, Hesychian by Nestle, and Alexandrian in common usage. The Alpha controlled text-type is called Syrian by Hort, Kappa (= Koine) by von Soden, A by Lagrange, Koine by Nestle, and Byzantine in common usage.)

As well as these two controlled groups, there is another group of manuscripts which was not rigorously controlled, called Delta (Kenyon). (The Delta uncontrolled text-type is called Western by Hort, Iota by von Soden, D by Lagrange, and Western in common usage.)

Finally, there are manuscripts and 'families' of manuscripts which preserve readings that we know, from other sources such as quotations from the Fathers, were early. Lake suggested that these families, taken together, showed that there existed another text-type, and Streeter suggested this text-type might have originated at the great library in Caesarea. It now seems unlikely that a standard edition was ever made at Caesarea, or, indeed, that there ever was one 'Caesarean' text. At best we can talk about a 'tribe' (Colwell), a collection of 'families', and this should be called Gamma (Kenyon).

So little has been done on the text of the epistles from this point of view (the great exception is the work of Zuntz) that we shall be wise not to attempt to assign any manuscripts to this 'tribe'. The value of mentioning the hypothesis is to warn ourselves not to write off every reading in a late manuscript as belonging to the Alpha text-type and therefore of little value. Not only might the Alpha text-type preserve a good early reading, but the late manuscript might in fact belong to the Gamma tribe.

(The Gamma tribe is called Caesarean by Lake and Streeter, Iota alpha-eta-iota by von Soden, and C by Lagrange. The two clearest families are named after the scholars who first recognized the relationship in manuscripts of the Gospels, Ferrar (family 13, as minuscule 13 is the first member of the family), and Lake (family 1, as minuscule 1 is the first member of the family).)

What are the manuscripts that have been grouped in the four ways mentioned above?

First, there are about 637 *Greek* manuscripts of *Romans* or parts of *Romans* in existence. Seven of these are written on papyrus, prepared from papyrus reeds cut into strips, laid side by side one way, overlaid side by side at right-angles to the first, and then hammered together and polished. The papyrus manuscripts variously date from about A.D. 200 to about 700. The rest are written on parchment, made from the skin of cattle, sheep, and goats, especially that of young animals. The skins were scraped, washed, smoothed with pumice, and dressed with chalk. They are divided into two classes, those written (like the papyri) in capital letters or 'uncials', dating from the fourth century to the eighth and ninth centuries, and those written in lower-case letters or 'minuscule' letters, dating from the ninth century to the fifteenth century, when printing was invented as a way of copying. There are twenty-three uncial manuscripts of *Romans* or parts of *Romans*, and about 607 minuscules.

As well as Greek manuscripts of *Romans*, there are manuscripts in other languages, the 'versions'. These translations were made very early in the history of the use of *Romans*, and they were copied and standardized in the same way as the manuscripts in the Greek line of transmission. The main versions are in Latin, Syriac, Coptic, Gothic, Armenian, Georgian, Ethiopic, and Old Slavonic.

Besides straight copies of *Romans*, or copies of *Romans* in which the verses are kept in order so as to provide the basis of a continuous commentary, we have numerous short extracts quoted by teachers of the Church in sermons or theological writings, and short sections that go to make up lectionaries for convenient use in worship.

Below there is a list of the manuscripts cited in the commentary. Most of the manuscripts belong to the Alpha text-type, which in general is not so good a text as the Beta, but none of the Alpha readings can be dismissed out of hand, since any one of them may represent an early reading which has a claim to be considered on its merits. Some of these manuscripts may turn out not to belong to the Alpha group, but to the Gamma tribe.

Our printed editions, upon which the RSV is based, usually follow the Beta text-type, as this in general represents a much better text than the Alpha text-type, which lay behind the Authorized Version of King James. No one would wish to reverse the decision to follow the Beta manuscripts, but no text-type can be recovered in its original form (for all copies are imperfect) and no established text was itself perfect, representing as it did an attempt to get behind a rising tide of imperfect manuscripts by scholars whose judgement was not always right and whose equipment was always defective.

No grouping of manuscripts, therefore, can absolve the critic from examining a seriously proposed variant and trying to decide whether or not it represents an original reading that explains the other variants. In doing so, he will work by rules-of-thumb, the two classical ones being, Prefer the harder reading, and Prefer the shorter reading. Of course both of these 'rules' can be shown on occasion to be wrong, but they are useful tests to apply to any particular problem.

Most scholars are prepared to discuss variants from any manuscript, whatever its grouping, but I have gone further and resorted to conjecture when no other solution to a problem seems open. In doing so, I have tried to imagine a reading which would best explain the other readings, and which would best explain the sense of the passage under consideration. This is a risky and precarious thing to do, but the history of the transmission of all ancient documents seems to require us to take such a risk; the risk is widely taken with non-Biblical manuscripts.

The manuscripts and versions below which are definitely assigned to text-types are:

Beta: P⁴⁶ ℵ A B P Ψ 33 1739 sa bo
Delta: D E F G Old Latin
Alpha: K L most minuscules

Note:

ℵ* = reading of original manuscript
ℵ = reading of a correction to the original

Papyrus

P⁴⁶   The Chester Beatty Papyrus (86 leaves, of which 30 are at the University of Michigan; part of a codex of 104 leaves containing originally *Romans, Hebrews,* 1 and 2 *Corinthians, Ephesians, Galatians, Philippians, Colossians,* 1 and 2 *Thessalonians*); about A.D. 200.

Uncials

ℵ   (Aleph, the first letter of the Hebrew alphabet; symbol given by Tischendorf, its discoverer) Codex Sinaiticus (originally at St Catherine's monastery, Mount Sinai; now in the British Museum; the only complete uncial manuscript of the New Testament); 4th century.

A   Codex Alexandrinus (gift of the Patriarch of Constantinople to Charles I, 1627; in British Museum); 5th century.

B   Codex Vaticanus (Vatican Library, Rome); 4th century.

C   Codex Ephraemi (erased and over-written with sermons of Ephraem, i.e. a palimpsest); 5th century.

D   Codex Claromontanus (contains only the Pauline epistles; Greek D facing Latin d; Bibliothèque Nationale, Paris); 6th century, or perhaps 5th.

E   Codex Sangermanensis (Leningrad; a copy of D of no independent value; Greek E facing Latin e); 9th or 10th century.

F   Codex Augiensis (used to belong to monastery of Reichenau near Constance, Augia Maior; now in library of Trinity College, Cambridge; Greek F in column next to Latin f); 9th century.

G   Codex Boernerianus (once owned by Professor C. F. Börner of Leipzig; now in Dresden; Greek G with interlineal Latin g; perhaps written by Irish monks in monastery of St Gall); 9th century.

K   Codex Mosquensis (Moscow; uncial text divided into paragraphs separated by minuscule comments); 9th century.

L   Codex Angelicus (Angelican library, Rome); 9th century.

P   Codex Porphyrianus (palimpsest overwritten in A.D. 1301 with a commentary of Euthalius; now in Leningrad); 9th century.

Ψ   Codex Athous Laurae (monastery of the Laura on Mount Athos); 8th or 9th century.

0220   (one leaf of *Romans*: 4.23–5.3; 5.8–13; bought in Cairo in 1950 by Professor L. C. Wyman of Boston); 3rd or 4th century.

Minuscules

1   (the oldest and best manuscript of the family which comprises 1, 118, 131, 209; called fam. I by K. Lake, after whom the group is sometimes named; Basel); 12th century.

33   (called 'Queen of the cursives' by J. G. Eichhorn; Bibliothèque Nationale, Paris); 9th century.

69   (written partly on parchment and partly on paper; now in Leicester; the only member of the family 13, the Ferrar group, to contain the Pauline epistles); A.D. 1468.

81   (one of the most important of the minuscules; British Museum); A.D. 1044.

88   (grouped with H 917 1834 1836 as 'Euthalian' by Zuntz, i.e. as belonging to the Caesarean standard edition, cf. Gamma tribe, above; at Naples); 12th century.

104   (British Museum); A.D. 1087.

201   (British Museum); A.D. 1357.

206   (Lambeth Palace); 13th century.

216   (Lambeth Palace); A.D. 1358.

255   (Berlin Staatsbibliothek, now lost); 12th century.

326   (Lincoln College, Oxford); 12th century.

336   (University of Hamburg); 15th century.

337   (Bibliothèque Nationale, Paris); 12th century.

385   (British Museum); A.D. 1407.

424   (Vienna); 11th century.

440   (Cambridge University Library); 12th century.

489   (Trinity College, Cambridge; written on paper); A.D. 1316.

491   (British Museum); 11th century.

614 (Milan; 'It contains a large number of pre-Byzantine readings, many of them of the Western type of text', B. M. Metzger, p. 64); 13th century.

623 (Vatican Library, Rome); A.D. 1037.

629 (Vatican Library, Rome); 14th century.

999 (Mount Athos); 13th century.

1319 (Jerusalem); 12th century.

1739 (Mount Athos; copied by a monk named Ephraim from a 'very ancient manuscript' of 'outstanding quality', except in *Romans*, where he followed Origen's *Tomoi* as far as they were preserved); 10th century.

1827 (written on paper; Athens); A.D. 1295.

1836 (in the foreword to Paul, Euthalius is called 'bishop of Soulkē', as in 203 506 1875; Grottaferrata, Italy; see note on 88 and Zuntz); 10th century.

1852 (Uppsala); 13th century.

1874 (monastery of St Catherine, Mount Sinai); 10th century.

1898 (Athens); 10th century.

1908 (Pauline epistles with commentary; The Bodleian, Oxford); 11th century.

1913 (palimpsest – part of the Pauline corpus, with commentary, written over older theological text in uncials; Leipzig); 13th century.

1927 (text of Paul with commentary; Moscow); 10th century.

1984 (text of Paul with commentary; Naples); 14th century.

2127 (Palermo); 12th century.

Old Latin

d   see Greek D above.

e   see Greek E above.

f   see Greek F above.

g   see Greek G above.

Latin Vulgate (standard Latin edition made about A.D. 382, probably by Jerome)

D Codex Dublinensis or the Book of Armagh (Trinity College, Dublin; in the Pauline epistles the text is predominantly Old Latin, Metzger); 8th or 9th century.

A Codex Amiatinus (Laurentian Library, Florence; best manuscript of the Vulgate; written at order of Ceolfrid, Abbot of Jarrow and Wearmouth, and sent as gift to Pope Gregory); A.D. 716.

G Codex Sangermanensis (now in Paris); 9th century.

M Codex Monacensis; 8th century.

O Codex Oxoniensis (Laud. Lat. 108 Oxford); 9th century.

T Codex Toletanus (Madrid); 8th century.

V Codex Vallicellanus (Rome); 9th century.

Z Codex Harleianus (British Museum); 8th century.

Syriac Versions

syr^h The Syriac version of the New Testament issued by Thomas of Harkel (Heraclea), bishop of Mabbug in A.D. 616, with marginal notes.

Joseph White. *Actuum Apostolorum et Epistolarum tam Catholicarum quam Paulinarum Versio Syriaca Philoxeniana.* Two volumes, Oxford, 1799, 1803.

syr^p The Peshitta Version, or Syriac Vulgate (prepared probably to supplant competing Old Syriac translations); early 5th century.

syr^pal The Palestinian Syriac Version (independent of other Syriac versions; preserved in Gospel lectionary and fragments); 5th century?

Coptic Versions

sa Sahidic Version (southern dialect of Coptic, the latest form of the ancient Egyptian language; translation made at various times; a number of fragments, the best of which is Codex A of the Pauline epistles, the Chester Beatty Mss., ed. Sir Herbert Thompson, Cambridge, 1932); made in 3rd century?; our manuscripts later: 6th century?

bo Bohairic Version (northern dialect of Coptic; many manuscripts, mostly late); made in 4th century?

Ethiopic Version

eth (curious agreements with P46 for readings with little or no other support in Pauline epistles); made in 6th century?; manuscripts, 13th century and much later.

Armenian Version

arm (well over 1,200 manuscripts of all parts of New Testament); made in 5th century; manuscripts, 8th century onwards.

NAMES OF WRITERS ON *ROMANS* AND OTHER NAMES MENTIONED, WITH NOTES

ALTHAUS, PAUL (1888–1966): Lutheran theologian, professor of systematic and New Testament theology, Erlangen, 1925. Follows Luther in general, but accepts A. Schlatter's view that Paul said God reveals himself in nature.

Der Brief an die Römer. Das Neue Testament Deutsch, 6, Göttingen, 1932; 2nd ed., 1966.

AMBROSIASTER (4th century): anonymous Latin commentator on Paul. Wrote first Latin commentary on the thirteen epistles of Paul, traditionally ascribed to Ambrose. Traditional authorship disproved by Erasmus, who gave name Ambrosiaster. Commentary practical, has a sense of history, avoids allegory. Good witness to Old Latin text.

A. Souter. *The Earliest Latin Commentaries on the Epistles of St Paul: A Study.* Oxford, 1927.

ANAXAGORAS (*c.*500–*c.*426 B.C.) of Clazomenae in Ionia: Greek philosopher. Taught in Athens. The universe is directed by a supreme independent force, Spirit or Intelligence (*Nous*). Explained solar eclipses.

ARTEMONIUS, pseudonym of Samuel Crell (1660–1747): Unitarian preacher and writer. Educated in Amsterdam, active in Germany, England and Holland. Supported by Pierre Bayle; Isaac Newton; Anthony Ashley Cooper, third Earl of Shaftesbury. Name Artemonius taken from Artemon (or Artemas) who taught in Rome *c.*235 and was excommunicated for adoptionism. Artemonius's views mentioned at length and attacked by Bengel.

AUGUSTINE (354–430): bishop of Hippo, North Africa, theologian, philosopher, exegete, preacher. See Peter Brown, *Augustine of Hippo, a biography*, London, 1967. Opponent of Pelagius. Often expounded *Romans*, but his most important work on *Romans* is *The Spirit and the Letter* (412), in which he teaches that the external letter of the Law kills whereas the internal gift of the Spirit imparts God's righteousness to man. 'By the law of works God says, "Do what I command": by the law of faith we say to God, "Give what thou commandest"' (xiii = 22). Augustine was claimed by both Roman Catholics and Protestants in support of their understanding of *Romans*.

The Spirit and the Letter, translated with an introduction by John Burnaby, *Augustine: Later Works*, Library of Christian Classics, VIII, London, 1955.

BARNIKOL, ERNST (1892–1968): professor of church history, Halle, 1929–60, New Testament scholar, historian of nineteenth-century New Testament scholarship. Holds that 1 and 2 *Thessalonians*, *Galatians*, *Philemon* were written by Paul, and that 1 and 2 *Corinthians*, *Romans*, *Philippians* are composite letters, based on Paul.

'Römer 13: Der nichtpaulinische Ursprung der absoluten Obrigkeitsbejahung von Römer 13, 1–7', *Studien zum Neuen Testament und zur Patristik: Erich Klostermann zum 90. Geburtstag dargebracht*. Texte und Untersuchungen, Berlin, 1961, pp. 65–133.

BARRETT, CHARLES KINGSLEY (1917–   ): Methodist New Testament scholar, professor of divinity, Durham, 1958.

A Commentary on the Epistle to the Romans. London, 1957; reprinted with minor changes, 1962.

From First Adam to Last: A Study in Pauline Theology. London, 1962.

BARTH, KARL (1886–1968): Swiss Reformed theologian. Taught that all men are chosen and loved by God and that, although individual men in their opposition to God are as such rejected by God, their decision to reject God is ultimately 'nothing', since Jesus Christ has followed them into their state of rejection: as God loved his Son, so he loves all men. 'Jacob is always Esau also, and in the eternal "Moment" of revelation Esau is also Jacob' (on Romans 9.11–13).

Der Römerbrief. Bern, 1919; 2nd ed., completely rewritten, 1922. English translation by Sir Edwyn C. Hoskyns, *The Epistle to the Romans By Karl Barth*, London, 1933. Barth also published a shorter exposition of *Romans*, 1956, English translation by D. H. van Daalen: *A Shorter Commentary on Romans*, London, 1959.

BAUER, BRUNO (1809–82): taught theology in Berlin, 1834, and Bonn, 1839; permission to teach withdrawn, 1842. Started as a rightwing Hegelian; moved to the left, although politically he became conservative. Romans 1.18–8.39 is the kernel of *Romans*, not by Paul, written before 1 *Corinthians* but at a late time when the idea of Grace was firmly established. To this kernel was added an epistolary introduction (1.1–17); a section by one who wrote as a Jew, who had an early draft of Luke's Gospel in his hands (9–11); the pile of pieces of advice written by someone who possessed 1 *Corinthians* (12–14); and the concluding chapters by a Pauline apologist who made Paulinism the periphery of the Jewish centre (like the writer of *Acts*) and who knew 2 *Corinthians* (15, 16).

Kritik der paulinischen Briefe: Drei Abtheilungen. Berlin, 1850–2. *Erste Abtheilung: Der Ursprung des Galaterbriefs*, 1850. *Zweite Abtheilung: Der Ursprung des ersten Korintherbriefs*, 1851. *Dritte und letzte Abtheilung*, 1852: Der Römerbrief, pp. 47–76.

BAUR, FERDINAND CHRISTIAN (1792–1860): professor of history, Faculty of Theology, Tübingen, 1826. Put forward the first comprehensive critical history of the growth of the New Testament. The history of the Church is the history of how Christianity broke free from Judaism to become a universal religion. The key figure is Paul. He founded Gentile Churches, free from the Law. This led to a clash with Jewish Christianity, represented by Peter. Paul wrote *Galatians* to emancipate Christianity from Judaism by casting off circumcision; he wrote the two letters to the Corinthians to assert that he was as much an Apostle as the Apostles called by Jesus himself; and he wrote *Romans* 'to remove the last remnants of Jewish particularism, by showing that it is but a stage, a stepping-stone to the universalism of Christianity, in which all nations should be embraced' (*Paul*, vol.i, p. 309). The Catholic Church gradually came into existence as a synthesis between the two sharply opposed positions of Peter and Paul. Paul wrote only *Romans*, 1 and 2 *Corinthians*, and *Galatians*; the rest of the letters under his name are by followers who were moving towards the final reconciliation with the followers of Peter. *Acts* is the work of a Paulinist who tried to make Paul as petrine and Peter as pauline as possible.

Paulus, der Apostel Jesu Christi. Sein Leben und Wirken, seine Briefe, und seine Lehre. Ein Beitrag zu einer kritischen Geschichte des Urchristenthums. Stuttgart, 1845; 2nd ed., ed. E. Zeller, 1867.

Paul The Apostle of Jesus Christ, His Life and Work, His Epistles and His Doctrine. A Contribution to a Critical History of Primitive Christianity. Two vols., London, 1873 ff.

BENGEL, JOHANN ALBRECHT (1687–1752): Lutheran New Testament scholar and textual critic, professor in seminary at Denkendorf, 1713, General-superintendent, Herbrechtingen, 1741, Alpirsbach, 1749. As textual critic of New Testament grouped manuscripts into Asian and African families; saw that the right question to put about various readings was, Which reading is more likely to have arisen out of the other?; and formulated the rule-of-thumb, Prefer the harder reading to the easier. Wrote a 'Gnomon' of the New Testament. (A gnomon is the pin on a sundial, the shadow of which indicates the time.) This consisted of short pithy comments. Uneasy about Romans 9: 'The ix. chap. must not be shut within narrower limits than Paul permits in this x. chap., which is more cheerful and more expanded.'

Gnomon Novi Testamenti, in quo ex nativa verborum vi simplicitas, profunditas, concinnitas, salubritas sensum coelestium iudicatur. Tübingen, 1742.

BENTLEY, RICHARD (1662–1742): classical scholar and textual critic, Master of Trinity College, Cambridge, 1700, for most of the time against the fellows' wishes. Exposed the spurious Epistles of Phalaris, edited Horace and Terence, proposed a critical edition of the New Testament, which was never completed. He saw the value of relying on the oldest manuscripts. He also made conjectural emendations where there was no textual evidence, a procedure he brought into disrepute by an edition of 'Paradise Lost' (1732, when he was 70 years old) in which he proposed more than 800 emendations.

BORNKAMM, GÜNTHER (1905–   ): Lutheran New Testament scholar, professor of New Testament, Heidelberg, 1949.

Das Ende des Gesetzes: Paulusstudien. Gesammelte Aufsätze I. Munich, 1952; 2nd ed., 1958. Contains important essays on Romans 1–3; 6; 7; 11.33–36, and on anacolutha in *Romans.*

Studien zu Antike und Urchristentum. Gesammelte Aufsätze II. Munich, 1959. Essays selected from the two collections translated by P. L. Hammer: *Early Christian Experience,* London, 1969.

Paulus. Stuttgart, 1969. *Paul.* Translated by D. M. G. Stalker, London, 1971.

BOUSSET, WILHELM (1865–1920): Lutheran New Testament scholar, professor in Göttingen (1896–1916) and Giessen (1916–20). One of the founders of the History of Religions school. Important studies on Judaism, Gnosticism, and early Christianity. Emphasized the influence of Hellenism and the Mystery Religions on the Church.

Kyrios Christos: Geschichte des Christusglaubens von den Anfängen des Christentums bis Irenaeus. Göttingen, 1913; 2nd ed., 1921.

Kyrios Christos: a History of the Belief in Christ from the Beginnings of Christianity to Irenaeus. Translated by John E. Steely. Nashville, 1970.

BÜCHSEL, FRIEDRICH (1883–1945): Lutheran New Testament

scholar, professor in Rostock, 1918. Interested in the Johannine writings, the history of piety, and Christology. 'All the mystical in Paul's piety finally expressed itself in something completely unmystical: the piety of a moral life.'

'"In Christus" bei Paulus', *Zeitschrift für die neutestamentliche Wissenschaft* 42 (1949), pp. 141–58. The quotation is from p. 155.

BULTMANN, RUDOLF (1884–   ): Lutheran New Testament scholar, professor in Breslau, 1916, Giessen, 1920, Marburg, 1921. His theories about the Synoptic Gospels, Paul and John are the starting point of most modern discussions. His proposal that the New Testament must be 'demythologized' in order to speak to modern man is still debated. He argued that Paul was the founder of Christian theology. Paul's Christianity had no direct contact with the Palestinian Church, but was based on Hellenistic Christianity. The key to Hellenistic Christianity is the new confession, 'Jesus is Lord'. Paul's conversion brought him under the judgement of the cross of Christ over all human accomplishment. Paul's theology is best understood as anthropology: man prior to the revelation of faith 'has always already missed the existence that at heart he seeks'; man under faith knows himself challenged to surrender his own righteousness (his own view of himself as able to accomplish anything) to God's righteousness by dying to self and rising with Christ. Faith is primarily obedience. Righteousness is both a matter of hope and a present reality. It is a gift, not simply a declaration by God that the sinner is righteous.

Exegetica: Aufsätze zur Erforschung des Neuen Testaments, ed. Erich Dinkler. Tübingen, 1967. Contains 'Das Problem der Ethik bei Paulus' (1924); 'Römer 7 und die Anthropologie des Paulus'* (1932); 'Jesus und Paulus'* (1936); 'Glossen im Römerbrief' (1947); 'Ignatius und Paulus'* (1953); 'Adam und Christus nach Römer 5' (1959); 'Dikaiosyne Theou' (1964). The last-named is in English in *Journal of Biblical Literature*, Vol. 83, pp. 12–16. Those marked with an asterisk are translated by Schubert M. Ogden, *Existence and Faith: Shorter Writings of Rudolf Bultmann* (New York, 1960), together with the article 'Paulus', *Religion in Geschichte und Gegenwart*, 2nd ed., Vol. IV (1930), columns 1019–45. His section, 'The Theology of Paul', in *Theologie des Neuen Testaments* was first published in Tübingen in 1951. English translation by Kendrick Grobel. *The Theology of the New Testament*, Volume I. New York, 1951.

CALVIN, JOHN (1509–64): reformer. Born in Picardy, had to flee from France. While in Geneva he was pressed to stay and lead reform of Church after the bishop had left. Insisted that faith is the special gift of God to his elect. Righteousness is offered to all, but accepted only by those enlightened by God with special grace. God attributes to the elect his accepted righteousness as if it were their own, and holds them as though they were absolutely perfect, although they are not. Those rejected by God are no more unworthy than the elect; although the justice of this rejection is beyond doubt, there is no higher cause for it than the will of God. Calvin's commentaries are noted for their 'lucid brevity'.

Commentarii in Epistolam Pauli ad Romanos. Strassburg, 1540. *Corpus Reformatorum* lxxvii (xlix).

The Epistle of Paul the Apostle to the Romans and to the Thessalonians. Translated by Ross Mackenzie. Edinburgh, 1961.

CELSUS (flourished 177–80?): eclectic Platonist philosopher, perhaps writing from Alexandria. Wrote a book called *True Word* to recall men to the old polytheism and the beliefs of their fathers from the dangerous novelty of Christianity. This book known to us from copious citations in Origen's *Contra Celsum.*

CHRYSOSTOM, JOHN (*c.*347–407): bishop of Constantinople. Chrysostom means 'golden-mouthed', a tribute to his preaching. Delivered homilies on *Romans* and many other books of the Bible in Antioch between 386 and 398. God touches the soul deadened by sin and relaxes the deadness. He himself is righteous and makes those that are filled with the putrefying sores of sin suddenly righteous. The predestinarian passages are explained as God's foreknowledge of which men will turn out to be virtuous: he knows the pearl, though it lies in the mud, and he adds grace to the noble-born free-will in order to make it approved (Homily xvi).

The Homilies of S. John Chrysostom, Archbishop of Constantinople, on the Epistle of S. Paul the Apostle to the Romans. Revised translation based on Field's text by W. H. Simcox, 3rd ed., London, 1893.

CICERO, MARCUS TULLIUS (106–43 B.C.): Roman orator, philosopher, statesman. Created a Latin vocabulary for the discussion of Greek philosophy and made Greek philosophy at home in Latin. Follower of the Academy (ultimately going back to Plato); certain knowledge not possible. Much more sympathetic to Stoicism than to Epicureanism, but defended teaching that men had free-will.

The Nature of the Gods. Translated by Horace C. P. McGregor with an introduction by J. M. Ross. Harmondsworth, 1972.

CLEMENT OF ALEXANDRIA (*c.*150–*c.*215): theologian. Born probably in Athens, studied and taught in Alexandria. Christianity expounded as a way of knowledge open to all according to their capabilities. Defended free will: 'he who would have virtue must choose it'.

COLWELL, ERNEST CADMAN (1901–   ): Methodist New Testament scholar, textual critic, professor, Emory University, 1939, vice president, 1951, president Southern California School of Theology, Claremont, 1957, professor of New Testament, 1968. Advocate of Hort's dictum, 'All trusty restoration of corrupted texts is founded on the study of their history'. Colwell's terminology is adopted in the discussion of the text of *Romans*, above.

Studies in Methodology in Textual Criticism of the New Testament. Leiden, 1969.

CRANFIELD, CHARLES ERNEST BURLAND (1915–   ): theologian of the Reformed Church, senior lecturer in theology, Durham, 1962. Has written many articles on *Romans* in preparation for his commentary for the new International Critical Commentary.

'Some Observations on Romans xiii.1–7', *New Testament Studies*, Vol. 6 (1960), pp. 241–9.

'Metron pisteōs in Romans xii.3', *New Testament Studies*, Vol. 8 (1962), pp. 345–51.

A Commentary on Romans 12–13. Scottish Journal of Theology Occasional Papers, 12. Edinburgh, 1965.

'On some of the Problems in the Interpretation of Romans 5.12', *Scottish Journal of Theology*, Vol. 22 (1969), pp. 324–41.

CRELL, SAMUEL (1660–1747): *see* Artemonius.

CULLMAN, OSCAR (1902–   ): Reformed New Testament scholar, professor, Strassburg, 1930, Basel, 1938, as well as Paris, 1949.

Les premières confessions de foi chrétiennes. Paris, 1943; 2nd ed., 1948. English translation by J. K. S. Reid, *The Earliest Christian Confessions*, London, 1949.

Der Staat in Neuen Testament. Tübingen, 1956; 2nd ed., 1961. English translation by F. V. Filson. *The State in the New Testament*, New York, 1957.

DAVIES, WILLIAM DAVID (1911–   ): Welsh Congregationalist New Testament scholar, professor Duke University Divinity School, 1950, Princeton, 1955, Union Theological Seminary, 1959, Columbia, 1960, Duke, 1966.

Paul and Rabbinic Judaism: Some Rabbinic Elements in Pauline Theology. London, 1948.

DEISSMANN, GUSTAV ADOLF (1866–1937): New Testament scholar, active in ecumenical movement, professor in Heidelberg, 1897, Berlin, 1908. Paul made the religion of Christ world-wide by going beyond the specifically Jewish appreciation of the Person of Jesus. Paul drew on his more Hellenistic experience. Christ is Lord; Christ is Spirit. 'Just as the air of life which we breathe is "in" us and fills us, and yet we at the same time live and breathe "in" this air, so it is with St Paul's fellowship of Christ: Christ in him, he in Christ.'

Die neutestamentliche Formel 'in Christo Jesu'. Marburg, 1892.

Paulus: Eine kultur- und religionsgeschichtliche Skizze. Tübingen, 1911; 2nd ed., 1925. English translation by Lionel R. M. Strachan, *St Paul: A Study in Social and Religious History*, London, 1912.

DENNEY, JAMES (1856–1917): Free Church of Scotland, theologian and New Testament scholar, professor of systematic and pastoral theology, Glasgow Free Church College, 1897, professor of New Testament, 1899. Justification by faith is the whole of Paul's gospel; Luther his true interpreter. *Romans* addressed to men of all times. Its polemic is anti-legal, against all custom, dogmatic tradition or clerical order in the Church. Christian liberty is liberty in which the will of God is done from the heart.

St Paul's Epistle to the Romans The Expositor's Greek Testament, edited by W. Robertson Nicoll. Vol. ii, London, 1900.

DIDYMUS OF ALEXANDRIA, 'The Blind' (*c*.313–98): theologian. Blind from infancy. Made director of Catechetical School by Athanasius.

DIONYSUS, in Greek mythology, son of Zeus. Legends about him played important part in Mystery Religions of Greece, which spread throughout the Hellenistic world.

DODD, CHARLES HAROLD (1884–1973): Congregationalist New Testament scholar, Rylands Professor of Biblical Criticism and Exegesis, Manchester, 1930, Norris-Hulse Professor of Divinity, Cambridge, 1935–49. Coined the term 'realized eschatology' to describe Jesus' teaching about the Kingdom of God: the timeless fact is embodied, so far as history can contain it, in the historic crisis which the coming of Jesus brought about. He interprets the thought of *Romans* according to the same pattern: Paul speaks of a crisis of divine judgement and grace falling upon the world, and repeated in every soul.

The Epistle of Paul to the Romans. The Moffatt New Testament Commentary. London, 1932.

EBELING, GERHARD (1912–   ): Lutheran theologian, professor of church history, Tübingen, 1946, professor of systematic theology, 1954, Zürich, 1956, Tübingen, 1965, Zürich, 1969. 'Church History is the history of the exposition of scripture'. Particularly interested in Luther as an exegete. God's Word comes to the man who admits that his whole existence is questionable. Faith is the passive acceptance of the radical question about himself. *See* Fuchs.

EPICTETUS of Hierapolis, Phrygia (*c.*60–140): Stoic philosopher. A slave, lame from youth, who gained his freedom. World governed by providence. Man should endure and abstain in order to be independent of external events.

EPIPHANIUS (*c.*315–403): bishop of Salamis, Cyprus. Wrote *Panarion* (the Refutation of all the Heresies). Supporter of monastic movement, great organizer, rigid and intolerant.

ERASMUS of Rotterdam (in Latin form, Desiderius) (*c.*1466–1536): editor, scholar, satirist. Illegitimate son of a priest. Entered order of Augustinian Canons, but rarely lived in a monastery. Studied in Paris. Visited England, Italy; lived in Basel and Freiburg-im-Breisgau. Attacked war, abuses in church. First to publish a printed Greek New Testament, 1516. Insisted that Luther agreed with Catholic Church on fundamentals. When compelled to attack him, unerringly chose Luther's denial of human free will. (Luther himself acknowledged this: 'You and you alone have seen the question on which everything hinges, and have aimed at the vital spot.') Expounded *Romans* in his *Paraphrases of the New Testament* so as to emasculate the doctrine of predestination.
  De Libero Arbitrio. Basel, 1524. Translated and edited by E. Gordon Rupp in collaboration with A. N. Marlow. *Luther and Erasmus. Free Will and Salvation.* Library of Christian Classics, XVII, London, 1969.

EUSEBIUS OF CAESAREA (*c.*260–*c.*340): bishop and church historian. His *Ecclesiastical History* is our main source for the early history of the church; contains invaluable long extracts from other authors.

EUSEBIUS OF EMESA (died *c.*359): bishop, exegete. Probably a disciple of Eusebius of Caesarea.

FEINE, PAUL (1859–1933): Lutheran New Testament scholar, professor in Vienna, 1894, in Breslau, 1907, and Halle, 1910. The centre of

Paul's work and thought is the gospel as witness to the historical revelation of God in Christ; everything follows from Paul's picture of Christ, and his faith in Christ. Attacked A. Schweitzer and Bousset.

Der Römerbrief. Eine exegetische Studie. Göttingen, 1903.

Theologie des Neuen Testaments. Leipzig, 1910; 2nd ed., 1911; 3rd ed., 1919; 4th ed., 1922.

Der Apostel Paulus: Das Ringen um das geschichtliche Verständnis des Paulus. Gütersloh, 1927.

FERRAR, WILLIAM HUGH (1834/5–71): textual critic, professor of Latin, University of Dublin. On the basis of Wettstein's observation of affinity between minuscules 13 and 69, Ferrar argued that 13, 69, 124, and 346 derived from a common archetype. Lake and others have added more to the list; see report in Metzger, pp. 61 f.

A Collation of Four Important Manuscripts of the Gospels: with a view to prove their common origin, and to restore the text of their archetype. Posthumously edited with an introduction by T. K. Abbott, Dublin, 1877.

FUCHS, ERNST (1903–   ): Lutheran New Testament scholar and theologian, professor in Tübingen, 1953, Berlin, 1955, Marburg 1961. True existence in faith is for man to know himself addressed by love. This is the 'speech-event' which frees a man from the past and gives him hope in the future. *See* Ebeling.

Die Freiheit des Glaubens: Römer 5–8 ausgelegt. Munich, 1949.

GIFFORD, EDWIN HAMILTON (1820–1905): schoolmaster and theologian. His commentary on *Romans* held by Sanday and Headlam (writing in 1895) to be 'on the whole the best as it is the most judicious of all English commentaries on the Epistle'.

The Epistle of St Paul to the Romans. With Notes and Introduction. Speaker's Commentary. London, 1881.

HARNACK, ADOLF (after 1914, von Harnack) (1851–1930): church historian, theologian, professor in Leipzig, 1876, Giessen, 1879, Marburg, 1886, and Berlin, 1888. Wrote an enormous number of books and articles the most important being *History of Dogma, The Mission and Expansion of Christianity in the First Three Centuries, What is Christianity?,* and *Marcion.* All but the last are translated into English. The gospel is the basis of culture because it frees men to be responsible in higher things. The history of the Church is the history of how the gospel was almost lost when it became entangled with Greek metaphysics, how it was revived when Luther dissolved the connection with dogma.

Marcion: Das Evangelium vom fremden Gott: Eine Monographie zur

Geschichte der Grundlegung der katholischen Kirche. 2nd ed. Leipzig, 1924.

HAWKINS, ROBERT MARTYR (1887–1968): Methodist New Testament scholar, professor, Vanderbilt University, 1928–1955. All Paul's letters have been modified to bring them into harmony with a later orthodoxy. Romans was written to a church intensely Jewish in sympathy, to commend to them Paul's hellenistic interpretation of the gospel. Chapter 2 is basic to Paul's position: Gentiles without the Law are able to be righteous. Paul adopts the language of the Mystery Religions and commends 'mystic enthusiasm' by which believers die and rise with Christ, live in Christ and in the power of the Spirit. Passages which assert the universal sinfulness of man and the universal atonement in the blood of Christ are secondary; passages such as 1.18–32; 3.9–20, 23–26; 15.8–13 are not by Paul. (In the book listed below, which I have not seen, he seems also, according to a review, to have argued that the predestinarianism in Romans 9–11 was not by Paul.)

'Romans: A Reinterpretation', *Journal of Biblical Literature*, Vol. lx (1941), pp. 129–40.

The Recovery of the Historical Paul. Nashville, 1943.

HEADLAM, ARTHUR CAYLEY (1862–1947): Church of England theologian, professor of dogmatic theology, King's College, London, from 1903, professor of divinity, Oxford, from 1918, bishop of Gloucester from 1923. Disliked ecclesiastical parties, worked for union with other Churches.

A Critical and Exegetical Commentary on the Epistle to the Romans. With William Sanday. The International Critical Commentary. Edinburgh, 1895; 5th ed., 1902.

HICK, JOHN HARWOOD (1922–   ): United Reformed Church, philosopher and theologian, professor in Birmingham, 1967. The nature which God has given man is a nature which will eventually lead him freely to respond to his maker.

Evil and the God of Love. London, 1966.

'The Problem of Evil in the First and Last Things', *Journal of Theological Studies*, new series Vol. XIX (1968), pp. 591–602.

'Freedom and the Irenaean Theodicy Again', *Journal of Theological Studies*, new series Vol. XXI (1970), pp. 419–22.

HILLEL, RABBI (at time of Christ): tolerant and lenient interpreter of the law. 'Be of the disciples of Aaron, loving peace and pursuing peace, loving mankind and bringing them nigh to the Law'.

HOFMANN, JOHANN CHRISTIAN KONRAD VON (1810–77): Lutheran theologian. His themes were *Heilsgeschichte* (salvation-history) and holiness. 'For me as theologian, I the Christian am the real subject-matter of my scientific discipline.'

HORT, FENTON JOHN ANTHONY (1828–92): Anglican theologian, New Testament scholar, textual critic, one of the translators of the Revised Version, fellow of Trinity College, Cambridge, 1852–7, of Emmanuel College, 1871, Hulsean professor, 1878, Lady Margaret's, 1887. Wrote the Introduction to the edition of the New Testament he revised with Brooke Foss Westcott:

The New Testament in the Original Greek. Vol. I. Text; Vol. II. Introduction, Appendix. Cambridge and London, 1881.

Prolegomena to St Paul's Epistles to the Romans and the Ephesians. Lectures. London, 1895.

IGNATIUS OF ANTIOCH (*c.*35–*c.*117): bishop. Wrote letters to Churches at Ephesus, Magnesia, Tralles, Rome, Philadelphia, and Smyrna, and a letter to Polycarp, bishop of Smyrna. Letters written while being taken to Rome to be martyred. These letters interpolated and added to. A Syriac manuscript containing only the genuine letters to Ephesus, Rome, and Polycarp published in 1845. Warns against Judaizers, docetic heretics. Eucharist is 'medicine of immortality'. Bishop's authority necessary for eucharist and marriage.

IRENAEUS (*c.*130–*c.*200): bishop of Lyons, theologian. Wrote in Greek to attack Gnosticism by showing that scripture (the writings of prophets and apostles), the Faith (as taught by the apostles and their immediate successors) and the bishops (the successors of the apostles' successors) agreed. God the Father is Creator; God the Son was incarnate to 'sum up' mankind, i.e. to restore man to life and fellowship with God. Quoted about 63 passages from Romans 1–14 in his book *Against Heresies*.

Adversus omnes Haereses. Edited by W. W. Harvey. Cambridge, 1857.

The Demonstration of the Apostolic Preaching. Translated from the Armenian with Introduction and Notes by J. Armitage Robinson. London, 1920.

W. Sanday and C. H. Turner, *Novum Testamentum Sancti Irenaei*. Oxford, 1923.

ISIDORE OF PELUSIUM (died *c.*450): monk and exegete.

JOSEPHUS, FLAVIUS (*c.*37–*c.*100): Jewish soldier and historian. Fought in Jewish War of A.D. 66; taken captive by Romans, 67; won Vespasian's favour and set at liberty, 69. Settled in Rome; given citizenship. Wrote *Jewish War* and *Antiquities of the Jews*.

JÜLICHER, ADOLF (1857–1938): Lutheran New Testament scholar and church historian, professor in Marburg, 1888–1923. Pointed out that Jesus's parables were not originally allegories. *Romans* written to defend Paul's gospel against unbelieving Judaism. The gospel is God's power unto salvation for *everyone* who believes. The righteousness of God describes a religious right-disposition which enables God to free him who possesses it from destruction. Paul could not entirely free himself from the Jewish idea that 'saved' required there to be also 'damned'.

Der Brief an die Römer. Die Schriften des Neuen Testaments neu übersetzt und für die Gegenwart erklärt. Vol. II, Göttingen, 1907; 2nd ed., 1917, pp. 223–335.

JUSTIN MARTYR (*c.*100–*c.*165): Samaritan philosopher who became a Christian, taught in Rome, and was scourged and beheaded for refusing to sacrifice. Wrote an *Apology* addressed to the emperor Antoninus Pius, his adopted son Verissimus ('the philosopher', Marcus Aurelius), his adopted son Lucius, the senate and people of Rome to recommend the Christian faith. Another apology (*The Second Apology*) later appended. Wrote a *Dialogue with Trypho, a Jew* to show that Christianity was the true heir of the Old Testament. Harnack dates the *Apology* a few years after 150 and the *Dialogue* between 150 and 160. Eusebius's *Chronicon* dates the *Apology* not later than 142. Justin never mentions Paul. He twice quotes the Old Testament in forms very close to those found in *Romans* (Dial.27 = Rom. 3.12, (11), 13, 16, 17; Dial.39 = Rom. 11.2–4).

KABISCH, RICHARD (1868–1914): Lutheran theologian, writer on education. The future eschatological hope is the dominant note in Paul's Gospel.

Die Eschatologie des Paulus in ihren Zusammenhängen mit dem Gesamtbegriff des Paulinismus. Göttingen, 1893.

KÄSEMANN, ERNST (1906–   ): Lutheran theologian and New Testament scholar, professor in Mainz, 1946, Göttingen, 1951, Tübingen, 1959. God's righteousness is his rule over the world which has been eschatologically revealed in Christ. It is the power of the Creator who makes a new creation out of nothing by justifying the ungodly and raising the dead. The only thing man can do is to obey. Important essays on *Romans*, particularly Chapters 3, 4, 6, 8, 9–11, 12, and 13, appear in

Exegetische Versuche und Besinnungen, Vol. I, Göttingen, 1960; Vol. II, 1964. *Essays on New Testament Themes*. London, 1964. *New Testament Questions of Today*. London, 1969.

Paulinische Perspektiven. Tübingen, 1969. *Perspectives on Paul*. London, 1971.

An die Römer. Handbuch zum Neuen Testament. Tübingen, 1973.

KENYON, SIR FREDERICK GEORGE (1863–1952): textual critic, Director and Principal Librarian, British Museum, 1909–30, professor of ancient history in the Royal Academy, 1918.

Our Bible and the Ancient Manuscripts. London, 1895; 3rd ed. 1911; 4th ed., revised, 1939; 5th ed., revised by A. W. Adams, 1958.

Handbook to the Textual Criticism of the New Testament. London, 1901; 2nd ed., 1912.

The Chester Beatty Biblical Papyri: Descriptions and Texts of Twelve Manuscripts on Papyrus of the Greek Bible. London, 1933 ff. Fasciculus III Supplement: *Pauline Epistles*. Text, 1936; Plates, 1937.

The Text of the Greek Bible: A Students Handbook. London, 1937; 2nd ed. 1949.

KIRK, KENNETH ESCOTT (1886–1953): Anglican moral theologian and New Testament scholar, professor in Oxford, 1932, bishop of Oxford, 1937. The righteousness of God is, first, the revelation that there is a God to whom sin is utterly hateful, who will judge and punish sinners according to their works; and then, by extension, the revelation that eternal life is promised to them that by patience in well-doing seek for glory and honour and incorruption (Rom. 2.7), however much they may fall by the way. Justification is 'relief from hopelessness'. Opposes the idea that righteousness is imputed, and says that Paul was not anxious to foster the idea that righteousness was imparted.

The Epistle to the Romans in the Revised Version with Introduction and Commentary. The Clarendon Bible. Oxford 1937.

KNOX, JOHN (1900–   ): Anglican (formerly Methodist) New Testament scholar professor Union Theological Seminary, New York, 1943–66, Episcopal Theological Seminary of the Southwest, 1966.

Commentary on Romans. The Interpreter's Bible. Vol. IX, New York, 1953.

KÜHL, ERNST (1861–1918): Lutheran theologian, professor in Marburg, 1893, Königsberg, 1895, Göttingen, 1910.

Der Brief des Paulus an die Römer. Leipzig, 1913.

KÜMMEL, WERNER GEORG (1905–): Lutheran New Testament scholar, professor in Zürich, 1932, Mainz, 1951, Marburg, 1952.

Römer 7 und die Bekehrung des Paulus. Leipzig, 1929.

His three essays 'Jesus und Paulus' (1937, 1948, 1964) are reprinted in *Heilsgeschehen und Geschichte: Gesammelte Aufsätze 1933–1964.* Edited by Erich Grässer, Otto Merk, and Adolf Fritz. Marburg, 1965.

KUSS, OTTO (1905–): Roman Catholic New Testament scholar, professor in Seminary, Regensburg, 1946, Paderborn, 1948, professor in University, Munich, 1960.

Der Römerbrief. First part (1.1–6.11), Regensburg, 1957. Second part (6.11–8.19), 1959.

LACHMANN, KARL (1793–1851): classical philologist, text critic. First to base a Greek text of the New Testament on the oldest manuscripts (1831, 1842–50). First to see that Mark's Gospel was source used in Matthew and Luke; 'De ordine narrationum in evangeliis synopticis', *Theologische Studien und Kritiken,* Vol. 8 (1835), pp. 570–90.

LAGRANGE, MARIE-JOSEPH (1855–1938): Biblical scholar, textual critic, of the Friars Preachers (Ordo Praedicatorum, the Dominican Order), co-founder of l'École Biblique, Jerusalem, 1890, and of *Revue Biblique,* 1892. The justice of God (Rom. 1.17) is the virtue of God communicated to men, consisting of the state of justice. It is given to men and is the principle which makes men die to sin in order to live to God in Christ.

Saint Paul: Épître aux Romains. Études Bibliques, Paris, 1915.

LAKE, KIRSOPP (1872–1946): Anglican Biblical and patristic scholar, textual critic, educated Oxford, professor Leiden, 1904, Harvard, 1914. On the basis of studies of family 1 (the Lake group) and family 13 (Ferrar), he moved towards the theory that there existed a local text at Caesarea, neither Alexandrian (Beta text-type) nor Western (Delta text-type).

The Text of the New Testament. Oxford Church Text Books. London, 1898. (1st ed. mentioned Caesarean possibility, a suggestion dropped in later editions, until revived under Streeter's influence.) 6th ed., revised by Silva New (later, Mrs Lake), 1928.

LEENHARDT, FRANZ-J. (1902–): professor, Geneva. The central theme of *Romans* is, paradoxically, the problem of the Church. Treatment of Chapters 9–11 is the touchstone of interpretation of the whole. The doctrine of justification by faith is the heart of the gospel; it is the reign of faith, which constitutes the life of the Church. Faith is the welcome man accords to God's initiative, to found a new humanity.

L'Épître de Saint Paul aux Romains. Commentaire du Nouveau Testament. Neuchatel, 1957. *Complément,* 1969. English translation by Harold Knight, *The Epistle to the Romans: A Commentary.* London, 1961.

LIDDON, HENRY PARRY (1829–90): Anglican theologian and Biblical scholar, professor, Oxford, 1870–82. 'In the Gospel the Righteousness which God gives ... is revealed as depending on Faith, and as producing the faith on which it depends.' 'Justification and sanctification may be distinguished by the student, as are the arterial and nervous systems in the human body; but in the living soul they are coincident and inseparable.' His commentary started as an Analysis, privately printed for distribution to students attending his lectures in 1875–6. Posthumously published from manuscripts dated 1878 and 1880, according to Liddon's intention.

Explanatory Analysis of St Paul's Epistle to the Romans. London, 1893.

LIETZMANN, HANS (1875–1942): Lutheran New Testament scholar and church historian, professor in Jena, 1905, Berlin, 1924. Brought to bear great learning in many fields on historical and exegetical problems. The 'righteousness of God' in Paul has an iridescent double meaning: it describes a divine property, which yet is also by grace granted to believing man. Often both meanings are simultaneously present.

An die Römer. Handbuch zum Neuen Testament, 8. Tübingen, 1906; 2nd ed., 1928; 3rd ed., 1933.

LIGHTFOOT, JOSEPH BARBER (1828–89): Anglican classical and Biblical scholar, professor in Cambridge, 1861 (Lady Margaret's, 1875), bishop of Durham, 1879. 'Christ's righteousness becomes our righteousness by our becoming one with Christ, being absorbed in Christ.' Two versions of *Romans*: a longer, to Rome; and a shorter, for a wider circle of readers. *Notes* on Romans 1.1–7.25 published posthumously.

'The Structure and Destination of the Epistle to the Romans' (articles reprinted from the *Journal of Philology,* 1869, 1871). *Biblical Essays.* London, 1893.

Notes on Epistles of St Paul from Unpublished Commentaries. London, 1895; 2nd ed., 1904.

LIPSIUS, RICHARD ADELBERT (1830–92): Lutheran theologian and historian, professor in Leipzig, 1859, Vienna, 1861, Kiel, 1865, and Jena, 1871. Paul's thought moves from the circle of Jewish ideas, the religion of the Law, to a new circle, the religion of the Spirit of God. He does not adopt Greek ideas, but makes the move on the basis of a deepening ethical understanding of the Hebrew contrast between spirit and flesh.

The satisfaction of the Law's requirements through the death of Christ is at the same time destruction (*Aufhebung*) of the whole religion of the Law; the atoning death of the Messiah at the same time the neutralization of the power of sin; the justification reckoned by grace at the same time the implanting by which one shares the death and life of the Reconciler.

Der Brief an die Römer. Hand-Commentar zum Neuen Testament. Freiburg i.B., 1891; 2nd ed., 1892.

LOHMEYER, ERNST (1890–1946): Lutheran New Testament scholar, professor in Breslau, 1920, removed because of anti-Nazism and taught in Greifswald, 1935, rector-designate, 1945, arrested and died in prison, 1946.

Grundlagen der paulinischen Theologie. Tübingen, 1929.

Probleme paulinischer Theologie. Darmstadt, 1954.

LOISY, ALFRED FIRMIN (1857–1940): French Biblical scholar, one of the founders of Modernism in France, excommunicated 1908, professor of history of religions, Collège de France, Paris, 1909–30. *Romans* consists of a short letter by Paul (1.1–17; 3.27–4.24; 9.1–13; 9.30–10.21; 15.8–33, passages themselves glossed by later hands) to which was added (a) a speculative section, written not before the end of the first century, to transform messianic faith into a theory of redemption (3.21–26; 5.1–8.39). This section had already been surcharged by (b) 7.7–25. Later were added (c) a section derived from Jewish sources (1.18–3.20; glossed by 2.14, 15); (d) 9.14–29, written after 150; (e) 11.1–36; (f) a moral part (not a unity; 13.1–7 comes from a later hand, and 13.8–12 depends on a Gospel tradition) (12.1–15.7); and (g) a section against Gnostic heretics (16.17–20). The doxologies provide evidence of surcharges and retouchings (15.13, 33; 16.16, 25).

'Les Épîtres de Paul', *Revue d'histoire et de littérature religieuses*, Vol. 7 (1921), pp. 76–125; 213–50.

Naissance du christianisme. Paris, 1933. English translation by L. P. Jacks, *The Birth of the Christian Religion.* London, 1948.

Remarques sur la littérature épistolaire du Nouveau Testament. Paris, 1935.

LÜDEMANN, HERMANN (1842–1933): Lutheran theologian, professor in Bern, 1884–1928. *See* A. Schweitzer.

Die Anthropologie des Apostels Paulus und ihre Stellung innerhalb seiner Heilslehre. Nach den vier Hauptbriefen dargestellt. Kiel, 1872.

LÜTGERT, WILHELM (1867–1938): Lutheran theologian and New Testament scholar, professor in Greifswald, 1895, Halle, 1901 (1912,

systematic theology), Berlin, 1929. *Romans* was written to a predominantly Gentile Christian Church in Rome to defend her against antinom-
ian Christianity. This explains Paul's positive attitude to the Law, and
explains why he gives his teaching about grace the form of teaching
about justification. His positive attitude to the Law is caught up in his
doctrine of grace. This also explains why he spends so much time on the
history of Israel; he is defending both the Law and Jewish Christianity
against Gentile Christianity.

*Der Römerbrief als historisches Problem. Beiträge zur Förderung christ-
licher Theologie.* Gütersloh, 1913.

LUTHER, MARTIN (1483–1546): reformer. As Augustinian monk
lectured on moral philosophy in the arts faculty at Wittenberg from
1508, on the Bible from 1509; on the *Sentences* of Peter Lombard at
Erfurt from 1509; on the Bible at Wittenberg from 1511, where he
became *Lectura in biblia* (professor of biblical theology) from 1512. We
have his own lectures notes on *Romans*, delivered between Easter 1515
and September 1516 (three semesters, lecturing on Mondays and
Fridays in term at 6 a.m.). After the break with Rome Luther often
preached from *Romans*, but only published one general treatment of the
epistle, his *Preface to St Paul's Epistle to the Romans* (1522; slightly
revised, 1546). The characteristic image of the pre-Reformation lectures
on *Romans* is the hospital; the sinner is both sick and healthy; actually
sick, but healthy by virtue of the sure promise of the physician whom
he believes. Although remission of sins is indeed true, there is no
removal of sins except in hope. In 1522 Luther's characteristic note is of
the joyful and free heart. Despite the fact that sins remain in Christians,
fighting against the Spirit, yet grace makes us to be fully and completely
reckoned justified before God. Grace is not divided nor given bit by bit;
grace brings us entirely into God's favour. Through faith a man
becomes sinless and obtains the desire to keep God's commands, in that
he gives God his honour and pays what he owes him. God's righteousness is the righteousness which counts with God, which he gives to some
man. No man can give himself faith or remove his own unbelief. In
answer to Erasmus's book *On the Freedom of the Will* (1524), Luther
wrote *On the Bondage of the Will* (1525). He argued that the predestinarian texts in Romans 9 could hardly be taken in Erasmus's sense.
Admitted that by the light of nature and the light of grace God was unjust, 'who crowns one ungodly man freely and apart from merits, yet
damns another who may be less, or at least not more, ungodly'.
Thought that God's justice would be vindicated by the light of glory.

Was probably the first theologian to be a thorough-going determinist. 'Free will is obviously a term applicable only to the Divine Majesty.'

Vorlesung über den Römerbrief 1515–1516. Kritische Gesamtaufgabe. Vol. 56. Weimar, 1938. English translation, to be used with caution. Wilhelm Pauck, *Luther: Lectures on Romans.* Library of Christian Classics, xv. London, 1961.

Vorrede auf die Epistel Sankt Paulus' zu den Römern. Kritische Gesamtausgabe. Die Deutsche Bibel. Vol. 7, Weimar, 1931, pp. 1–26. English translation, *Luther's Works: American Edition.* Vol. 35, Philadelphia, 1960. pp. 365–80.

De servo Arbitrio. Kritische Gesamtausgabe. Vol. 18, Weimar, 1908. Translated and edited by Philip S. Watson in collaboration with B. Drewery. *Luther and Erasmus: Free Will and Salvation.* Library of Christian Classics, xvii. London, 1969.

LYONNET, STANISLAUS (1902–   ): Roman Catholic Biblical scholar, member of Society of Jesus, professor in seminary, Lyon-Fourvière, 1938–40, professor of Armenian and Georgic languages, Pontifical Biblical Institute, Rome, 1942, of scripture, 1950. The righteousness of God is the saving activity of God which accomplishes the promises of grace, and overcomes the obstacles to man's restoration.

Quaestiones in Epistulam ad Romanos I. 2nd ed., Rome, 1962.

Les étapes de l'histoire du salut selon l'épître aux Romains. (Dust jacket: 'les etapes *du mystère* du salut' etc.). Paris, 1969.

MANEN, WILLEM CHRISTIAAN VAN (1842–1905): theologian of the Dutch Hervormed Kerk, church professor of exegesis and systematic theology, Groningen, 1884, state professor for New Testament exegesis and the history of early Christian literature, Leiden, 1885. The Epistle to the Romans is a compilation made by a Paulinist of the right wing and of 'catholic' sympathies. He used treatises or parts of treatises written by the Pauline school, which espoused a Christian gnosis. It is unlikely that this school had any direct connection with Paul himself.

Paulus II. De Brief aan de Romeinen. Leiden, 1891. German translation by G. Sclager: *Die Unechtheit des Römerbriefes.* Leipzig, 1906.

'Romans (Epistle)', *Encyclopaedia Biblica.* Edited by T. K. Cheyne and J. Sutherland Black. London, 1899–1903. Columns 4127–45.

MANSON, THOMAS WALTER (1893–1958): Presbyterian New Testament scholar, professor, Mansfield College, Oxford, 1932, Rylands professor, Manchester, 1936. *Romans* written from Corinth in two forms, one to Rome and the other to Ephesus.

'St Paul's Letter to the Romans – and Others'. *Bulletin of the John Rylands Library*, Vol. 31 (1948), pp. 224–40. Reprinted in *On Paul and John*, London, 1963.

MARCION (? –c.160): theologian, New Testament scholar, founder of a Church. Born in Sinope, Pontus. Shipowner. Went to Rome c.138–9. Excommunicated, 144. Gave his followers a systematic theology, *The Antitheses*, and a canon of scripture, *The Apostle* (an edition of ten letters of Paul, excluding the Pastorals), with brief prefaces, *The Prologues*, and *The Gospel* (an edition of Luke's Gospel). Distinguished two 'Gods', 'the good God' of Jesus, and 'the righteous God' of the Old Testament, who, though not evil, causes harm. Only Paul preserved the gospel, which the other apostles, who were 'false brothers', distorted. Made a sharp distinction between Law and Gospel. Probably would baptize only virgins, widows, the celibate, and divorced. His edition of *Romans* can be approximately recovered from the writings of Tertullian and other opponents. For example, he did not have the reference to 'come of the seed of David according to the flesh', 1.3; the word 'first' in 'to the Jew first', 1.16; the citation from Habakkuk with its introduction, 'as it is written', 1.17; 1.19–21; 3.31–4.25; 8.19–22; 9; 10.5–11.32; 13.1–7; 15; 16. Not all of these deficiencies are equally certain. *See* Harnack.

MARCUS AURELIUS (121–80): Roman philosopher, emperor from 161. Put down his meditations in Greek, probably gradually accumulated over a period of ten to fifteen years. Mild Stoicism. 'With your whole will surrender yourself to Clotho to spin your fate into whatever web of things she will' (iv.34).

The Meditations of the Emperor Marcus Antoninus. Edited with Translation and Commentary by A. S. L. Farquharson (1871–1942). Two volumes, Oxford, 1944.

METZGER, BRUCE MANNING (1914–): Presbyterian New Testament scholar, textual critic, bibliographer, professor, Princeton Theological Seminary, 1954. Advocate of the eclectic method of textual criticism. 'Choose the reading which best explains the origin of the others.'

The Text of the New Testament: Its Transmission, Corruption, and Restoration. Oxford, 1964; 2nd ed., 1968.

MICHEL, OTTO (1903–): Lutheran New Testament scholar, professor in Halle-Wittenberg, 1938, Tübingen, 1940. Defends Luther's reading of *Romans* against Schlatter's criticism. The starting point remains the preaching of the gospel, but the revelation of the eschatalogical 'wrath of God' is embedded in the preaching of the gospel. The preaching of the gospel leads necessarily to the indictment of mankind.

Paulus und seine Bibel. Gütersloh, 1929; 2nd ed., photographic reproduction of 1st with a new supplement, Darmstadt, 1972.

Der Brief an die Römer. Kritisch-exegetischer Kommentar über das Neue Testament. Begründet von H. A. W. Meyer. 1st ed., 1955; 2nd ed., 1957; 3rd ed., 1963; 4th ed., 1966.

MICHELSEN, J. H. A.: Kampen.

'Kritisch onderzoek naar den oudsten tekst van "Paulus' brief aan de Romeinen"', *Theologisch Tijdschrift*, Vol. 21 (1886), pp. 372–86; 473–90; Vol. 22 (1887), pp. 163–203.

MOFFATT, JAMES (1870–1944): Presbyterian New Testament scholar and church historian, professor United Free Church College, Glasgow, 1915, Union Theological College, New York, 1927.

A New Translation of the New Testament. London, 1913; final revision, 1935.

MOULE, HANDLEY CARR GLYN (1841–1920): Anglican theologian, principal of Ridley Hall, Cambridge, 1880–99, professor, Cambridge, 1899, bishop of Durham, 1901. The righteousness of God 'is "*God's* righteousness", as being provided by Him and availing with Him'.

The Epistle of Paul the Apostle to the Romans, with Introduction and Notes. The Cambridge Bible for Schools. Cambridge, 1879.

MOULTON, JAMES HOPE (1863–1917): Methodist, professor of Hellenistic Greek and Indo-European philology, Manchester, 1908.

A Grammar of New Testament Greek Vol. I: Prolegomena. Edinburgh, 1906; 2nd ed., 1906. Continued and completed by W. F. Howard and Nigel Turner.

MÜLLER, CHRISTIAN: Lutheran New Testament scholar.

Gottes Gerechtigkeit und Gottes Volk: Eine Untersuchung zu Römer 9–11. Göttingen, 1964.

MUNCK, JOHANNES (1904–65): Danish Lutheran New Testament scholar, professor, Aarhus, 1938. There was no ultimate conflict of aims between Paul and the Jewish Christians: both wanted the salvation of Jews and Gentiles. Paul thought the conversion of the Gentiles was necessary before Israel would return. Paul worked on the principle of 'representative universalism'; the response of a part would stand for the response of the whole. When all the Gentiles had heard, the end would come.

'Israel and the Gentiles in the New Testament'. *Journal of Theological Studies*, new series, Vol. II (1951), pp. 3–16.

Paulus und die Heilsgeschichte. Aarhus, 1954. English translation by Frank Clarke, *Paul and the Salvation of Mankind*. London, 1959.

Christus und Israel, eine Auslegung von Röm. 9–11. Aarhus, 1956.

MURRAY, JOHN (1898–   ): Presbyterian theologian, ordained in The Orthodox Presbyterian Church, U.S.A., 1937; professor of systematic theology, Westminster Theological Seminary, Philadelphia, 1937. The righteousness of God is contrasted not only with human unrighteousness but with human righteousness. It is 'God-righteousness', characterized by the perfection belonging to all that God is and does. The gospel is God's righteousness supervening upon our sin and ruin. Rejects the attempts to interpret election in Romans 9 in corporate terms.

The Epistle to the Romans: The English Text with Introduction, Exposition and Notes. Two volumes, Grand Rapids, Michigan, 1960, 1965; bound as one volume, 1967.

NABER, S. A. (1828–   ?): philologist, professor, Amsterdam, 1878. *See* Pierson.

NACHMAN BEN ISAAC, RABBI (died *c*.356): said to have cited Habakkuk 2.4 as the one commandment necessary, Makkoth 23b. See discussion in Paul Billerbeck, *Kommentar zum Neuen Testament aus Talmud und Midrasch*, Vol. III, Munich, 1926, pp. 542 f.

NOCK, ARTHUR DARBY (1902–63): classical scholar, historian of Hellenistic religion, professor, Harvard, 1930.

Conversion: the old and the new in religion from Alexander the Great to Augustine of Hippo. Oxford, 1933.

NYGREN, ANDERS THEODOR SAMUEL (1890–   ): Lutheran theologian, philosopher of religion, professor, Lund, 1924, bishop of Lund, 1948. Emphasizes the unity of *Romans*. Righteousness from God comes into the world through Christ. The age to come has begun in the midst of men. He who believes in Christ already, in this life, shares in the new age.

Pauli brev till Romarna. Stockholm, 1944; 2nd ed., 1947. English translation by Carl C. Rasmussen, *Commentary on Romans*, London, 1952. German translation, Göttingen, 1951.

ORIGEN (*c*.185–*c*.254): Alexandrian theologian, Biblical scholar, spiritual writer. Interpreted the Bible literally, morally, and allegorically, the last being the highest sense. Defended human free will. God is only *said* to harden some men; the hardening follows as a result of the inherent wickedness in such men: wax is melted and mud dried by the same heat. Believed all souls would eventually be saved. The word of God is the soul's physician, working slowly but surely. Origen's commentary on *Romans* was written in Greek, of which fragments on Romans 1 and 9 are preserved in *The Philocalia of Origen* made by Gregory Nazianzen and Basil. A Latin rendering, compressed and rather free, was made by Rufinus of Aquileia (*c.*345–410).

The Philocalia of Origen: The Text Revised with a Critical Introduction and Indices. J. Armitage Robinson. Cambridge, 1893. English translation by G. Lewis, Edinburgh, 1911.

'Notes on the Manuscripts and Editions of Origen's Commentary on the Epistle to the Romans in the Latin Translation by Rufinus', by Miss C. P. Hammond. *Journal of Theological Studies.* New Series Vol. XVI (1965), pp. 338–57.

ORPHISM: a mystic Greek cult, connected with Orpheus. Rites of purification and initiation. Flourished 6th century B.C.; revived under Roman empire.

OSIANDER, ANDREAS (1498–1552): Lutheran theologian, professor in Königsberg, 1550. Inaugural lecture, *De iustificatione.* The sinner is reckoned righteous by God because Christ dwells in him. Osiander in this way avoided the charge that God was a liar in calling sinners righteous, but at the cost of threatening the foundations of Lutheranism.

OVID (Publius Ovidius Naso) (43 B.C.–A.D. 18): Latin poet, exiled A.D. 8. Guide to Greek mythology and Roman legend.

PALLIS, ALEXANDER (1851–1935): Greek merchant and scholar, naturalized British subject, 1898. *Romans* was an irenic letter by a Jew in Alexandria to the Church at large written between A.D. 70 and the end of the century. Not by Paul, lacking the spontaneity, unconventionality, and ruggedness to be found in his letters to the Corinthians and Galatians. The original simple letter interpolated by later theologians, who added: 1.19–31; 3.21–31; 4.17; 5.3, 4, 5, (6), 7, (8), 11, (15), 18, 19; 6.5–11, 14–23; 7.1–25; 8; 9.8–33; 10; 11.6, 7, 11, 12, 21, 22; 13.1–14; 14.8b, 9, 16–23; 15.1–13, 23, 24, (28); 16.1–20.

To the Romans: A Commentary. Liverpool, 1920.

PELAGIUS (*c.*360–after 418): British or Irish lay monk, theologian and exegete. Came to Rome *c.*400 and remained there till 410 (fall of Rome to Alaric); went to North Africa, attacked by Augustine, went to Palestine, condemned by councils at Carthage, Mileve (both 416), Carthage (418), Ephesus (431), and the Second Council of Orange (529). When he came to Rome wrote a commentary on the thirteen epistles of Paul. Heard a bishop cite Augustine's prayer, 'Give what you command and command what you will' (*Confessions* 10.40), and attacked the idea as immoral. Taught that the same law of Christian behaviour, in all its rigour, should be followed by every baptized member of the church.

Pelagius' Expositions of 13 Epistles of St Paul. Edited by A. Souter. Text and Studies, IX. 1–3. Cambridge, 1922–31. Reprinted by A. Hamman, *Patrologia Latina, Supplementum* I (1958), columns 1110–1374.

PHILO (*c.*15B.C.–*c.*A.D.50): Jewish theologian, philosopher, and exegete of Alexandria. Wrote in Greek. Collected Hellenistic Jewish philosophical and exegetical traditions to show that Judaism was the true religion of mankind. Kept the Law, but saw behind the regulations a spiritual and heavenly truth.

Philonis Alexandrini Opera quae supersunt. Edited by Leopold Cohn and Paul Wendland, with Sigofred Reiter. 6 vols. Berlin,, 1896–1915. Vol. VII, Leisegang's Index, 1930. Translated by F. H. Colson and G. H. Whitaker with Ralph Marcus, Loeb Classical Library. 10 vols., 2 supplements, London, 1929–62.

PIERSON, ALLARD (1831–96): Dutch Lutheran theologian, became agnostic ('abstentionist'); professor in Heidelberg, 1870–4, professor of aesthetics and modern languages, Amsterdam, 1877–95. With Naber put forward the hypothesis that *Romans* was edited by a Bishop Paul of the second century from fragments, some of which were pre-Christian Jewish of a liberal kind. Bishop Paul loved the church and her unity above all.

Verisimilia. Laceram conditionem Novi Testamenti exemplis illustrarunt et ab origine repetierunt A. Pierson et S.A. Naber. Amsterdam, 1886.

PLATO (*c.*427–348 B.C.): Greek philosopher. Pupil and interpreter of Socrates. Taught in Athens in the Academy. There is an unchanging reality, the world of Ideas or Forms, behind the changing appearance of the world.

PYTHAGOREANS AND NEO-PYTHAGOREANS. Followers of Pythagoras (*c.*580 B.C.–). Ascetic, held transmigration of souls. Cult revived under early Roman empire; fused with Orphism.

QUINE, WILLARD VAN ORMAN (1908–): philosopher, professor in Harvard. Questions whether the absolute distinction between analytic statements (statements like 'The number of the planets is necessarily greater than seven') and synthetic statements (statements that might or might not be true) is possible to maintain.

From a Logical Point of View, Cambridge, Massachusetts, 1953; 2nd ed., 1961.

Word and Object. Cambridge, Massachusetts, 1960.

QUMRAN writings: documents, mainly in Hebrew, found hidden in caves above the Wadi Qumran and northwards, on the west coast of the Dead Sea. They date from the second century B.C. to the first century A.D.

iQS Serek hajjaḥad in cave 1, Qumran. The Scroll of the Rule or The Dead Sea Manual of Discipline.

iQS a Serek ha'edā in cave 1, Qumran. The Rule Annexe (to The Scroll of the Rule) or The Messianic Rule.

4QFlor Florilegium in cave 4, Qumran. A Midrash on the Last Days; Biblical passages with commentary.

G. Vermes, *The Dead Sea Scrolls in English*. Harmondsworth, 1962.

SANDAY, WILLIAM (1834–1920): Anglican New Testament scholar, professor in Oxford from 1882.

With Arthur C. Headlam, *A Critical and Exegetical Commentary on The Epistle to the Romans.* The International Critical Commentary. Edinburgh, 1895; 5th ed., 1902.

SCHELKLE, KARL HERMANN (1908–   ): Roman Catholic New Testament scholar, professor in Tübingen, 1950.

Paulus Lehrer der Väter: Die altkirchliche Auslegung von Römer 1–11. Düsseldorf, 1956, 1959.

SCHLATTER, ADOLF (1852–1938): Lutheran New Testament scholar and theologian, professor in Greifswald, 1888, Berlin, 1893, Tübingen, 1898. Criticized Luther and Calvin for starting from man instead of from God, and substituting God's mercy for his righteousness. God's righteousness is the righteousness of the Creator, who reorders men's relations to himself and makes them believers. The proclamation of Christ in the gospel gives men fellowship with Christ.

Gottes Gerechtigkeit: Ein Kommentar zum Römerbrief. Stuttgart, 1935.

SCHLICHTING, JONAS (1592–1661): German Unitarian theologian, under influence of Socinianism from Poland.

SCHOEPS, HANS JOACHIM (1909–   ): Jewish scholar, professor for Religions – und Geistesgeschichte, Erlangen, 1950.

Paulus: Die Theologie des Apostels im Lichte der jüdischen Religionsges-

chichte. Tübingen, 1959. Revised for English translation. Translated by Harold Knight. *Paul: The Theology of the Apostle in the Light of Jewish Religious History*. London. 1961,

SCHULZ, DAVID (1779–1854): Lutheran theologian, professor in Halle, 1809, Frankfurt/Oder, 1809, Breslau, 1811. Fought for freedom from the old Lutheran confessions.
   Die christliche Lehre vom Glauben. 1834.

SCHWEITZER, ALBERT (1875–1965): Alsatian theologian, New Testament scholar, philosopher, musician, historian of music, medical doctor, missionary. In the year of his last medical examinations published a survey of the interpretations of Paul from the break of the spell of Reformation dogma down to his own day. Took seriously the observation of Lüdemann and Otto Pfleiderer that there were two different anthropologies and views of salvation in Paul's writings, the Jewish and the Hellenistic. According to one, man was forensically justified and saw himself in a religious subjective-ideal relation to God; according to the other, man was freed from the flesh and the Holy Spirit was bestowed on him, and he entered into an ethical objective-real relation to God. Schweitzer denied that Paul moved away from his Jewish roots into Hellenistic religious ideas, but insisted that the later development, which was Paul's distinctive position, was based on a heightening of Jewish ideas, 'the future hope raised to the highest degree of intensity'. He called Paul's view 'the mystical doctrine of redemption through the being-in-Christ'. He expounded Paul in a book written during his second return to Europe in 1927–9, on the basis of a draft which went back to 1906.
   Geschichte der paulinischen Forschung von der Reformation bis auf die Gegenwart. Tübingen, 1911. English translation by W. Montgomery. *Paul and his Interpreters: A Critical History*. London, 1912.
   Die Mystik des Apostels Paulus. Tübingen, 1930. English translation by W. Montgomery. *The Mysticism of Paul the Apostle*. London, 1931.

SCOTT, CHARLES ARCHIBALD ANDERSON (1858–1941): Presbyterian New Testament scholar, professor Westminster College, Cambridge, 1907–32.
   Christianity According to St Paul. Cambridge, 1927; 2nd ed., 1932.
   'The Epistle to the Romans'. *Abingdon Commentary*, New York, 1929.

SEEBERG, ALFRED (1863–1915): Lutheran New Testament scholar, brother of the historian of dogma Reinhold, professor in Dorpat, 1895,

Rostock, 1908, Kiel, 1914. Argued that a Christological baptismal creed was used by missionaries within the first twenty years of the Church's existence, and lies behind the New Testament writings.

Der Katechismus der Urchristenheit. Leipzig, 1903. Reprinted with an introduction by Ferdinand Hahn, Munich, 1966.

SEEBERG, REINHOLD (1859–1935): Lutheran theologian, historian of dogma, professor, Dorpat, 1885, Erlangen, 1889, Berlin, 1898.

Lehrbuch der Dogmengeschichte I, Leipzig, 1895; 3rd ed., 1920. II, 1898; 4th ed., 1930. III, 1913; 4th ed., 1930. IV, 1, 1917. IV, 2, 1920. Revised by the author and translated by C. E. Hay, *Text-Book of the History of Doctrines,* 2 vols. Grand Rapids, Michigan, 1952.

Aus Religion und Geschichte. I. Leipzig, 1906. II, 1909.

SEMLER, JOHANN SALOMO (1725–91): Lutheran theologian, New Testament scholar, and historian, professor of history and Latin poetry, Altdorf, 1751, of theology in Halle, 1753. Fought on one side against the old orthodox theory of verbal inspiration in favour of an historical and critical approach to the Bible; and, on the other side, against rationalistic attacks on Christianity in favour of a gospel of the grace of God, in which Christ's death and resurrection bring men their redemption. Semler, although in general sympathetic to Luther's theology, was sharply critical of his answer to Erasmus in *De servo arbitrio.* Semler's numerous short exegetical and critical notes on passages in the New Testament laid the foundation of modern critical study.

Gottfried Hornig. *Die Anfänge der historischen-kritischen Theologie: Johann Salomo Semlers Schriftverständnis und seine Stellung zu Luther.* Göttingen, 1961.

SEVERIAN (flourished *c.*400): bishop of Gabala, opponent of Chrysostom, exegete.

SOCRATES (469–399 B.C.): philosopher in Athens. Taught by asking questions. Sentenced to death for introducing strange gods and corrupting youth with his teaching.

SODEN, HERMANN FREIHERR VON (1852–1914): Lutheran textual critic, professor of New Testament, Berlin, 1893. With financial support from a rich Berlin lady, produced the fullest collection of variant readings in the New Testament yet available. His theory of the history of the text has won little support, and unfortunately his references are not always accurate.

Die Schriften des Neuen Testaments in ihrer ältesten erreichbaren Textgestalt hergestellt auf Grund ihrer Textgeschichte. I. Teil: Untersuchungen.

Three parts. Berlin, 1902, 1907, 1910. II. Teil: Text mit Apparat. Göttingen, 1913.

SPITTA, FRIEDRICH (1852–1924): Lutheran New Testament scholar, historian of church music, professor in Strassburg, 1887, Göttingen, 1919. Showed importance of Hellenistic-Jewish literature for understanding New Testament. Isolated sources in *Romans*.

Zur Geschichte und Litteratur des Urchristentums. Dritter Band, erste Halfte: Untersuchungen über den Brief des Paulus an die Römer. Göttingen, 1901.

STOICS: followers of Zeno of Citium, Cyprus, who came to Athens and began to teach in the Painted Porch, the Stoa, in 302 B.C. Became the dominant philosophy in the Hellenistic world, the empire conquered by Alexander the Great. Popularized in the Roman empire by Seneca, Marcus Aurelius, and Epictetus. The universe was seen as one great city, ruled by one Supreme Power (Destiny, Zeus, Providence, the Universal Law, Nature). History is cyclical: at the end of every world-period the universe is reabsorbed into the divine Fire, and then would start again an exact repetition of its course. God's design was good, and was to be submitted to. Everything is determined. The body did not matter, only the mind, a spark of the divine. Happiness consisted in virtue, and in submitting to whatever came to pass.

STREETER, BURNETT HILLMAN (1874–1937): Anglican New Testament scholar, textual critic, Queen's College, Oxford. *See* Lake.

The Four Gospels: A Study of Origins treating of the manuscript tradition, sources, authorship, and dates. London, 1924; 4th impression, revised, 1930.

STUHLMACHER, PETER (1932–   ): Lutheran New Testament scholar, professor Erlangen, 1968, Tübingen, 1972.

Gerechtigkeit Gottes bei Paulus. Göttingen, 1965.

TACITUS, PUBLIUS (?) CORNELIUS (*c.*55–*c.*117): Roman historian. Wrote *Histories* and *Annals*, neither of which has been preserved in full.

TALBERT, CHARLES H. (1934–   ): Baptist New Testament scholar, associate professor of religion, Wake Forest University, 1969.

'A Non-Pauline Fragment at Romans 3.24–26?', *Journal of Biblical Literature*, Vol. LXXXV (1966), pp. 287–96.

TERTULLIAN, QUINTUS SEPTIMIUS FLORENS (*c.*160–*c.*220): North African theologian. Lawyer, converted to Christianity in 195 or 196. Became Montanist *c.*207. First theologian to write in Latin. Most important works: *Apologeticum* and *Against Marcion*.

THEODORE OF MOPSUESTIA (*c*.350–428): bishop, Antiochene theologian and exegete. Rejected allegorical interpretation of scripture.

THERAPEUTAE: members of Jewish monastic community in Egypt described by Philo in *De vita contemplativa*.

THOMAS AQUINAS (*c*.1225–74): theologian, philosopher, of the Friars Preachers (Ordo Praedicatorum, the Dominican Order). Wrote commentary on *Romans* between finishing his *Summa contra Gentiles* and beginning the *Summa theologiae*, between 1261 and 1264. Insisted both that God infuses grace in the ungodly who are justified, and that a movement of free will towards God in faith also takes place.

TISCHENDORF, KONSTANTIN VON (1815–74): Lutheran textual critic, professor of New Testament, Leipzig, 1845. Discovered numerous manuscripts of the New Testament, above all ℵ.
   Novum Testamentum Graece. Ad antiquissimos testes denuo recensuit apparatum criticum omni studio perfectum apposuit commentationem isagogicam praetexuit Constantinus Tischendorf. Editio octava critica maior. 2 vols., Leipzig, 1869, 1872.

VENEMA, HERMANN (1697–1787): Reformed theologian, professor in Franeker, 1724. Advocated strictly philological approach to the Bible.

WEISS, BERNHARD (1827–1918): Lutheran theologian and New Testament scholar, professor in Königsberg, 1857, Kiel, 1863, Berlin, 1877. Above all a text-critic and master of exegetical questions.
   Der Brief an die Römer. Kritisch-exegetischer Kommentar über das Neue Testament begründet von H. A. W. Meyer. Göttingen, 1881; 2nd ed., 1899.

WEISS, JOHANNES (1863–1914): Lutheran theologian and New Testament scholar, son of Bernhard, professor in Göttingen, 1890, Marburg, 1895, Heidelberg, 1908. Emphasized importance of eschatology in understanding New Testament.
   Das Urchristentum. Published and completed by Rudolf Knopf. Göttingen, 1917. English translation, *The History of Primitive Christianity.* Translated by Frederick C. Grant, Arthur Haire Forster, Paul Stevens Kramer, and Sherman Elbridge Johnson. 2 vols., New York, 1937. Reissued as *Earliest Christianity: A History of the Period* A.D. *30–150.* Edited with new introduction and bibliography by F. C. Grant. New York, 1959.

WEISSE, CHRISTIAN HERMANN (1801–66): philosopher, amateur

New Testament scholar, professor in Leipzig, 1828–37, 1845. One of the first to establish that Mark's Gospel was used as a source in the Gospels of Matthew and Luke, 1838, and that John's Gospel employed written discourse courses, 1856. Argued that only 1 *Corinthians*, 2 *Corinthians*, 1 *Thessalonians*, and *Philemon* are pure examples of Paul's writings (2 *Corinthians* being a compilation). *Galatians* and *Colossians* have been interpolated, a process which possibly began with Paul's permission. *Romans* and *Philippians* are compilations, continuously interwoven with interpolations. The interpolator had the highest respect for Paul's actual words and omitted only the introductions to several letters when they were being combined into one. The theory was stated in 1855; a reconstruction was published posthumously in 1867. Details in Lipsius's commentary on *Galatians*, *Romans*, and *Philippians*.

Philosophische Dogmatik oder Philosophie des Christenthums. 3 vols. Leipzig, 1855, 1860, 1862.

Beiträge zur Kritik der paulinischen Briefe. Edited with an introduction by E. Sulze. Leipzig, 1867.

WELLHAUSEN, JULIUS (1844–1918): theologian, biblical scholar, Arabist. Studied in Göttingen, professor of Old Testament in Greifswald, 1872, Privatdozent for Semitic languages in Halle, 1882, professor in Marburg, 1885, Göttingen, 1892–1913. Dominated Old Testament scholarship of his day. Reconstructed the history of Israel on the basis of a sharp distinction between sources in the Pentateuch. Devoted last 15 years of his life to a critical analysis of the Gospels.

WETTSTEIN, JOHANN JAKOB (1693–1754): Basel theologian and textual critic. Removed from posts in Church and university because of his textual criticism and alleged rationalism, 1730. Went to Amsterdam; on rehabilitation by church in Basel, taught at Remonstrant College, 1734. Edition of New Testament drew attention to readings of old manuscripts; he was first to designate uncials by capital, Roman letters minuscules by Arabic numerals. Collected classical, patristic, and rabbinic parallels to New Testament words and ideas.

Prolegomena ad Novi Testamenti Graeci editionem accuratissimam e vetustissimus codicibus manuscriptis denuo procurandam. Amsterdam, 1730.

Novum Testamentum Graecum editionis receptae cum lectionibus variantibus, codicum mss., editionum aliarum, versionum et patrum nec non commentario pleniore ex scriptoribus veteribus Hebraeis, Graecis et Latinis historiam et vim verborum illustrante opera et studio Joannis Jacobi Wetstenii. 2 vols., Amsterdam, 1751–2.

WILES, MAURICE FRANK (1923–   ): Anglican theologian and patristic scholar, professor, King's College, London, 1967, Oxford, 1970.

The Divine Apostle: The Interpretation of St Paul's Epistles in the Early Church. Cambridge, 1967.

WINDISCH, HANS (1881–1935): New Testament scholar, professor in Leiden, 1914, Kiel, 1929, Halle, 1935. Full of common sense.

WREDE, WILLIAM (1859–1906): Lutheran New Testament scholar, professor in Breslau, 1893. Paul is the founder of a second Christian religion.

Paulus. Tübingen, 1905; 2nd ed., 1907. English translation by Edward Lummis. *Paul.* London, 1907.

ZAHN, THEODOR (1838–1933): Lutheran New Testament scholar, professor in Göttingen, 1871, Kiel, 1877, Erlangen, 1878, Leipzig, 1888, Erlangen, 1892–1909. Defended authenticity and historicity of New Testament books with wide and exact learning. Text critic and historian of canon.

Der Brief des Paulus an die Römer. Kommentar zum Neuen Testament. Leipzig, 1910; 2nd ed., revised by Friedrich Hauch, 1925.

ZIESLER, JOHN A. (1930–   ): Methodist New Testament scholar, born in New Zealand, St Matthias College, Bristol.

The Meaning of Righteousness in Paul: A Linguistic and Theological Enquiry. Cambridge, 1972.

ZUNTZ, GÜNTHER (1902–   ): classical scholar, textual critic, professor of Hellenistic Greek, Manchester, 1963–9.

The Text of the Epistles: A Disquisition upon the Corpus Paulinum. The Schweich Lectures of the British Academy 1946. London, 1953.

Addendum

BLACK, MATTHEW (1908–   ): Presbyterian biblical scholar, professor, St. Andrews, 1954.

Romans. New Century Bible. London, 1973.

MORE ABOUT PENGUINS
AND PELICANS

Penguinews, which appears every month, contains details of all the new books issued by Penguins as they are published. From time to time it is supplemented by *Penguins in Print*, which is a complete list of all titles available. (There are some five thousand of these.)

A specimen copy of *Penguinews* will be sent to you free on request. For a year's issues (including the complete lists) please send 50p if you live in the British Isles, or 75p if you live elsewhere. Just write to Dept EP, Penguin Books Ltd, Harmondsworth, Middlesex, enclosing a cheque or postal order, and your name will be added to the mailing list.

In the U.S.A.: For a complete list of books available from Penguin in the United States write to Dept CS, Penguin Books Inc., 7110 Ambassador Road, Baltimore, Maryland 21207.

In Canada: For a complete list of books available from Penguin in Canada write to Penguin Books Canada Ltd, 41 Steelcase Road West, Markham, Ontario.

The Pelican New Testament Commentaries

THE GOSPEL OF ST MARK
D. E. Nineham

THE GOSPEL OF ST LUKE
G. B. Caird

THE GOSPEL OF ST JOHN
John Marsh

THE GOSPEL OF ST MATTHEW
John Fenton

PAUL'S FIRST LETTER TO CORINTH
John Ruef